PREMIERE®
to go

ISBN 0-13-027739-8

90000

9 780130 277398

to go series

PREMIERE

to go

Dennis Chominksy

Prentice Hall PTR, Upper Saddle River, NJ 07458
www.phptr.com

Library of Congress Cataloging-in-Publication Data

Chominisky, Dennis.
   Premiere to go/Dennis Chominsky
     p. cm. — (To go series)
   ISBN 0-13-027739-8
     1. Motion pictures—Editing—Data processing. 2. Adobe Premiere. I. Title. II. Series.
   TR899.C478 2000
   778.5'235'0285369—dc21

                                                 00-060694

Editorial/Production Supervisor: *Kerry Reardon*
Project Coordinator: *Anne Trowbridge*
Acquisitions Editor: *Tim Moore*
Editorial Assistant: *Julie Okulicz*
Manufacturing Buyer: *Maura Zaldivar*
Manufacturing Manager: *Alexis Heydt*
Marketing Manager: *Debby vanDijk*
Art Director: *Gail Cocker-Bogusz*
Interior Series Designer: *Rosemarie Votta*
Cover Designer: *Anthony Gemmellaro*
Cover Design Director: *Jerry Votta*

© 2001 Prentice Hall PTR
Prentice-Hall, Inc.
Upper Saddle River, NJ 07458

Prentice Hall books are widely used by corporation and government agencies for training, marketing, and resale.
The publisher offers discounts on this book when ordered in bulk quantities.
For more information, contact

   Corporate Sales Department
   Prentice Hall PTR
   One Lake Street
   Upper Saddle River, NJ 07458
   Phone: 800-382-3419; FAX: 201-236-7141
   E-mail (Internet): corpsales@prenhall.com

Printed in the United States of America

10 9   8   7   6   5   4   3   2   1

ISBN 0-13-027739-8

Prentice-Hall International (UK) Limited, *London*
Prentice-Hall of Australia Pty. Limited, *Sydney*
Prentice-Hall Canada Inc., *Toronto*
Prentice-Hall Hispanoamericana, S.A., *Mexico*
Prentice-Hall of India Private Limited, *New Delhi*
Prentice-Hall of Japan, Inc., *Tokyo*
Pearson Education Asia, Pte. Ltd.,
Editora Prentice-Hall do Brasil, Ltda., *Rio de Janeiro*

This book is dedicated to Tara.
Thanks for being so supportive.

CONTENTS

CHAPTER 2
SOURCE MATERIAL: GETTING IT STRAIGHT 25

CHAPTER 5

CHAPTER 6
FINE-TUNING USING TRIM MODE 125

CHAPTER 7

CHAPTER 9

CHAPTER 10

INTRODUCTION

It's amazing to walk down the street and see just how many people have video cameras. From tourists creating memories of their trip to a proud new parent capturing his child's precious moments (usually the first fifteen years of non-stop archives), people are capturing more events on video than ever before. For those who choose to enter into the world of television and multimedia, advances in technology have produced an explosion of video opportunities that were not possible even a decade ago.

Whether you are gathering your videos for personal reasons or pursuing a career in the video industry, producing the best quality movies is no longer a task just for the specialists. A new revolution in digital software has resulted in a world where hundreds of thousands of people are looking for a way to put together the best possible video to communicate their story. Programs like Adobe Premiere have made editing for these individuals a much more pleasurable experience. Premiere is simple to use. There is virtually no learning curve, yet it is powerful enough to cut broadcast quality movies on it. Adobe Premiere is the leading video editing software on the market today. It comes packaged with all the tools you need to get started editing your raw footage right away. No other package lets you work with so many different types of source materials and output to just about any type of media, whether it be analog tape or digital computer files.

There are so many types of productions that you can edit in Premiere, it would take a series of volumes to cover all of the topics that I would like to include in this book. This book covers some of the basic (but important) features and concepts of Premiere, but also takes many of these aspects and puts them into real-life editing situations.

From tips to try to warnings to avoid, this book contains information that every user will find beneficial. Take the time to do some experimenting on your own. The ideas presented in this book are only examples. Take them and turn them into a masterpiece video of your own. Don't expect George Lucas to be knocking down your door after your first project, but remember, keep trying out new ideas. Push the envelope in Premiere. You'll be surprised at what it can do.

WHO SHOULD READ THIS BOOK

This book is written for people who have some video basics and background. This is not an intro to video 101, although some of the topics covered are for beginners to Premiere. Those of you who have edited before and are ready to bring your skill up to the next level will get the most out of this book. This book is intended for users who:

◆ Are In A Hurry—producers and editors who want and need information fast.

◆ Already Know The Basics—this is not an Introduction to Premiere book.

◆ Expect Real Insight—the examples are from real projects. The Tips, Tricks, and Warnings will really give you the perspective you are looking for in a book.

◆ Want To Improve The Quality Of Their Work—serious individuals who take pride in developing new projects while learning every step of the way.

Throughout the course of this book I will introduce different types of features people are integrating into their video productions today. It would be great to fill up a book with the best and wildest projects that have ever been edited, but if they don't warrant any practical use for you, then I have wasted your time.

HOW THIS BOOK IS WRITTEN

This book is laid out in a way that focuses on some very specific topics within Premiere. You can utilize this book as a quick reference, jump-right-in-and-get-the-answer-you-need type of book. There are a few sections that do apply a bit more of a basic overtone. The reason for this is that with a program as powerful and dynamic as Premiere, with the ability to incorporate so many different media types, you need to understand how to put together and use these examples and understand how to produce a complete package, from start to finish. By analyzing the examples in this book and formulating your own versions when creating your projects, you will begin to expand the capabilities you can offer to your clients and pick from a multitude of tools to incorporate into your next Premiere movie.

Each chapter contains a variety of icons indicating points of interest that will help you while developing your applications. These icons include Notes, Tips, and Warnings.

Notes contain related information that will make understanding the point being discussed more clear.

 Tips are suggestions that can save you time and energy while developing your program. Some tips contain recommendations about other topics that will help develop your skills.

 These are cautions. I highly recommend you read them to make yourself aware of possible problems or pitfalls you may encounter while programming.

WHAT YOU WILL NEED

I will assume that if you are flipping through the pages of this book, you are interested in using Premiere or are already editing in Premiere. My recommendation to get the best out of this book is to own or have access to a copy of Premiere 5.1 so that you can walk through the procedures step by step while working in front of your computer. Most topics cover material that applies to other versions (even in other editing packages).

The first, and most obvious, thing you will need is a computer. Whether you work on Macintosh or Windows, just about all of the features apply to both platforms. Keep in mind that your original Premiere movies are cross-platform. Whichever system you choose, load it up with as much memory as possible. This will make your editing time more enjoyable, leaving you more time to be creative and not waiting for your computer to process information.

The last thing you will need is a video capture board. Without this, you will not be able to digitize or output any footage to tape. There are so many brands out there, most of them being able to produce broadcast quality images. Check the specs on each board and each manufacturer. Some have different input connections, some can output only certain qualities, and others need a computer system loaded with enough stuff that you can also fly the space shuttle. Look around and get the best board for your types of projects.

GOING BEYOND THE BOOK

One thing that makes this book unique is that you can take it beyond the text and images printed on this page. If you need to contact me regarding the topics covered in this book or have suggestions and ideas that you would like to see in the next version, let me know. I have discovered while writing this book that the more you learn about a program, the more you still have to go. If you want to ask a question or show off some of the neat things you have created using Premiere, e-mail me at dennis@pfsnewmedia.com.

OUTLOOK TOWARD THE FUTURE

I have been in the video editing industry a long time. I used to do it the old-fashioned way. Never again. The advancements with computer-based nonlinear editing systems have convinced me to continue along this route. With the emergence of HDTV and interactive television just around the corner, many new opportunities will arise for video producers and editors. If you're looking for a challenging career that demands both a creative touch with a technical insight, video is the industry for you. With the promise of 500 plus channels, we're all going to need some interesting content to fill these slots. Keep editing.

EXPANDING THE APPLICATIONS

As Premier makes editing easier, more people will begin adopting its power and performance. Its flexibility allows for such a wide array of users to begin editing whatever type of content is needed. There will definitely be more:

◆ Video for the Web—including integration with animations, interactivity, and high-performance digital media capabilities.

◆ Corporate Presentation—a shift from the over-indulged talking head presentation to something with more impact.

◆ DVD Home Movies—high quality imagery and breath-taking sound make DVDs such a better product than its analog cronies.

◆ Enhanced CD—all music CDs released from the record companies will have video clips, interactive games, bios, and possibly even concert footage clips to go along with the music tracks.

◆ Kiosks—the trend for information kiosks will be popping up everywhere, in schools, in restaurants, and maybe even on sidewalk corners.

All of these things exist right now in some fashion but will continue to increase at a rapid growth rate as Adobe Premiere introduces more features and easier ways for producers and editors to put these types of applications together.

TO SUM IT UP

This book tells it like it is. Real-life examples. Real-life applications. With the way technology makes editing clean and simple, more people will be using Premiere because of its flexibility that will suit their specific needs when producing movies. The great part about Premiere is its versatility. It's hard to stop at the basics. More and more, producers are pushing the limits of the software technologically and creatively, putting together some of the most amazing video programs ever produced. Once again, I encourage you to read this book, use it as a stepping stone, and then let your creativity take it one step further. Remember, your only limitations are the ones you let stand in your way. Don't let bells and whistle overshadow your message. Keep it interesting.

ACKNOWLEDGMENTS

I did it again. Fortunately, writing a second book is a bit easier than the first. I guess if you can complete one book in your lifetime, thats a tremendous goal. If you get the opportunity to write a second one, you should count your lucky stars. Thanks to everyone who has helped me continue my writing career. To all my family and friends, I could not have done it without your support. I especially want to thank Mom, Dad, JP, and Diana. Your encouragement has always kept me going. To the newest member of my family, Tara, your love and patience have been more than I could have ever expected. To Dee and John Friend, thanks for being one of the best cheering sections (and part time publicity directors). I wanted to give a special thank you to my grandmothers, "Gram" Kohn, "Nanny" Chominsky, and "Grandma" Hunt...now your names will be in print around the world.

To the crew at PFS New Media, you have all contributed in different ways. Most of the ideas in this book have come from the projects that have come in and out our door. To all my friends who I still owe a few drinks to for being M.I.A. for the past few months, thank you Sean (Conn.), Kim (LA), Joe and Jen, Ruben, Brad, Chris (Topher), Patrick and Ineke, Andrea, Dinger, Janine and Phillip, Andy and Richelle, and the rest of the gang. And of course my nocturnal buddy, Monty, who passed away in the middle of this book. This one's for you.

STARTING A PROJECT AND MAINTAINING IT

I guess this should be the chapter everyone reads. No matter what type of project you're working on, you need to have a well thought-out plan. This plan can come in many forms, including storyboards, scripts, and outlines. Whichever form you choose to work from, you need to be very specific and detailed. By "specific" and "detailed," I don't mean just which visuals you plan on using, but also, just as important, the scope of the project, overall length, and distribution formats. Many of these factors need to be decided before you begin to digitize clips or add any transitions. Let's look at Premiere's opening setup screen and project setting preferences.

NEW PROJECT SETTINGS WINDOW

The first thing you see when you launch Premiere is the New Project Settings Window. This window lets you customize your project for achieving optimal end results. The top pull-down menu determines what parameters are available in the Project Setting Window (Figure 1-1). The default setting is for the General Settings. Here you can control the Editing Mode. This allows you to select either Video For Windows (.AVI format) or QuickTime (.MOV). The Advanced Settings button may become active depending upon which type of capture card you have installed.

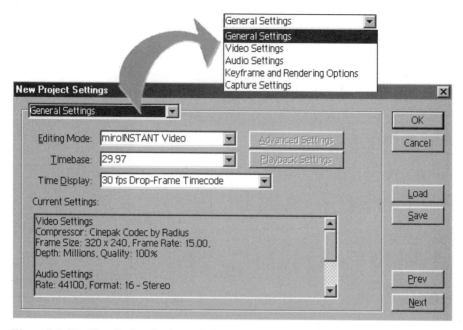

Figure 1-1 The New Project Settings window allows you to customize the overall setup of your project.

The settings you set in the Project Settings Window affect how your video appears inside Premiere and when you output to tape directly from the timeline. There are additional quality settings if you export your movie as a digital computer file.

The next options work somewhat hand-in-hand. The Time Base option sets the time position of the timeline or sequence of edits. The Time Display determines the frame rate at which you will play your movie. The standard frame rate for video in America is approximately 30 frames per second (fps). That means that if we broke up your video clip into still frames, you would get 30 individual frames for each second of video that goes by. Displaying this many images per second is what gives the illusion of movement, bringing your image to life.

American video standards, known as NTSC, runs at 30 fps. Film runs at 24 fps. Most European countries use a system called PAL, which runs at 25 fps. If you intend to distribute video tapes in other countries, check to see each country's standard format.

The next aspect to consider is whether or not you're working in drop frame or non-drop frame. This becomes relevant for those of you editing projects for broadcast television. Without going into too much detail, video actually runs at a rate of 29.97 frames per second. Therefore, with longer format broadcast television, a video clip playing at 30 frames per second would actually run longer over time because of the extra small percentage of time. To accurately allow producers to calculate exact time durations of clips for broadcasts, drop frame actually "drops" a calculated frame over the course of a specific amount of time.

VIDEO SETTINGS

The next selection in the top drop-down menu is Video Settings. Here some different parameters appear. Click on the Compressor drop-down menu to display the various choices (Figure 1-2). This is the real heart and soul that will determine the quality of your video clips. Each of these compression selections uses its own compression algorhythms to maximize the amount of hard drive space it takes to capture and play your clips. These compression formulas are known as codecs, which stands for compressor/decompressor. Which compression formats and how well they perform will depend on a number of things. The main aspect is the speed of your hard drive. In other words, can your hard drive spit out the data fast enough in order to play back the video

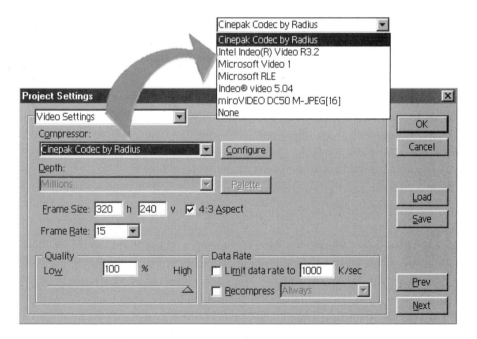

Figure 1-2 Premiere includes a variety of video compression formats.

stream? Most computers are not equipped to reproduce full-screen, full-motion video. The amount of data it would take to continuously display a full screen image, 30 of them every second, would just get bottlenecked and cause the video to play back at a slower rate, skip frames, lose sync, or even cause your system to crash. These files would be too large for the computer's throughput. I will discuss compression formats in more detail in the Chapter 10, Outputting Your Work.

Throughput is the computer's ability to output a specific amount of data in a given time. The higher the overall system's throughput (bus speed, memory, etc.) the better quality video you will be able to play back (more frames per second, fewer artifacts, larger window size).

You can also click on the Next and Previous buttons to cycle between the setting windows.

The compression format you select will determine whether or not you have access to Depth option (color palette). Microsoft Video 1 and None will give you the chance to select the palette bit depth. The more colors, or high bit depth, the more accurately the computer can capture them. You have probably seen a low bit-depth image. The colors are generally not the exact match and similar colors are usually blurred together. Selecting an 8-bit, or 256-color depth rate would be ideal for reducing the file size if you are editing strictly for distribution on the web. If you are outputting to tape, try to use the highest bit depth rate available to maximize image quality.

Next you must select the size of your video clips. This will determine the Frame Size (size of the screen) by number of pixels (Figure 1-3). {show clip height and width dimensions} Make sure the check box marked Aspect 4:3 is highlighted. This keeps the video clip you are digitizing in the proper viewing aspect ratio. With this option selected, whatever value you enter in the first field, Premiere will automatically calculate the proper value in the second field.

Once again, the compression format you selected in the previous step will determine if the Quality and Data Rate options are available. The higher the Quality setting and the Data Rate, the better quality image you will get. Well, if that's the case, whyever use a lower setting? For one thing, higher quality images require more data to be recorded about the clip. This means filling up hard drive space very quickly. However, unless you have unlimited amounts of hard drive space, long format video projects are going to require a great deal of hard drive space. The other factor is throughput. If your computer is not capable of outputting large streams of information continuously, your video output will most likely get bottlenecked. This will either cause the playback to skip frames, slow down the playback rate, or even freeze up completely. If you are outputting to tape, I recommend using the highest bit-depth rate available to maximize image quality.

Figure 1-3 Enter the desired Frame Size (in number of pixels).

Many people (including myself) usually get confused between Time Base Option and Time Display Option the first time you use Premiere. Simply put, Time Base Option is the output frames per second, whereas Time Display Option is the preview/editing display frames per second within Premiere.

The best way to achieve maximum quality is to run a few tests on your system. Digitize a few clips at different quality settings and rates and see how they each play back. If they all look fine, then you know your system is capable of handling the highest quality video settings.

AUDIO SETTINGS

The next screen allows you to select the Audio Settings. Just like video, the higher you set the audio rate, the better quality audio sample you'll capture. (Figure 1-4). What this setting means is that at 44 kHz, the computer is capturing 44,000 samples of the incoming audio source per second. Compare that to 11 kHz capturing 11,000 samples per second. The more samples per second mean a more accurate reproduction of the original sound file.

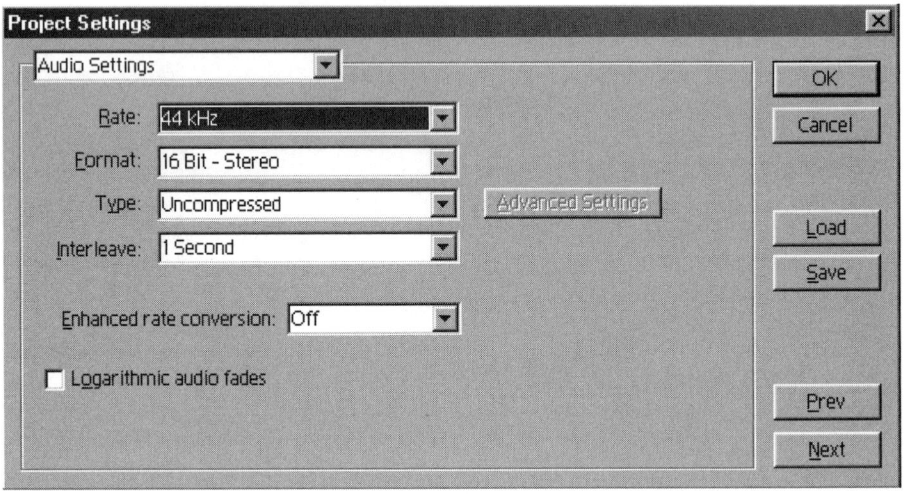

Figure 1-4 The Audio Settings window.

The computer will capture up to the same quality only as your original source material. If your source audio is coming from a third generation mono audiocassette being played on a small boom box, your initial audio file is not going to come out sounding like the New York Philharmonic Symphony. Remember a simple rule: Garbage in, garbage out.

If you are not sure of the projects file output or whether it's going to be used for more than one application, capture the audio at the highest quality. You can resample the audio to a lower quality (for output on a CD-ROM or Web site), but you cannot resample to a higher quality. Audio files take up much less space than video files. Therefore you can store long lengths of high quality audio without taking up much hard drive space.

The next option is the Format setting. Just like video, the higher the bit rate, the better the quality. The better the quality, the more hard drive space it takes up. Capturing your files in stereo allows you to play back the audio files with their natural pan settings. It is almost impossible to separate individual elements recorded with a mono signal. Mono signals mix both the left and right tracks together to form one complete mix.

Keeping elements as separated as possible allows you to have more control over their individual settings and characteristics (changing their volume, pan setting, or even applying effects).

Depending upon the final output of your project, you most likely want to work without any compression on your audio. If you are producing a project for CD-ROM or the web, you may want to consider using one of the audio codecs to reduce the overall size of your audio file.

The interleave setting determines how often Premiere needs to read the audio information for playback. A one-second interval means that every second Premiere reads that particular frames set of audio data. This may bog down your system and cause it to play back at a slower speed or break up. By increasing the interleave value, the computer will load longer lengths of data and play it back from the systems memory. This, however, requires more RAM. The Enhance Rate Conversion setting determines the resampling rate versus quality issue. Set to Off, Premiere is able to resample audio very quickly yet can sacrifice quality. The Better setting tries to accommodate both resampling time and quality, finding a compromise somewhere down the middle of the road. The Best setting focuses on producing the highest quality resampled audio, but it takes the longest amount of time to do its work.

The Logarithmic Audio Fades check box is more a matter for your ear. This setting determines how audio fades sound during playback. Selecting this option gives the audio fades a more natural sound, whereas deselecting this option produces very linear fades. But like all things that are better, it does take more processing time to calculate the natural audio fades. I think this one is worth waiting for.

KEY FRAME AND RENDER OPTIONS

The first three options are self-explanatory. These check boxes shut off the audio filters, video filters, and audio rubber banding during playback of your timeline (Figure 1-5). This allows you to play back your edited timeline without those filters or effects and without having to go in and remove them from your project. The actual filters still remain in your timeline but are not processed during playback of your movie.

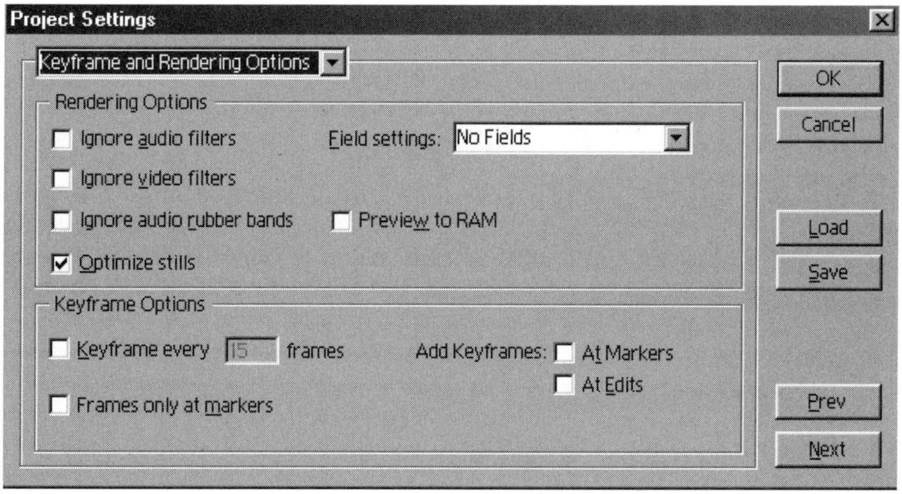

Figure 1-5 The Keyframe and render Options window.

Optimizing Stills is a process that I am not a big fan of. This option allows Premiere to use one long clip of a still image instead of reproducing multiple frames of that same clip over and over for the duration of the still clip. Field settings are going to apply to the type of display hardware you are using to show your final movie. As with most things, test to see which setting works for the applications you are using. If you are previewing your clips on a computer monitor, keep the No Fields as your default setting. If you are displaying your clips on a television monitor, you may need to switch over to one of the field settings (either Upper or Lower).

SAVING PROJECT SETTINGS

Back in the old days of analog video editing, an editor, producer, or lowly intern had to manually set and write down all of the settings and adjustments made for each and every project. Fortunately, we live in a digital age where computers remember everything for us. This holds true with the project settings in Premiere. You can go in and customize your settings and then save them. This allows you to rapidly recall the settings used for a particular project or apply saved-templated settings you created for various applications. This saves you the time of having to go through all of these options every time you begin to work on a project. For example, you may choose to create a setting for outputting a project to videotape. This setting may have the various parameters set for reproducing the highest quality. You may also create a setting for maximizing content for the web. To save a project's settings:

❶ Customize all the parameters throughout the Project Settings Window.

❷ Enter a name for these settings in the Save Project Settings Window (Figure 1-6).

❸ Option: Enter a description to help identify what type of project these settings would work best.

❹ Click OK.

To recall a previously saved project settings group:

❶ Open the New Projects Setting Window.

❷ Click the Load button.

❸ Select from one of the default or customized settings you created (if applicable) from the Load Project Settings window (Figure 1-7).

❹ Click OK.

You can also choose to delete a setting from this window by simply highlighting the setting name and clicking the Delete button. A prompt will appear reaffirming that you want to permanently delete the selected setting.

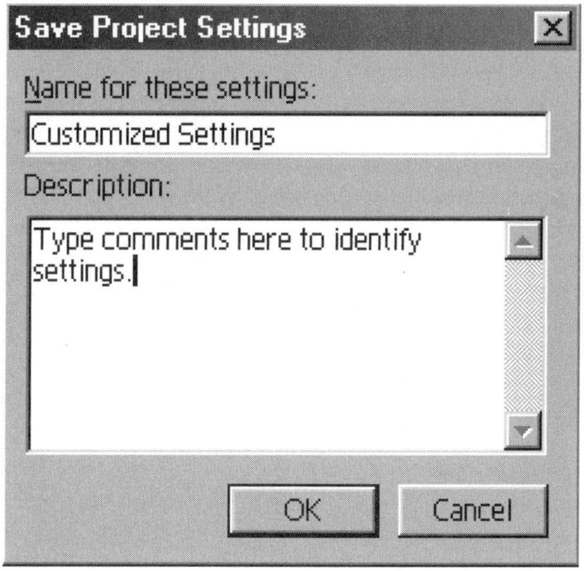

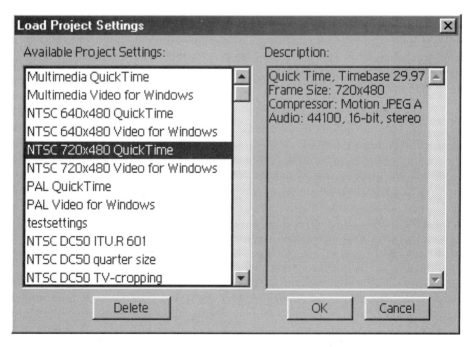

Figure 1-6 The Save Project Settings Window allows you to save your customized settings to use for other projects.

Figure 1-7 The Load Project Settings Window contains your customized and standard default project settings.

SAVE, SAVE, AND RE-SAVE

Here's the first main point I want to drill into you when working on any project. It will probably be the last thing I remind you of as well. It is so important and too many editors ignore it until it's too late. Let's face it, when you're on a roll, the last thing you want to think about is breaking the rhythm you're in to save your project. What could be worse than editing a masterpiece all day long and just as you're about to output your project...CRASH. Your system locks up. The only thing you can do is reboot. You guessed right. You've lost everything—all because you didn't save your work.

I cannot stress enough to periodically save your work. The best times are when you are at some sort of resting point, after editing a complicated section, before you make any changes, or before you set out to render your entire timeline. These, of course, are only a few examples. Save as often as you feel comfortable. To save your project:

❶ Select Save from the File menu.

❷ Type in a name for the project. Windows users should include the .ppj extension after the file name (i.e., TestMovie.ppj).

❸ Select the location where you want to save the file.

SAFEGUARD YOURSELF WITH AUTO SAVE AND ARCHIVES

For those of you like me who like to work at warp speed, getting as many edits done as fast as possible, this next tip is for you. Thanks to Premiere's Auto Save feature, now you can blaze ahead without the fear of losing too many edits if you unexpectedly quit out of the program. You can set Premiere to automatically interrupt you for a brief moment and force a Save Your Project. You can control the interval at which Premiere auto saves your work. You can also set whether Premiere saves your project to the existing file and location or saves it as a new archive. Archived files are automatically saved in the Project-Archives folder inside the main Premiere folder. To set up the Auto Save feature:

❶ Select Preferences from the File menu.

❷ Select Auto Save/Undo from the pop-up menu.

❸ In the Preference window, make sure the Automatically Save Project option is selected (Figure 1-8).

❹ Enter the numeric value in minutes for when you want Premiere to perform the auto save.

To set the number of archived files of a given project:

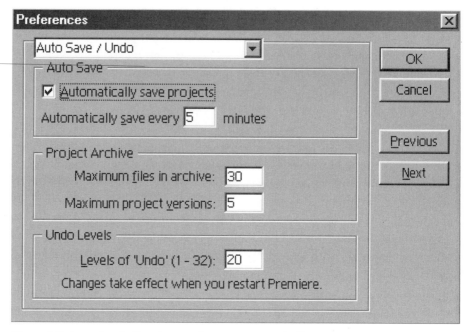

Figure 1-8 An option in Premiere can be set to automatically save your work at whatever time interval you select.

❶ In the Preference window, enter the maximum number of files you want archived in the Project Archive field.

❷ Enter the number of maximum project versions in the respective field.

❸ Click OK.

CREATING A BIN

This is where you begin to map out your project. Think of bins as the storage area where you are grouping your files. They are used to organize your media into whichever categories you desire. The clips and files you see in Premiere's project window and bins are only reference icons for the media clips. These icons do not contain the actual media but are the tools used to retain all of the source's information and location in order to display the image or play the audio when called upon. You can create as many bins as you need to organize your project. You can even create bins inside of bins. To create a bin:

❶ Click on the Project Window (or an existing bin) to select it.

❷ Select Create from the Project menu.

❸ Select Bin from the submenu.

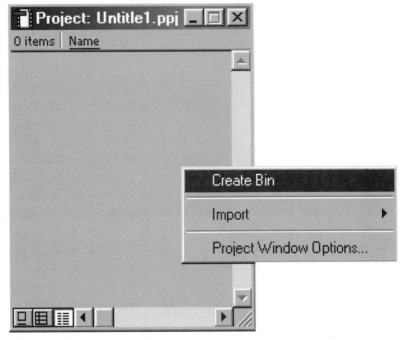

Figure 1-9 Quickly and easily create Bins in the Project Window.

❹ Enter a name for the bin in the Create Bin window that appears.

❺ Click OK.

Or

❶ Click on the Project Window (or an existing bin) to select it.

❷ Right click (Windows) or Option click (Macintosh) to open an options menu (Figure 1-9).

❸ Enter a name for the bin in the Create Bin window that appears.

❹ Click OK.

CREATE A UNIQUE NAMING STRUCTURE

The quickest way to waste time and mess up a project is to be lazy about naming your files within the project. Properly naming each and every file, bin, title, etc. is crucial for locating the right clip easily and accurately. Here are some suggestions that make organizing and editing a breeze:

◆ Do not name your clips:

Shot 1

Shot 2

Shot 3

◆ Instead, be descriptive:

Motorcycle driving into sunset

Overhead shot of horses running

Pan shot across bridge

◆ Use a shorthand method for labeling shots:

Close Up = CU

Extreme Close Up = ECU

Wide Shot = WS

(This will help group similar shots and offer a better description of the shot without lengthy titles).

◆ Create a bin and name it for every type of file you'll be working with (Graphics, Titles, Audio, Video, Sequences, Animations, etc.) (Figure 1-10).

◆ Create a bin and name it for each tape that is used. Therefore, if you shot three tapes of original source footage, create three bins within the Video Bin named for each source tape.

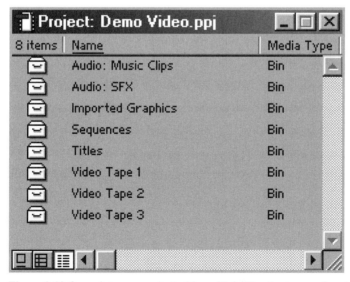

Figure 1-10 Organize your project with multiple Bins to store and sort your source material.

Make sure that the name you give a source tape bin appears on the actual tape itself for easily identifying which tape has which clips. Use a grease pencil or permanent marker to identify each tape. This will be important to quickly identify a tape when Batch Digitizing footage for your project or needing additional footage from that same tape (Figure 1-11).

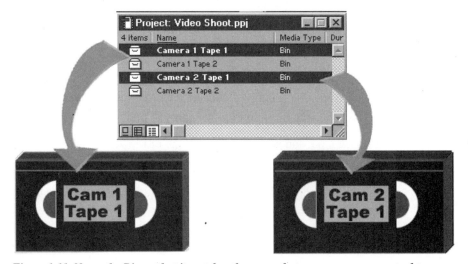

Figure 1-11 Name the Bin so that it matches the name that appears on your actual tapes.

IT'S MORE THAN JUST A NAME

One thing that many editors do not take full advantage of is all the useful information that is contained within each clip. The Bin Window Options allow you to customize the information that appears in each bin (Figure 1-12). You can select from the various options to display any or all of these statistics in the text view of your bin. (Figure 1-13). These statistics make identifying and sorting each clip very helpful. Some statistics that can really save you time while working on a project include:

◆ View timecode information to identify similarly named clips.

◆ Check the duration of a clip.

◆ Check the file size and other characteristics.

◆ Enter comments about each clip.

◆ Check the number of times a clip has been used in your sequence.

◆ Display file location (path) on the storage device.

◆ Display the source tape or reel name.

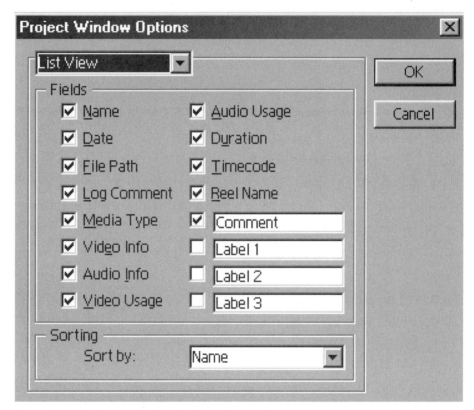

Figure 1-12 The Project Window Options window allows you to customize the Project and Bin information that is displayed.

2 items	Name	Media Type	Duration	Video Info	Audio Info
	CU_product.mov	Movie	00:04:25	320 × 24..	22Khz – 8 Bit – Mono
	WideAngle.mov	Movie	00:13:10	320 × 240	22Khz – 8 Bit – Mono

Figure 1-13 The Project and Bin windows display the information that you select in the Project (Bin) Window Options window.

To open the Project or Bin Window Options window:

❶ Select the Project window or desired Bin window.

❷ Select Project Window Options (or Bin Window Options) from the Window menu.

Or

Right click (Windows) or Option-click (Macintosh) the desired window to display a pop-up menu. Select Project Window Options (or Bin Window Options).

If you are working inside the Project window, the display choice will read Project Window Options. If you have a Bin window open, the display choice will read Bin Window Options. These windows contain the same information.

You can use this information to pinpoint the exact shot you are looking for while editing a project. You can click on the heading of each column to change the priority of the particular column from top to bottom. You can even change the order of the columns and the way they appear. To rearrange the order for grouping your own customized layout:

❶ Make sure you are viewing your clips in the bin in List View.

❷ Click and hold the mouse button on the column you wish to move. The cursor should change to a closed hand icon.

❸ Release the mouse button once you have positioned the heading where you would like it.

You can also sort the clips by each of the different statistical options:

❶ Click on the bin to select it.

❷ Select Bin Window Options from the Window menu or Right click (Windows) or Option-Click (Macintosh) on the bin and select Bin Window Options from the pop-up menu.

❸ Select the category you want to sort in the Sort By pop-up menu (Figure 1-14).

The Thumbnail View only allows information of comments and labels, whereas the Icon View does not allow for any information at all.

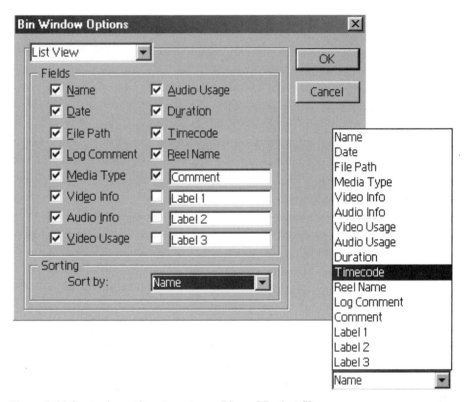

Figure 1-14 Customize settings to sort your Bin and Project files.

SEARCHING THROUGH THE STATS

Think of the List Bin statistics options as a large and useful database resource. What this means is that now you can use it to search and sift through all the clips to find your specific shot. That is why it is so important to properly label each clip that you digitize or import. To use the search feature capabilities:

❶ Click on a bin to select it.

❷ Right click (Windows) or Option-click (Macintosh) on the bin and select Search from the pop-up menu. The Project/Library Search window appears (Figure 1-15).

❸ Select which category heading you want to search through in the first Find entry field.

❹ Select whether you are searching for whether the information is or is not contained in the search.

❺ In the last field, enter the name or description of the clip you are looking for.

❻ You can narrow the search even more by entering information in both of the category heading fields.

❼ Click Find to begin the search.

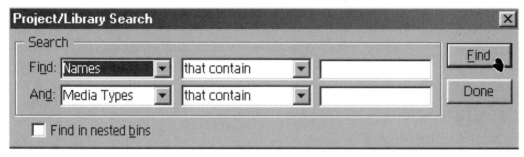

Figure 1-15 The Project/Library Search Window allows you to perform customized searches based on various criteria.

 Be sure to select Find In Nested Bins. This option allows Premiere to search into bins that have been created and stored in other bins (Figure 1-16).

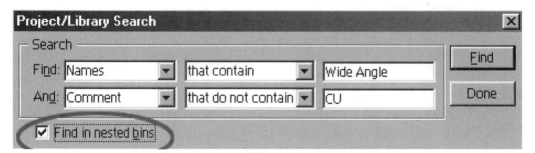

Figure 1-16 The Find In Nested Bins searches bins that are located inside or are a subset of other bins.

SO WHERE ARE THESE FILES KEPT ANYWAY?

The best advice I can give you when starting a project in Premiere is to be neat and organized. Once you save and name these files, you will have a much easier time locating the correct files. But where do they actually live? You should start off by creating a general project folder to keep the contents of the entire project (or as much as possible) in one area. You might do this for every unique storage drive you'll be using during the project. Here are a few ideas to stay organized:

◆ Create a folder on your internal hard drive for all of your project settings and related files for that specific project.

◆ Create a general folder on your media disks to keep all of your digitized audio, video, and graphic clips. Use a naming structure that is easily identifiable (i.e., "ProjectName_MediaFiles") (Figure 1-17).

◆ Inside your general media folder for each project, create subfolders to organize the various media categories (Figure 1-18).

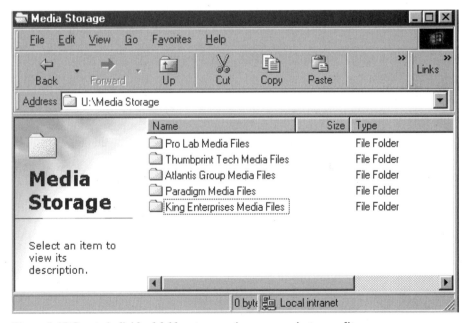

Figure 1-17 Create individual folders to organize every project you edit.

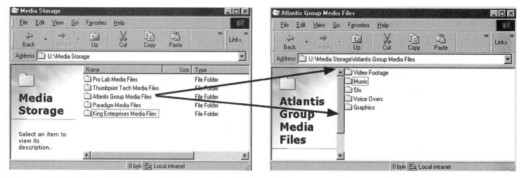

Figure 1-18 Create sub-folders within a project folder to better sort various media types.

ARCHIVING PROJECT FILES AND RELATED MEDIA

You might be expecting this to be in the last chapter. However, properly backing up your work is something that needs to be considered from the very beginning and utilized throughout every stage of your project. One of the great advantages of computer-based nonlinear editing systems is the ability to pick up and return to a project at any point with the computer remembering everything for you. Whether it's two days or two months, all of your settings are there where you last left off. This is very useful because many times clients need to make changes to a project or make an altered version of a previous version several months later. The problem occurs if you need the hard drive space to work on other projects or if your computer crashes and deletes the necessary files. What's an editor to do? To prevent this situation from happening, every night or at the end of a project, back up all of your files related to a project, including the media files. Restoring a project from a single archived tape is much better than trying to recreate the project from scratch (believe me, I've learned from my mistakes). The following are the items you need to back up your projects:

◆ DAT drive or DLT drive (Jaz drive optional for small projects)

◆ Properly formatted media tapes or disks (DAT, DLT, etc.)

◆ Archiving Software (ArcServe, Backup Exec, Mezzo, Retrospect)

◆ SCSI cable

Any time you are connecting SCSI devices, be sure that the SCSI ID Numbers are unique. Duplicate SCSI ID Numbers will cause one or more of those devices not to function properly.

DELETING FILES

This one is self-explanatory. Throughout the course of every project, you will need to delete files from your project. To delete a clip, bin, or library from a project:

❶ Select the item you wish to delete.

❷ Hit the Delete key.

> **As with most computer-based editing systems, Premiere's clips work as reference points to the original media. Therefore, deleting a clip in the project window does not remove the media from the hard drive.**

To permanently remove digitized or imported media (source files) stored on a hard drive:

❶ From the Desktop level, select the hard drive containing the media or files you wish to delete.

❷ Open the folder you created that contains the project's media files.

❸ Select the individual files you wish to delete.

❹ Hit the delete key.

GETTING RID OF UNWANTED SOURCE FOOTAGE

Many times when we digitize media on the fly (hitting Record while the source media is playing, not being controlled by specific in- and out-points), the result is usually unwanted media before and after the desired portion. Because video especially takes up tremendous amounts of hard drive space, you are probably going to want to delete the unnecessary footage surrounding your clip. Besides running out of hard drive space faster, having a great deal of excess footage will also become a problem when it comes time to back up your project for archiving and storing on the shelf. Keeping that unwanted footage for every clip may cause you to need extra back-up storage tapes (usually DAT or DLT tapes), which can get expensive.

> **Always leave some room on each side of the portion of the clip you are using. These "handles" may come in very handy if you need to trim the clip or add a transition.**

Premiere automatically makes a duplicate of your project when you select to trim a project. Each in- and out-point becomes the starting and ending point for those clips, removing the unwanted portions before the set-in point and after the set-out point. You can choose to keep handles for each clip. Handles are the extra amount of footage (already digitized) you choose to keep before a given in-point and after the out point on each clip used in your project. Any clips that were not used in your project are not copied to the new duplicate version of your project.

 Premiere copies only clips used in the project's sequence. It does not bring over any clips not used in the sequence, even if they have in- and out-marks.

To remove unwanted source footage:

❶ Make sure the project you want to trim is currently open.

❷ Select Utilities from the File menu.

❸ Select Project Trimmer from the pop-up window.

❹ Select Create Trimmed Batch List from the Project Trimmer window (Figure 1-19). This can be used for redigitizing timecoded source material at a later time.

❺ Select Copy Trimmed Source Files. This creates new copies of the source material from the marked clips plus their given handle.

❻ Enter a numeric value for the number of frames you want to keep as the handles for each marked clip.

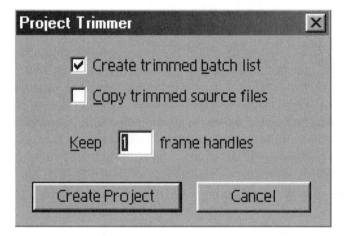

Figure 1-19 The Project Trimmer window allows you to save only the portions of your source materials used in your timelines plus any desired handles.

If you're working in NTSC formats (used by American television standards), there are 30 frames per second. Therefore, if you want to save 2-second handles on each side of your marked clips, enter the value of 60 in this field. PAL formats work on 25 frames per second.

❼ Click Create Project.

Remember to save your original project before trying to create a trimmed version. If you did not, an error message will appear prompting you to save the original project first (Figure 1-20).

❽ Type and name the new version and select a destination. It cannot be saved in the same location as the original file.

❾ Click OK.

❿ Type in a name and a destination for the Batch List file.

⓫ Click OK.

Once your material has been copied and checked, you can delete the original project and its related media. I highly recommend doing this for the first time with a test project, just to make sure you are comfortable with the procedure.

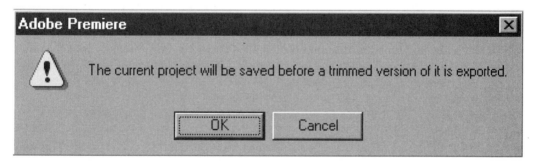

Figure 1-20 Message window indicating that you must save your project before creating a trimmed version.

CREATING A CROSS-PLATFORM MOVIE

Which platform should you start working on? Macintosh? Windows? Fortunately, Premiere is inherently a cross-platform format. This means that you can move your raw Premiere movie between different platforms, as long as there is a version of Premiere available for that given platform. That means that you can take a Premiere 5.1 movie project started on a Windows platform, move it over, and finish it on a Macintosh. There are a few points to keep in mind:

◆ Make sure that file formats are cross-platform compatible (.AVI video clips may not play on a Macintosh, depending upon which version of QuickTime you are running).

◆ Any fonts used must have a cross-platform equivalent (Helvetica on the Macintosh correlates with Arial on a Windows Platform).

◆ Most of Premiere's file settings can be transferred between platforms, except Filter Factory and Transition Factor settings (.PFF), command sets (.PFN), transition sets (.PFX), convolution kernel settings (.CVL), and Level filter settings (.LVL).

◆ Files must be compliant with each platform file-naming structure (number of characters and spaces allowed in a file name).

To avoid cross-platform naming incompatibilities, I recommend using a traditional 8.3 naming structure. This means limit the name of your file to eight letters with a three-letter file type extension.

SUMMARY

This chapter is one of the most critical. You need to understand all of the settings and how they affect one another in order to get the desired end result you're looking for. You can live without special effects and titles. You may be editing for personal use, so audio sweetening is not necessary. But if you want your footage to look good on a video tape, you need to understand what it takes to get it there. Don't let the technical jargon scare you. Play around and make a few tests for yourself. See what results you get from the different settings. Once you get what you want, you're all set.

chapter 2

SOURCE MATERIAL: GETTING IT INTO PREMIERE

T his is where it all begins. If you cannot get your audio, video, and other source material into Premiere, it's going to be an awfully quick edit session. You can pack up and go home now. This chapter is going to make sure that this scenario doesn't happen to you. Bringing source material into Premiere is fairly easy. There are several different ways to start getting your source materials into the system. It just depends on what type of media your source material is on and what type of hardware you have in your system. I'm going to go into some detail covering the most common ways that editors get their source material into Premiere.

COPYRIGHT ISSUES: DON'T BREAK THE LAW

Gathering source footage is essential for starting a video (or audio) editing session, but you need to be careful with what you use. Copyrighted material (whether from television broadcasts or some other person's property) cannot be used freely. I do not recommend trying to use any copyrighted material unless you get express written consent from the licensing agency that owns or has rights to the footage. To avoid any headaches, the best solution is to just produce your own footage. Grab a camera and shoot what you need. If you do not have the means to get the scenes you're looking for, there are many companies that lease stock footage.

ONLINE VS. OFFLINE

With the transition from linear tape-to-tape editing studios to computer-based nonlinear editing systems, editors just coming into the industry are somewhat unfamiliar with the terms Online and Offline editing. Improvements in the quality of video captured, edited, and output from a computer, along with prices continuously falling on equipment, have made it possible for more people to be in control and perform their own online editing sessions (finishing your project on the same computer you do your offline edit). Premiere is one of these programs capable of being integrated into a consumer editing system for home movies or powerful enough to be used in professional environments (Figure 2-1).

Online editing studios were generally filled with millions of dollars worth of professional tape deck, switchers, edit controllers, and special effects generators. The cost to put a system like this together and the time and knowledge to get the setup working properly were enormous. Therefore, studio owners needed to charge high prices to rent out a room like this for the day in order to recoup some of their investment. The only way to allow people to edit videos yet not sell off their first born was to configure

Figure 2-1 Premiere is being used in today's top professional nonlinear edit studios.

lower-priced equipment setups that offered a chance to create a rough version of their project with minimal features. This is what is referred to as offline editing, where you save time and money rough-cutting a project and then finish it at an online studio. Generally with offline editing, you are not editing your final master at the highest quality with all of the finishing touches added to the project.

With the advent of computer-based editing, producers and editors began using these applications to edit their movies. The one major problem was the quality of the video. The systems were not capable of capturing and playing back high quality video at full screen, full motion. This resulted in footage that was very pixilated (Figure 2-2). The video sources had to be compressed (using various Codecs) in order to play back the footage. Today, drastic changes in technology allow producers to edit their final versions directly on a computer, providing the same (if not better) quality and features that were offered in those pricey studios.

Codec stands for Compression / Decompression. Codecs, such as Cinepak and MPEG, are small engine-like applications that mathematically reduce the file size of your source footage. One drawback is that the image quality is generally reduced as well.

The methodology has changed to some degree. Now people generally associate the difference with online and offline editing simply to which resolution you are using when digitizing your source footage. Low resolutions are equated to offline editing, while working with high resolutions are used for finishing your online mix. The advantage to editing a project at low resolution first is that you are not filling up your hard drives with high quality source footage that may not be used in your final edit. The ideal editing situation, if you have time-coded source material and remote edit control of your decks (not available on consumer decks), is to digitize your source material at low resolution, rough-cut your sequence, and finally redigitize only the portions of the clips used in your sequence at high resolution.

MAKING SENSE OF RESOLUTION, COMPRESSION, AND QUALITY

There are several factors that determine the quality of your final image when you output from Premiere. The settings you select during the digitizing process are the overall deciding factors. The controls you have available on your system partially depend on the type of video and audio capture card installed in your computer. These controls are usually designed to be integrated within Premiere (since many video capture cards come bundled with a copy of Premiere). Your video capture card may offer some of the following control features found on my Pinnacle miroVIDEO DC-50 board (or others not present in this list):

1:1 (Uncompressed)

4:1 Compression

50:1 Compression

Figure 2-2 Low-quality, highly compressed video shows a great deal of pixilation.

◆ The main Video for Windows Capture Options window allows you to select additional settings such as Video Format, Video Input, Video Display, and Compression (Figure 2-3).

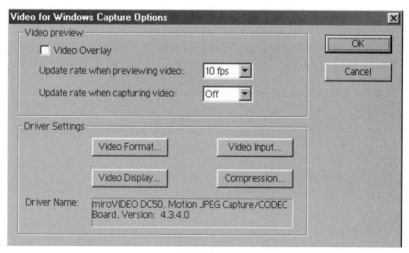

Figure 2-3 Each Manufacturer of Capture Cards offers slightly different ways for accessing input controls.

◆ The Video Format window allows you to set the Capture resolution (frame size and pixel type) along with overall quality settings (Compression ratios and Data Rates) (Figure 2-4).

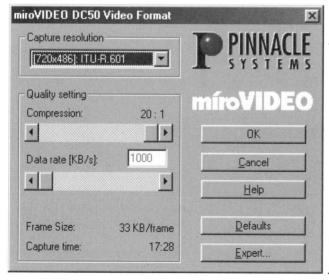

Figure 2-4 The DC-50's Video Format window sets the overall look and feel for incoming footage.

◆   The Video Input window is where you determine which input connection is being used to capture the video signal (Composite, Component, S-Video, etc.) and their format standard (NTSC is the one used in the United States). You also have controls to adjust the signal's brightness, contrast, saturation, sharpness, and hue (Figure 2-5).

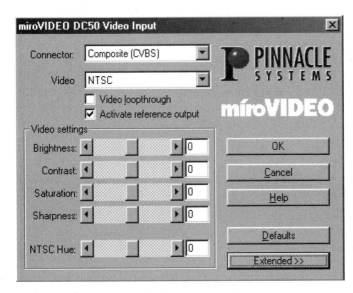

Figure 2-5 Different Capture Cards allow you to choose between different input connections.

◆   Each Input type may have some advanced settings. These controls greatly affect the way the image looks as it is being captured into your system (Figure 2-6).

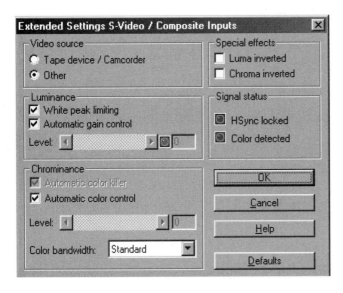

Figure 2-6 High-quality clips are a result of low compression ratios (2:1) and higher data rates. Low-quality images result from the opposite settings.

◆ High-quality capture boards should have an area to test the performance of your system. This screen shows a great deal of useful information, helping determine if your system can achieve the quality and quantity of source material. The test results should indicate the amount of free hard disk space, speed at which it can read and write files, and an overview of the other settings checked that will determine the input and playback capabilities of your system (Figure 2-7).

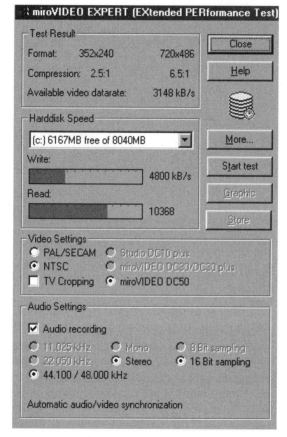

Figure 2-7 Testing the capabilities of your system.

If you do not see a signal coming into your Capture Monitor, check the video input selection to make sure you are reading from the right connection. Think of this as a mini patch bay, so you can minimize the amount of times you have to physically switch wires and connectors.

The greater the amount of compression, the lower the quality of the image will be once digitized. Therefore, an image compressed at 50:1 is going to produce a very pixilated, low-quality image (Figure 2-8). The file size, however, is relatively small due to the amount of compression. This amount of compression would be used if you were trying to edit a rough cut, focusing on conserving hard drive space. If you are working with time-coded material and have control over your source decks through Premiere, you can go back and redigitize the portions of the clips used in your timeline at a lower compression ration (higher quality image). Using a compression ratio of 2:1 is going to produce a very clean, high-quality image (Figure 2-9). Because the computer is barely compressing the footage and actually recording the fine details of the image, the file size is going to increase astronomically. These high-quality, low-compression images are usually used as you are finishing resolutions for online quality.

Uncompressed video files (1:1) have absolutely no compression applied to their file. The image quality is superb but requires an extremely high-end computer system to store and play back files of that caliber.

To learn more about codecs and compression formats, check out two Web sites, CodecCentral.com and Terran.com. Each site offers valuable information about codecs and other compression technologies available for digital media.

DIGITAL MEDIA
VS. ANALOG MEDIA

Depending on the equipment used for capturing source material, you may find yourself working with different types of media during your project. There are two general types of media that you can use as your source material: digital and analog.

Digital media is created and saved as a digital file format that can be read by your computer. You can transfer your audio and video information the same way you transfer the data of a text document on some type of disk, As you shoot using a digital camera, the information is stored as a complex series of ones and zeros (digital information). This digital file format can be transferred to your computer and read by Premiere. Analog media cannot be read by your computer and must be digitized into the system (which then creates a digital file format that your computer can understand). Your computer must have a capture card in order to get analog audio or video into Premiere.

One advantage of digital media is that there is no loss of quality when making copies of copies. The fact that you are just transferring file information means that the quality should remain the same from the first copy to the last. Analog signals lose quality when transferring over several generations.

Figure 2-8 A Highly compressed, low-resolution image.

Figure 2-9 A minimally compressed, high-quality image.

TYPES OF FORMATS

The following is a brief list of analog audio and video formats:

◆ Beta SP

◆ Hi-8

◆ 3⁄4"

◆ SVHS

◆ VHS

◆ Audio Cassette

The following is a brief list of digital audio and video formats:

◆ DigiBeta
◆ DVC Pro
◆ Mini DV
◆ Digital-8
◆ DAT
◆ Compact Disc

 You can also digitize from any of the digital media formats listed above. The advantage to transferring the media is that it generally takes less time and provides a more accurate replica of the original source.

DIGITIZING AUDIO AND VIDEO (WITHOUT DECK CONTROL)

Once you have set the general properties of your project (see Chapter 1), it's time to start bringing in your source material into Premiere. If your system does not have playback control of your source deck, you can manually control your deck and watch the video source footage in a small Movie Capture window once you select the Movie Capture feature. The following procedure is a basic overview of the process for setting up your system for digitizing media without source deck control:

❶ Connect your source deck to your capture card. See the setup instructions for your particular capture card or other related hardware for more details on properly connecting audio and video equipment to your system.

❷ Open the Project Settings window (Figure 2-10).

❸ Select the desired Capture Format. Depending upon your capture card installed, the capture formats available to you may vary.

❹ Select the Capture Video check box if you want to digitize the video source connected to your capture card. Deselect this box when digitizing just audio.

❺ Select the Capture Audio check box if you want to digitize the audio source connected to your capture card. Deselect this box when digitizing just video.

❻ Adjust the remaining settings to customize the properties of the video and audio files that you are digitizing into Premiere.

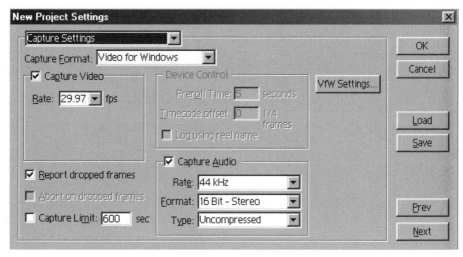

Figure 2-10 The Project Settings window.

❼ Select Capture from the File menu.

❽ Select Movie Capture from the pop-up menu.

❾ Use the controls on your source deck to play, rewind, fast-forward, or stop your tapes.

Always allow extra time for your tape sources and hard drives to get up to speed when capturing footage. If you start playing your source material right from the portion you want to capture, you may wind up missing the first few seconds of the clip while the system transfers into capture mode.

❿ Click the Record button in the Movie Capture window (Figure 2-11).

⓫ Click the mouse or press the Escape key to stop digitizing. Again, allow a few extra seconds after your desired outpoint. These handles may be beneficial for trimming and transitions.

⓬ With the Clip window selected, choose Save As from the file menu to specify the filename and location for this digitized media clip.

Depending on your capture hardware, settings may appear under various windows.

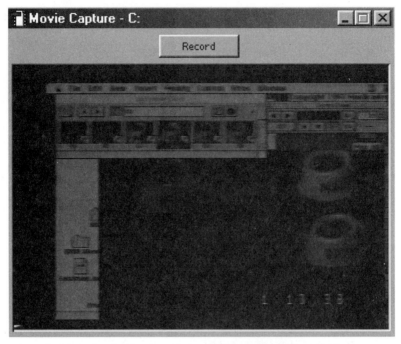

Figure 2-11 The Movie Capture window displays images being digitized.

CAPTURING AUDIO ONLY

Premiere is known for its professional digital video editing capabilities. But don't overlook its high-end nonlinear audio-editing capabilities either. Premiere provides a streamlined process for capturing audio by itself.

◆ To capture Audio Only on a Windows system, you need to digitize via the movie capture feature or use a separate audio capture application, such as Sound Forge or Microsoft Windows Sound Recorder. These applications will allow you to digitize and create wave files (.WAV). You must then import them into Premiere as a secondary step.

◆ To capture Audio Only on a Macintosh (as long as it has a/v inputs), you can capture audio directly from Premiere.

Audio Only clips are displayed in Premiere with a waveform icon (Figure 2-12). Premiere (Windows and Macintosh versions) can import many different types of digital audio files, including:

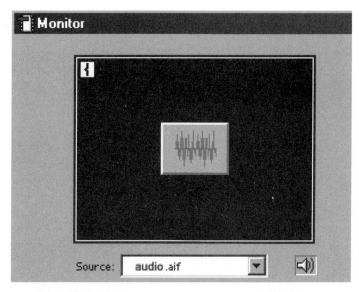

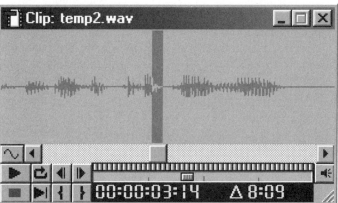

Figure 2-12 Audio clips are displayed with a waveform icon in Premiere.

♦ .AVI
♦ .MOV
♦ .AIFF
♦ .WAV

The Macintosh version can also import Sound Designer I and II file formats.

COMPARING AUDIO FILE SIZE TO QUALITY

It's somewhat impossible to gauge the exact file size of an audio clip, but there are a few ways to determine ways of reducing file size without jeopardizing too much in the way of quality.

It's important to understand how audio is captured. The quality of the audio is determined basically by the sample rate. With audio, digital audio (from DATs) is rated as the highest quality, recorded at 48kHz, or 48,000 samples per second. These samples are "snapshots" of the audio signal. The higher the number, the more detail about that source is being recorded. The lower the number, the longer the time intervals are when sampling your sound. This means that the computer basically fills in the intervals between samples, resulting in a less accurate representation of the original source signal.

A good way to describe what is taking place with the Sample Rate is to image a connect-the-dots-game (Figure 2-13). Notice the more accurate definition between points over the course of one second. The more samples that are taken, the better quality reproduction that signal will have. Where is the cutoff? Well, that depends on you. The lower the sample rate is, the smaller the file size. The higher the sample rate is, the better the quality sound file. Each project you produce will determine the individual specifications. I recommend to always capture at the highest sample rate (best quality). You can always scale it down (44kHz to 11.025khz), but you can never go in the reverse direction. Look at Chapter 10 to find out more about output options and signal qualities available through Premiere.

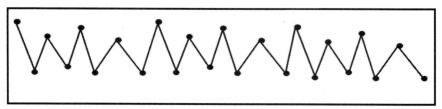

Exploded View of Audio Sample Rate 22.050 kHz

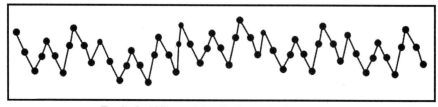

Exploded View of Audio Sample Rate 44.1 kHz

Figure 2-13 Sample Rate is similar to a connect-the-dots game. The higher the sample rate, the more accurate the detail it captures.

Other factors to be aware of when capturing audio are the Bit Depth settings and the Stereo settings. Bit Depth is the number of bits per sample. The two most common are 8-bit and 16-bit. Similar to sample rate, the higher the number, the better quality sound file you will have. You can also choose to digitize your audio in Mono or Stereo. Stereo tracks create a sense of perception and space. This is usually created by having two tracks (as opposed to one track in mono) and panning one track to the left speaker and one to the right speaker. You have more control over panning your sound tracks to the left, center, or right. Having separate tracks also offers more control over changing levels, pans, and other beneficial factors. Just like everything else in life, the better the quality, the larger the file size will be.

Unless free hard-drive space is absolutely at a minimum, always capture your audio at the highest quality. The highest quality audio files are still only a fraction of the file size of the same length video clip.

CAPTURING SOURCE MATERIAL (WITH DECK CONTROL)

There are so many advantages to working on a system when you can control your source deck from your computer through controls within Premiere. Among the benefits, the most important one is that you can now batch digitize your footage from an offline, low resolution to your finishing online, high resolution. This is assuming that most professional decks that offer remote control access also work with the ability to play and record timecode from your source tapes. Having deck control with timecoded source material also allows you to log your clips and digitize them all at once. Logging is the process of creating a list of tape names and marking in points (starting time codes) and out points (ending time codes). When you choose to actually digitize these clips, Premiere takes over, controlling your decks to find the desired In Points and digitizing the duration of the clips that you have previously selected. Another feature that comes with using remote controlled timecoded source material is an Edit Decision List, or EDL (See Chapter 10 for EDLs).

Premiere works with third-party plug-ins and hardware that allow you to control any professional tape deck with remote control capability.

There are several different types of remote control software and hardware applications on the market that work with Premiere. Many even come with the capture card you purchase. My miroVIDEO DC50 capture card by Pinnacle came with Pipeline Recorder, a plug-in application that allows you to control professional, remote controlled decks from Premiere.

To digitize audio and video from a remote controlled source deck:

❶ Select Preferences from the File menu.

❷ Select Scratch Disk/Device Control from the popup menu.

❸ Under Device Control, select the desired control option installed on your system from the pull down menu (Figure 2-14).

❹ Click OK.

❺ Select Capture from the File menu.

❻ Select Movie Capture from the pop-up menu.

❼ Enter in the name of the tape that is in your source deck. This will be used when identifying which tape a clip came from when batch digitizing your footage.

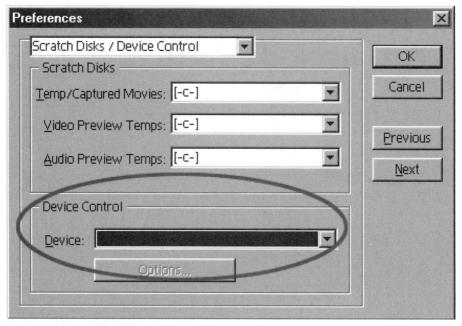

Figure 2-14 The Scratch Disk/Device Control window allows you to select the type of device control installed on your system.

Always clearly name each tape. Create a system to help you (or other editors working on your project) easily locate and identify any tape associated with a clip you digitized in Premiere. (Figure 2-15). This will make batch digitizing headache free.

Figure 2-15 Always enter a unique name for and clearly label each tape used in a project. Create your own naming structure if necessary.

⑧ Use the Control Interface to locate the In-Points and Out-Points of the clip you want to digitize.

⑨ Click Auto Record.

⑩ With the Clip window selected, choose Save As from the file menu to specify the filename and location for this digitized media clip.

It is important to save each clip after Premiere completes the capture process. Digitized clips exist as unsaved temporary files in the capture disk you have selected in your Preferences>Scratch Disk/Device Control window.

Premiere can then control the deck, find the desired starting position, and record the exact duration of the clip you marked. You will notice your deck rewind to a spot a few seconds before the marked In-Point of your clip. This allows the deck enough time to get up to speed in order for Premiere to accurately capture your clip.

LET THE COMPUTER WORK FOR YOU

In the last section we covered digitizing media from device-controlled decks. Therefore, if you have already done the basic leg work of digitizing the clips at a low resolution or have just logged the clips without any media associated with the files, let Premiere take control and batch digitize, or Batch Capture, your clips for you at high resolution. All you have to do is put in the correct tape when Premiere prompts you to insert the tape.

 Batch Capture digitizes media from the source tape names via device controlled decks. Premiere prompts you to insert one tape at a time. This is why I stressed the importance of properly naming and labeling your source footage tapes.

You can use the device control to view and mark your clips or enter the information in manually. This step is referred to as logging your clips or creating a Batch List (or Timecode List). To log your shots:

❶ Select Capture from the File menu.

❷ Select Batch Capture from the popup menu. The Batch Capture window should appear (Figure 2-16).

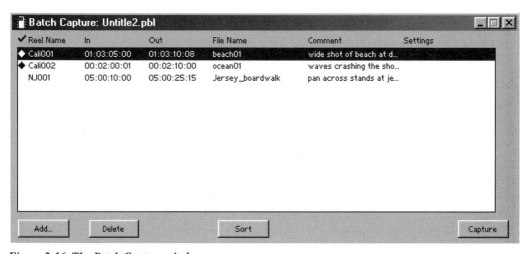

Figure 2-16 The Batch Capture window.

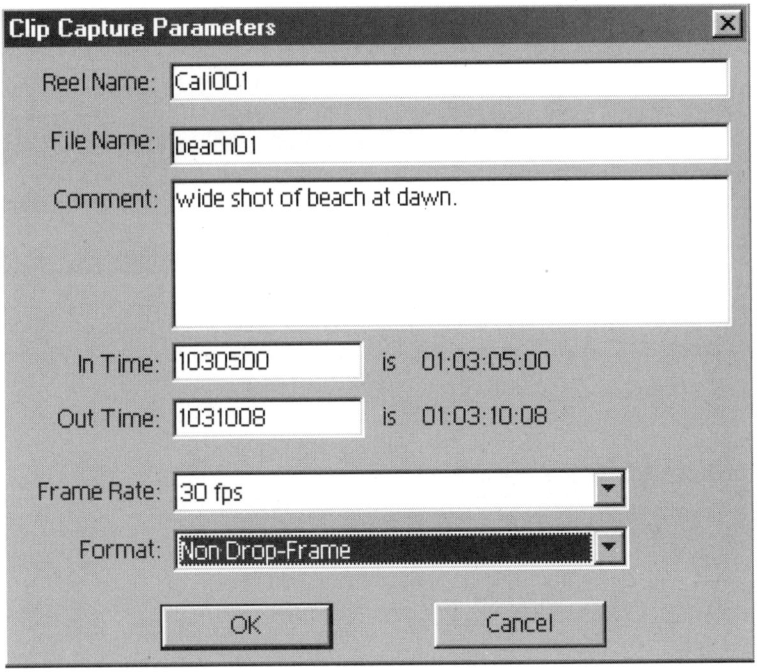

Figure 2-17 The Clip Capture Parameters window.

❸ Click the Add button in the lower left corner of the window. The Clip Capture Parameters window should appear (Figure 2-17).

❹ Type in the information for each file. Again, remember to give each one of your source tapes a unique name.

❺ Click OK.

❻ Repeat steps 3 through 5 for each clip that you want to add to the list.

❼ Save the list when you have finished entering all of your clips. Once it is saved, you do not have to capture the footage right then. You can open it at any other time when you choose to digitize your footage.

Once you log all of your clips into the Batch Capture window, you can still select which clips will get digitized. The far left-hand column has a check mark. This column indicates the capture status for each clip. If the column is empty, it means that the clip has not been captured. A check mark indicates that the clip has been digitized. A diamond indicates that the clip is marked to be digitized when you click the Capture button in the lower right portion of the window. Finally, an "X" indicates that there was an error during capture mode and was not digitized properly (Figure 2-18).

⬛ Batch Capture: Untitle2.pbl		
✔ Reel Name	In	Out
◆ Cal 001	01:03:05:00	01:03:10:08
◆ Cal 002	00:02:00:01	00:02:10:00
X NJ 01	05:00:10:00	05:00:25:15

Figure 2-18 Various symbols indicate the status of clips, whether they have been digitized or not.

REDIGITIZING THE CHOSEN FEW

If you have timecoded source material coming from a device-controlled deck, you may want to consider rough cutting your video in a low (offline) resolution first (see the section on offline editing above). A typical project usually entails digitizing more source material than what is actually used in your edited sequence in your timeline. Therefore, there is no reason to redigitize any footage at a higher (online) resolution other than the footage used in the timeline. This maximizes the amount of hard drive space left available for other projects.

> When redigitizing only the portions used in the timeline, Premiere creates a new project with the redigitized, higher resolution footage. It does not replace what currently exists on your system.

To automatically redigitize clips from a batch list:

❶ Open a project (if not already open).

❷ Select Utilities from the File menu.

❸ Select Project Trimmer from the pop-up menu.

❹ Check off Create Trimmed Batch List.

❺ Make sure Copy Trimmed Source Files is not checked.

❻ Enter the number of frames to add as handles during the recapture.

❼ Click Create Project.

❽ Save the new project when prompted.

❾ Save the Batch List file when prompted.

❿ Click the Capture button in the Batch Capture window.

For best results, make sure that you have the source deck and tapes properly set up and connected before clicking the Capture button.

IMPORTING STILL GRAPHICS

Bringing still images you've created with Photoshop or any other graphics program is easy. Still graphics can be used in just about any type of video production, whether used as full screen, forefront images or hidden subtly as part of the background. I personally recommend using Photoshop even for titles and backgrounds. Premiere's features are limited compared to the flexibility available with other graphics packages.

 The duration and aspect ratio settings for graphics that you import into Premiere are set under the General/Still Image preference setting (Figure 2-19).

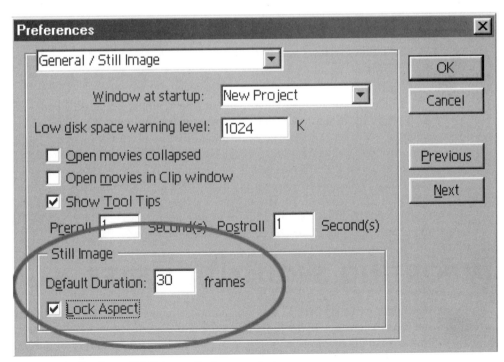

Figure 2-19 The General/Still Image Preference window.

To import individual graphics or entire folders of graphics into Premiere:

❶ Click on the bin to select where you want to bring in the graphic file.

❷ Select Import from the File menu.

❸ Select File (or Folder) from the pop-up menu.

❹ Locate the desire file (or folder) and click Open.

To import multiple files at once, you can either hold down the Control key or Shift key to select groups of files or (for Macintosh Users) select Import>Multiple to continuously select files to import.

Premiere can recognize the following still image file types:

◆ Photoshop (.PSD)

◆ Illustrator (.AI)

◆ Graphic Interchange Format (.GIF)

◆ Joint Photographics Experts Group (JPEG) (.JPG)

◆ Picture (.PICT or .PIC)

◆ Targa (.TGA)

◆ Tag Image File Format (.TIF)

Windows versions can also import PCX (.PCX) and Windows Bitmap (.BMP).

Premiere, Illustrator, and Photoshop (all Adobe products) integrate very well with each other. Adobe Illustrator files, when imported directly into Premiere, are converted from their native vector-based format into a pixel-based image, known as Rastorization. You can import an entire Photoshop file into Premiere or bring in just certain layers of a file. This is beneficial in many ways. The most interesting feature I find is that Premiere will preserve any transparency, or alpha channel, associated with that layer in Photoshop. This means that by importing in that layer (with the alpha channel) and placing it over an image or video clip on a lower channel, you will be able to see the remainder of the clip around the image (Figure 2-20).

IMPORTING SEQUENTIAL FILES

It would take a long time to edit a thousand individual frames together, creating the illusion of animation. If you use certain programs that can output individual sequential frames (like 3D Studio Max or Infini-D), you can import these files as one unit into Premiere as an animation file. The most important part is that each clip be properly numbered to show Premiere the proper order of the files.

Photoshop

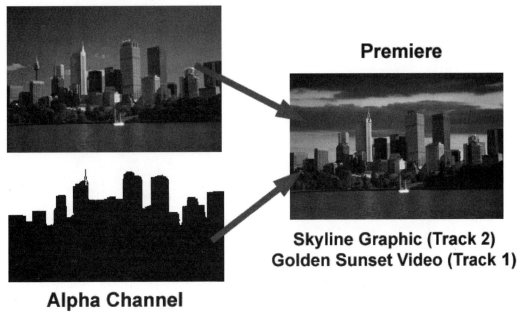

Alpha Channel

Figure 2-20 Premiere maintains any alpha channels associated with still images during import and editing.

Example:

filename001.bmp
filename002.bmp
filename003.bmp

To import the series of individual frames:

❶ Select the bin in which to store the imported file.

❷ Select Import from the File menu.

❸ Select File from the pop-up menu.

❹ Find the first numbered file in the sequential grouping.

❺ Click OK.

❻ Check the Import Numbered Stills check box at the bottom of the Import window (Figure 2-21).

❼ Click Open.

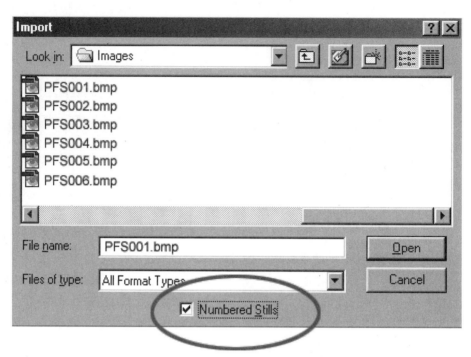

Figure 2-21 Check the Import Numbered Stills to import an animated sequence of frames as a single clip in Premiere.

SUMMARY

By now, you can see that there are many different ways to get source material into Premiere. This chapter also explains the flexibility and versatility of Premiere. The point is that no matter what type of source material you have, there are probably ten different ways to get that material into Premiere. Most of your controls and settings are from the capture card hardware and software you install on your system. If there's any place to spend a bit more money, you might as well put it into a high-end capture card. After all, if you don't capture high quality source material to begin with and take the proper time to set it up the correct way, your output video will be of poor quality.

chapter 3

TIDBITS AND TECHNIQUES: THINGS YOU SHOULD KNOW

This is the type of chapter that I wish the books I read (and still reference) contained: a cornucopia of useful information and helpful details that never seems to fit anywhere but I warn you that this chapter is going to jump around, from one topic to another. The importance of this chapter is for each reader to pick and choose the information that he or she can benefit from, whether a novice or a pro. I equate this chapter to the techniques that every editor will need to know (or at least find helpful) at some point in his or her career.

THE CONCEPT OF INSERT VS. OVERLAY EDITING

Understanding how to edit in Premiere is essential. If you can't build your timeline, the rest of this book will be useless. There are several ways to add the desired portion of your source footage into your timeline. The basic process involves:

- ◆ Digitize your footage
- ◆ Load a clip into the Source window
- ◆ Set a Mark In Point
- ◆ Set a Mark Out Point
- ◆ Edit the desired portion into your timeline

Once you set your In and Out Points, you can perform one of two possible methods for adding the footage to your timeline. You can drag your marked clip directly into the timeline area.

❶ Click and hold onto the Source window.

❷ Drag your mouse over to the timeline window.

You should see a gray area appear once your cursor is over an available track (Figure 3-1). The duration of the marked clip determines the width of the clip being added to the timeline. You cannot drag a clip into the timeline if a clip already exists in that portion of the timeline. Therefore, you cannot accidentally overwrite any clips you have edited into your timeline.

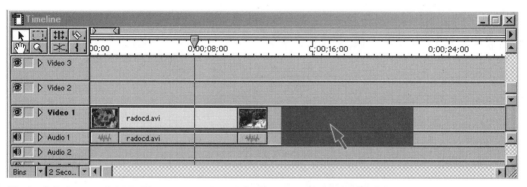

Figure 3-1 A gray place-holder appears when dragging source material directly into the timeline.

If you are dragging a source clip that contains both audio and video, you will not be able to add it to your timeline if one of those tracks is occupied. The video portion will not be added (even if that track is empty) if there is an audio clip in that location (Figure 3-2).

The other alternative to dragging a clip is to use one of the two edit buttons. (Figure 3-3) The two types of editing features are Insert Editing and Overlay Editing. Understanding the difference between the two is important. If you choose the wrong one, you could wind up ruining your entire sequence.

OVERLAY EDITING

The most often used form of editing is Overlay editing. It works by simply covering up whatever is in the timeline at the position where you want to place that clip, based on whichever tracks you have selected. If the timeline is empty or you are adding clips to the end of a sequence, Overlay just adds that footage without disrupting any other clips in the timeline (Figure 3-4).

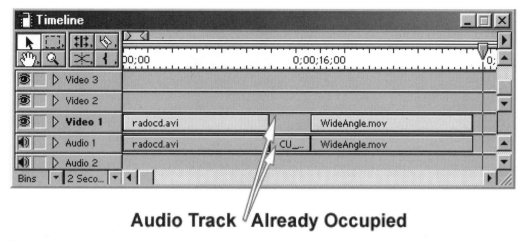

Audio Track Already Occupied

Figure 3-2 A source clip with audio and video cannot be added if even one of the tracks is occupied in the timeline.

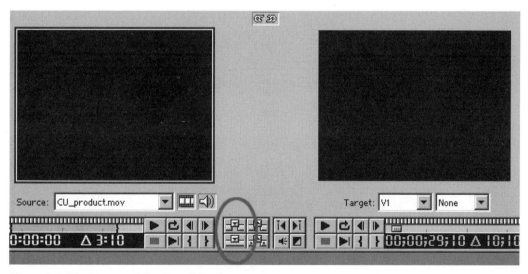

Figure 3-3 The Insert and Overlay editing buttons.

Overlay editing does not change the overall duration of your sequence, but can change the duration of any clips in the timeline if they get covered up (by any portion) of the clip being added.

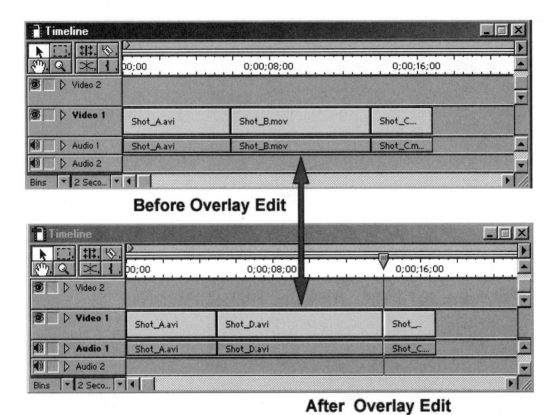

Figure 3-4 Overlay editing covers just whatever is in the timeline without shifting anything else in the selected tracks.

INSERT EDITING

Insert editing is used for a different purpose. One of the great benefits of editing on a computer is its ability to edit nonlinearly. That means that you can edit your movie in any order and add shots wherever and whenever. If you've ever edited on a linear system, you know that your edit master is only as good as your last edit. You cannot go back and add another shot in the beginning of your program and expect all the other shots to just slide on down. That is impossible to do when working on linear tape. With a computer, it's a different story. You have the ability to go in and add a shot at any point in time to any portion of your edited sequence. You add this new clip into the sequence while pushing all of your other clips farther down the timeline by the exact duration of the clip that is being added (Figure 3-5). To envision how insert editing works, imagine taking your film strip (edited sequence), cutting it at a particular frame, separating those pieces, and adding a new clip in between those old edit points.

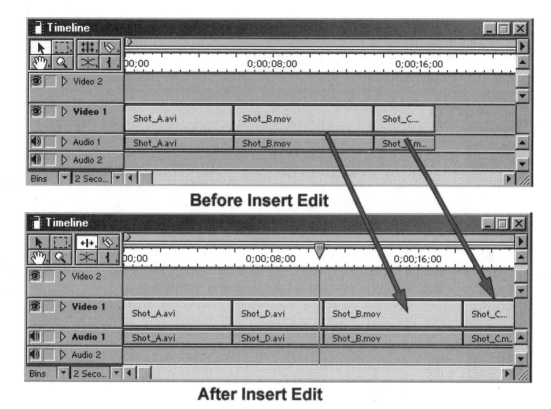

Figure 3-5 Insert editing shifts everything on the selected tracks farther down in the timeline.

Insert Editing does alter the overall duration of your sequence in the timeline. It does not affect the duration of any other clips in the timeline, just their location.

Warning: Insert editing is a common cause of knocking your timeline out of sync. When adding a clip, be sure to have all of the necessary tracks selected. If you have synced audio and video clips in your timeline and you just insert a video clip, you will knock all of the synced clips out of sync for the remaining duration of your sequence.

ONE, TWO, AND THREE POINT EDITING TECHNIQUES

Since we're covering the various methods for editing your source footage into your timeline, I should probably cover some other time-saving techniques. You do not always have to use all four editing marks to edit a shot into your timeline (the In and Out points on the source side and the In and Out points on the record side).

> To clear a marker from either the Source monitor or Edit monitor, park on the marker you want to remove and select Clear Marker from the Clip menu or hit Control-Alt-C (Windows) or Command-Option-C (Macintosh) on your keyboard.

◆ One Point Editing: This is usually done during a "rough cutting" session. If you are just trying to add clips to your timeline without setting in and out points, you can use you just use the playback indicator as you single mark. Just place the playback indicator anywhere in your timeline and click on one of the edit buttons (Insert or Overlay – depending on what else exists in your timeline). The playback indicator will act as the in point in your timeline and carry the full duration of the clip in your source monitor down into the timeline (since there were no marks in the source monitor).

◆ Two Point Editing : This technique is usually used to match two points, one in the source monitor and one in the timeline. Two points work well when trying to match up a starting point in the source monitor and a starting point in the timeline (or edit monitor). The rest of the duration, from the mark in point in the source monitor until where the clip ends, is added to the timeline when the insert or overlay edit buttons are pushed.

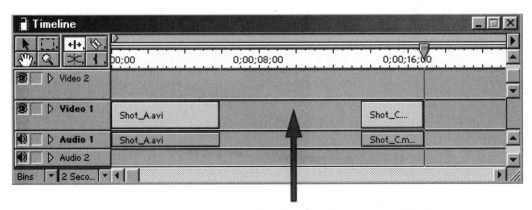

Figure 3-6 The Lift feature removes the clip(s) on the selected track(s), leaving a blank space in the timeline.

♦ Three Point Editing: This is the most common method of editing that I have seen editors use. It is quick and convenient (faster than measuring where to put the fourth edit point) while still giving you the accuracy to determine the exact starting and ending frames for either the source clip or the timeline. Premiere automatically edits in the fourth point. Therefore, you can mark any combination of the source clip's In point or Out point and the In point or Out point in your timeline. With experience you'll learn which circumstances determine which marks to use.

THE CONCEPT OF LIFT VS. EXTRACT

As an editor you are in a powerful position. You can give (add clips to the timeline) just as easily as you can take (remove clips from your timeline). Lift and Extract work is the complete inverse of Insert and Overlay.

With Lift, you mark the portion of your timeline (with In and Out points and the desired tracks) that you wish to remove. In contrast to Overlay's covering up whatever was in the timeline without altering any of the shots outside of that marked area, Lift does just the opposite. Lift actually removes the portion that is marked without affecting any of the shots outside of the marked area (Figure 3-6). This leaves a blank area in your timeline, holding the duration of the area where the clip(s) previously existed.

Extract works in the opposite manner of Insert. Again, Insert editing adds a clip to your sequence and pushes everything on those tracks farther down in the timeline. Extract removes the marked area of a timeline and shifts everything that was on the selected tracks back, butting up the new edit points so that there is no blank area left in the timeline from where the segment was removed (Figure 3-7).

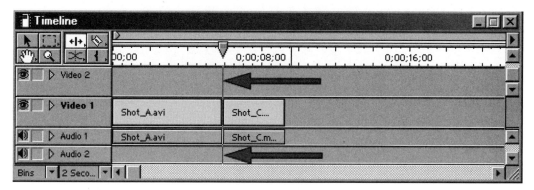

Figure 3-7 The Extract feature removes the marked portion of the selected track(s) and shifts everything back so that no blank space is left in the timeline.

Careless Extracting can knock your timeline out of sync. Be sure to have the correct tracks selected before extracting a segment from your timeline.

SAVING TIME SELECTING SOURCE CLIPS

Although it seems simple, I have been surprised by the number of editors that I've come across who didn't know this feature exists or how to use it to save time. The feature that I refer to is the Source Menu (selection pull-down menu) under the Source monitor. This shows a list of the clips that you have previously viewed in the source monitor since you opened the project (Figure 3-8).

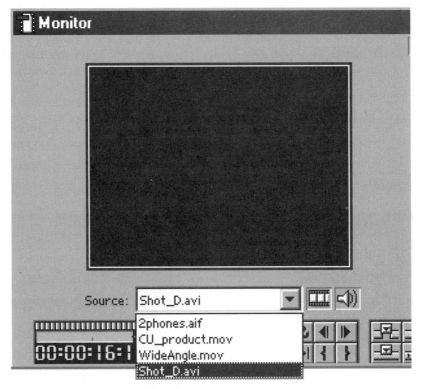

Figure 3-8 The Source Menu displays the clips that you have already loaded into the Source Monitor, allowing quick access to those clips.

This menu saves you time by not having to rummage through multiple bin windows looking for a clip you just viewed a few seconds ago. One situation where I find this pull-down menu extremely helpful is when I am cutting back and forth between a few clips. By selecting from the quick and convenient menu, I do not have to keep going back to my bins to grab the shot I just used. I can just keep selecting from the list the (let's say) three or so clips whose source footage I am continuously editing as I jump back and forth between them.

USING THE NAVIGATOR WINDOW

Another feature I find myself relying on is the Navigator window (Figure 3-9). It is one of the underrated features in Premiere that can save you a great amount of time. It can be used to:

◆ Give you a bird's-eye view of your timeline, showing you all of the clips and segments in your timeline, positioned by each track layer.

◆ Jump anywhere in your timeline with a simple click of the mouse. Just click in the Navigator window to jump to that particular area of your timeline and watch the main timeline window update to the position that you just selected.

◆ Quickly zoom your view of the timeline in and out, allowing you to see more detail or zoom out wide to see the entire timeline in one view. Drag the slider bar or click on the Zoom in or Zoom out buttons next to the slider.

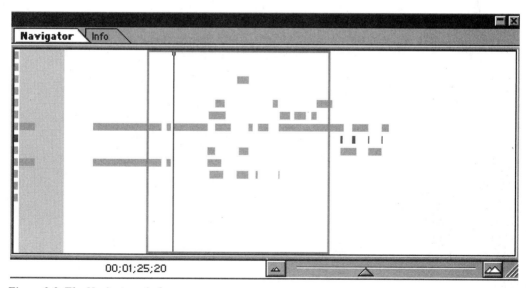

Figure 3-9 The Navigator window.

◆　Quickly identify the exact timecode location of the playback indicator. You can type in a timecode number and have the playback indicator jump directly to that timecode number.

◆　Stretch the Navigator window by dragging the bottom right portion of the window to open it as wide as you want. This way you can view more of your timeline without having to scroll.

PREVIEW BEFORE YOU EDIT

The great thing about computer based nonlinear editing systems, especially the ones like Premiere with multiple levels of Undo, is the fact that you can edit something to see how it looks and just as easily undo it if you don't like it. Another quick technique that allows you to see how a source clip would compare to your sequence is known as Ganging your shots. For instance, if you wanted to get an idea of where the source clip would be in relationship to where your shot would appear in your timeline (from given starting points), you would Gang the two clips. To use the Gang feature:

❶　Select the starting frame of your source clip.

❷　Select the starting frame in the timeline.

❸　Click the Gang button (Figure 3-10). When the chain icon is broken, the clips are not ganged together.

❹　Drag the jog tread, shuttle slider, Previous Frame button, or Next Frame button on the controllers to compare frames from the timeline to the source window. Each window should update by the same number of frames that you move.

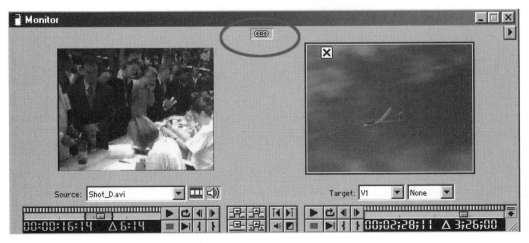

Figure 3-10 The Gang Button links source and program clips, allowing you to view how each one updates in relation to the other.

Note: Using any other controls than the ones listed here will turn off the Gang feature.

CREATING A "DO NOT ERASE" PROJECT

One thing that takes up a great deal of time is digitizing certain elements that I normally reuse in the majority of my projects: bars and tone, countdown, slate, common sound effects, my company logo, and certain background animations. Digitizing these items for every project became cumbersome, boring, and a complete waste of valuable time. There had to be a better way.

I created a project with all of the elements that I consistently used over and over again. I left this project on the hard drives, never removing it or deleting it. This way I could always bring it into any project I was working on and never have to redigitize the basics again. I named this project "Do Not Erase."

To bring another project (i.e., the Do Not Erase project) into your current project:

❶ Select Import from the File menu.

❷ Select Project from the pop-up menu or use the keyboard shortcut Control-Alt-Shift-I (Windows) or Command-Option-Shift-I (Macintosh).

❸ Select the existing Premiere movie from the Import window. The existing project's bins should appear in your current project window.

 You can even go as far as locking the files on the hard drive level so that you never accidentally erase the footage from the hard drive.

FIXING A TALKING HEAD SHOOT-GONE-BORING

Producing Talking Head videos for corporate clients are generally boring to begin with. Have you ever experienced, besides the boring content, that the camera person set up his camera in the same angle and position in respect to the on-camera talent. For instance, all of his shots were taken from the left side of the person speaking. That means all of the shots have the person looking off camera in the same direction. Talk about a cure for an insomniac.

A quick little fix is to vary the direction of the camera, even though you cannot reshoot the video. As long as the person (or scene) doesn't have any numbers or wording visible, you can flip-flop the shot to make it appear that the camera actually shot the person from a different angle (Figure 3-11). Yes, I know you can always pick up

Figure 3-11 Use the Horizontal Flip filter to make a shot appear from a different angle.

subtle hints about the shot being backwards, but the majority of your audience will never know what was done or pick up on the fact that the person on-screen normally wears a watch on the other hand, etc. With Talking Heads it's very hard to pick up on the flip, yet it makes such a difference in the continuity and flow of the video.

To reverse the angle of a shot:

❶ Click on the clip in the timeline that you want to change.

❷ Select Filter from the Clip menu or hit Control-F (Windows) or Command-F (Macintosh) on the keyboard.

❸ Select Horizontal Flip from the Available Filters window.

❹ Add it to the Current side of the window.

❺ Click OK.

MAKING ABSTRACT BACKGROUND LOOPABLE

There have been so many times when I needed a clip to use as a background, whether it was under a title or wherever. I'm talking about clips like water rippling on a lake or some other type of abstract imagery that does not show any type of true direction. It seems that no matter how long the clip I seem to have (duration wise), I always need it to be just a bit longer. Usually, if you edit that clip in twice, you'll notice the edit point. It will appear that there is a slight jump cut.

You can create a second clip, using the same exact footage, only rendered out backwards. By creating a clip using the same footage playing in reverse at the same speed (−100%), edit the clip into your timeline playing in the original direction, then match the clip to play in reverse, creating a nice even flow and avoid a jump cut. If you need even more time, you can then match in the original clip and keep repeating this pattern.

This technique does not work well for video footage that has a distinct direction to it, such as people walking down a street. It would look eye-catchingly wrong to have someone start off walking forward and then backward.

CREATING A COUNTDOWN IN PREMIERE

One thing that you will probably want to add to your edited master tape, especially if you're outputting for broadcast is a countdown. A countdown is used to indicate where your program begins. There are typically two seconds worth of black (with no audio) before the actual start of your movie. This really applies to live television, giving the

Technical Director and other crew members enough time to switch sources or fade in the material from tape without seeing anything on screen or hearing any sound (in case they fade in a bit early). Therefore, when you create a countdown, you usually see the two-second mark flash in for a split second and then go directly to black. That is also why you never see a one-second mark in a countdown. This two-second indicator mark is commonly referred to as a "Two Pop", since you see and hear the two second mark pop in and out for a duration of one frame (1/30 of a second in NTSC standards).

Premiere has the ability to generate a countdown. To use the internal countdown:

❶ Select Create from the Project menu.

❷ Select Universal Counting Leader from the pop-up menu. The Universal Counting Leader window should appear (Figure 3-12).

❸ Set any color attributes in the video portion of the screen.

❹ Set the audio attributes in the audio portion of the screen.

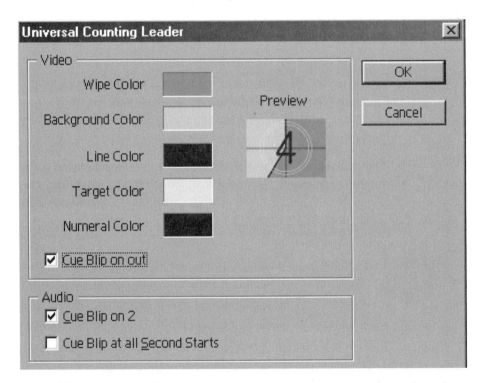

Figure 3-12 The Universal Counting Leader window for creating standard countdowns in Premiere.

Notice how the audio section contains two choices. You can add an audio blip at the two-second mark (the "Two Pop") or add an audio blip at every second. This helps the person cueing up the tape get a feel for when the program is going to start.

BUILDING YOUR OWN CUSTOM COUNTDOWN

I personally like to go one step further than the generic Premiere countdown. I like to create my own custom countdowns for a number of reasons. As I mentioned earlier in this chapter, I would create a custom countdown and save it in the DO NOT ERASE project; this way it's available anytime I need a countdown.

Creating a countdown can be as simple or as complex as you wish. Whether you choose to use still graphics or create a custom 3D animation, make sure that the end result is still the same... that the countdown is timed correctly and indicates when the program is about to begin. To create a countdown, include the following:

◆ Time out your graphics or animations to be exactly one second in duration (ten down to three). The "Two" second graphic should only appear for one frame.

◆ Put audio blips for the duration of only one frame on the first frame of each identifiable second graphic. (Figure 3-13).

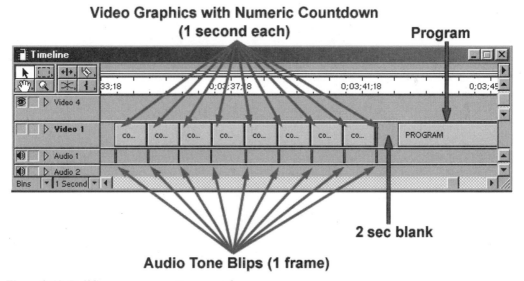

Figure 3-13 Building your own custom countdown.

◆ If you use animation, make sure you clearly identify which frame is the starting frame of each second during the countdown. It can be as simple as making the number icon change color for a single frame with the audio blip.

By creating custom countdowns, I can give one last indicator that the person has my tape. Any good marketing or advertising person will tell you to get your logo in front of as many people as possible. Here's another opportunity. (Figure 3-14).

Figure 3-14 Sample shot of one of my company's custom countdown screens.

See Chapter 10 for more details on preparing your program for output.

SUMMARY

I know this chapter covered many different topics, but I think you'll find each one beneficial. Having these topics explained just makes working on a project that much easier. Once you get the grasp of these ideas, they'll probably become second nature and you'll never have to read this chapter again. But making sure that you understand these concepts is why I included them in this book. There are probably a million more tidbits and techniques that you'll come across yourself. Send them to me and I'll try to include them in the next edition of the book. Check out the Web site at www.phptr.com/togo to find out a few more techniques that you might find valuable when you start your next video project.

chapter 4

IMAGE EFFECTS WITHIN TIMELINE SEGMENTS

This is what you've all been waiting for. The technical part of digitizing audio and video clips and properly managing them in your bins is boring. Adding the sizzle to your sequence...that's exciting. So let's not waste any time. This chapter is going to cover a variety of techniques to improve your edited sequence, segment by segment.

STACKING UP THE CLIPS

You have all seen the results of some creative editing using multiple layers of video clips. Vertical layering of clips allows you to display multiple images on-screen at any given moment. This may be as simple as superimposing two different video clips or as complex as a combination of superimpositions, graphics with alpha channels, text and titles flying by the camera, and picture-in-picture images floating smoothly across the screen. To layer clips in your timeline:

❶ Select the source footage in the Source Monitor.

❷ Mark the In and Out points in your timeline.

❸ Select the desired video track using the Target track selector located under the Program Monitor or click directly on the track name in the timeline (Figure 4-1).

❹ Use one of the Edit Buttons (Insert or Overlay) to add the clip to the timeline.

❺ Go back and place In and Out Marks at the same positions as your previous edit.

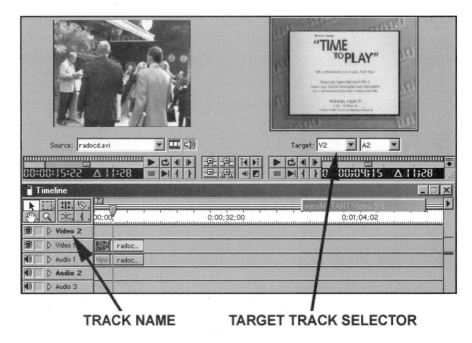

TRACK NAME   TARGET TRACK SELECTOR

Figure 4-1 Use the Target Track Selector or click on the Track Name itself to select the track where you want to edit in the source material.

❻ Select the desired video track using the Target track selector (generally a higher track than your previous edit).

Premiere allows you to go crazy to your heart's content and add up to 96 layers of video. (I seriously doubt you'll ever need more than that). In order to add more than the default two video tracks visible in the timeline:

❶ Click on the little triangle located in the top right corner of the Timeline window.
❷ Select Track Options from the pop-up menu (Figure 4-2).
❸ Click the Add button in the Track Options window (Figure 4-3).
❹ Enter the number of the video track you would like to add to your current timeline.
❺ Click OK.

You do not need to select all of the tracks now. If you are not sure how many tracks will be used for the project, you can add tracks at any point by repeating the above process. You can also choose to name each track. To name any track in the timeline:

❶ Click on the little triangle located in the top right corner of the Timeline window.
❷ Select Track Options from the pop-up menu.

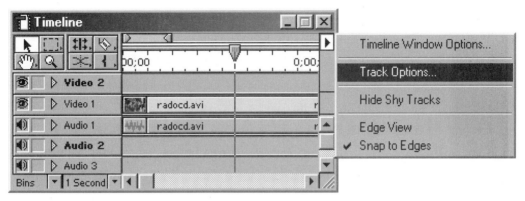

Figure 4-2 You can access the Track Options from the Timeline window.

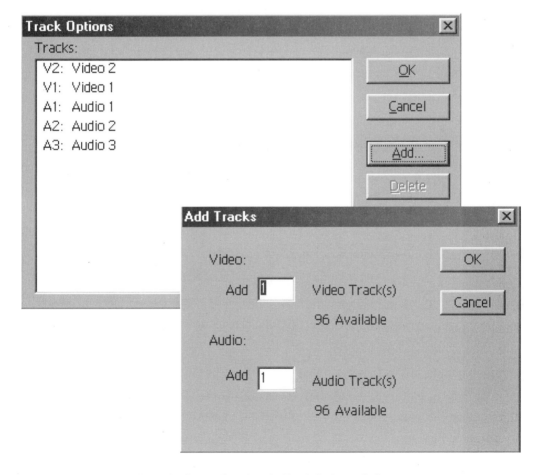

Figure 4-3 Add new audio and video tracks using the Track Options window.

❸   Select the track that you wish to name.

❹   Click the Name button in the Track Options window.

❺   Enter any alphanumeric name in the text field in the Name Track Window.

❻   Click OK.

VIEWING MORE THAN ONE TRACK

In Premiere (or just about any nonlinear editing system), once you add a video clip to Track 2, it automatically covers the portion of the clip below in track 1 when played. Think of the playback indicator line as a camera, reading the images from the upper-most track on down as it moves across the timeline (Figure 4-4). In order to see the clip below, we must alter the clip on the upper track by adding an effect (i.e., picture-in-picture) or change the level of opacity.

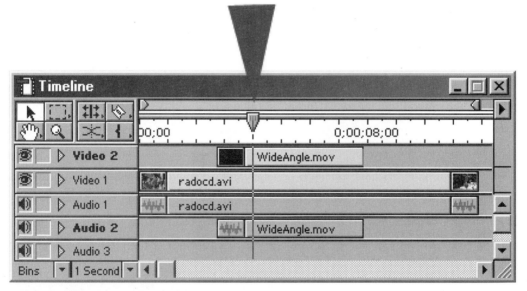

Figure 4-4 When no effects are added, Premiere plays back the video clip on the highest track, covering any clips in lower tracks.

Changing the level of opacity of a clip is a common effect used, most often referred to as a superimposed image. When two images are superimposed at 50 percent you would see full-screen portions of both clips equally (Figure 4-5). Just like most effects, you can control the "amount of effect" you are applying to the clip.

Figure 4-5 The clip in the middle represents the combination of the other two images superimposed together.

To superimpose the entire portion of two layered video clips:

❶ Place one video clip in Track 1.

❷ Place another video clip in Track 2.

❸ Click the triangle located next to the track name on Track 2 to expand the tracks view (Figure 4-6). Notice the Opacity bar underneath the track in the timeline.

❹ Hold the Shift key down and drag your mouse up and down to change the opacity level of the entire clip. A percentage indicator will appear to show you the amount of transparency or opacity you are applying to the clip.

The lower the percentage you make the clip on Track 2, the more visible the clip in Track 1 will become. But there will most likely be times when you do not want the clip to remain at one transparency level for the duration of the entire clip. The next section covers how to control the level for each frame, if desired.

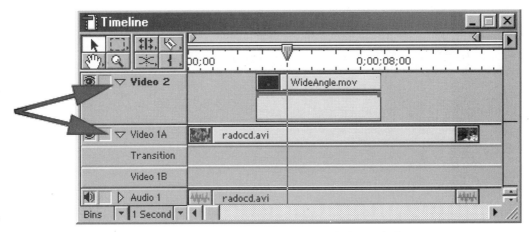

Figure 4-6 Clicking on the triangle next to the track name expands the track view.

USING KEYFRAMES TO CUSTOMIZE TRANSPARENCY

In order to vary the amount of transparency, whether it's just a simple dissolve-like effect from 0 percent to 100 percent or customizing each frame for some off-the-wall effect, you need to set these different variables using Keyframes. Keyframes are markers that contain a specific set of instructions at a specific point in time. In other words, when the playback head comes across a keyframe, it will know exactly how the effect is to be displayed during playback. Keyframes hold information such as size, position, opacity, and rotation, among other characteristics. If you want to vary the transparency of a clip at different points of the clip's duration, you will need to add keyframes at those particular points in the timeline.

To use keyframes to adjust the individual transparency levels of these keyframes:

❶ Layer two tracks of video and expand the view of Track 2 as described in the above example.

❷ Click on one of the little red boxes on the transparency line. The cursor should change to a finger icon.

❸ Move the box up or down to change the level of transparency at that specific point in time.

Hold the Shift Key while dragging the keyframe box to specify an amount as a percentage.

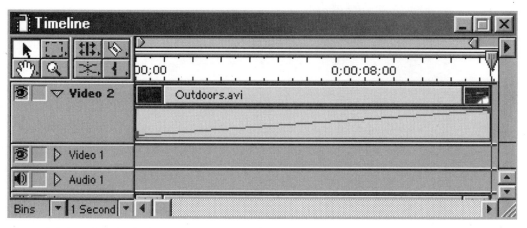

Figure 4-7 Lowering the first keyframe creates a smooth fade-in from completely transparent to fully opaque.

Notice the ramping effect that occurs when you lower the position of only the first keyframe. (Figure 4-7). Lowering the first keyframe all the way down will give you a nice smooth fade-in of the image on Track 2.

 All effects always need a minimum of two keyframes, one at the beginning and one at the end of the clip. You cannot delete these keyframes.

To add more keyframe throughout a clip:

❶ Click and hold the mouse anywhere (other than on the first or last keyframes already present) on the transparency line.

❷ Drag the mouse up or down to change the transparency level at that position. Premiere automatically adds in the new keyframe.

❸ Drag the keyframe left or right to adjust the degree of change (amount of transparency level and rate of change) between the keyframes on either side of the one you are adjusting (Figure 4-8).

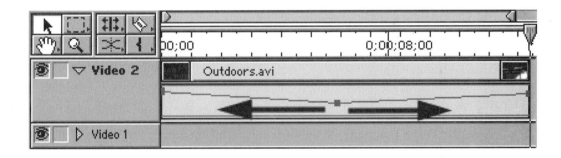

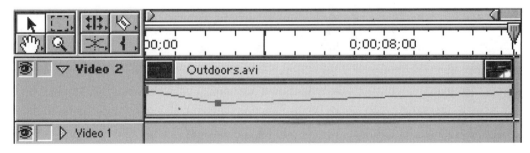

Figure 4-8 Drag the keyframe to adjust the amount of time it takes to change levels between the surrounding keyframes.

You can go back and fine-tune the position of any keyframe at any point of your editing session.

FADING IN AND FADING OUT

A very common effect used in all types of programs is to have one shot slowly fade in, remain superimposed over the original shot, and then slowly fade back out. With the use of adding a couple of keyframes, you can quickly achieve this effect.

❶ Add a clip to Track 1.

❷ Add a second clip to Track 2. This shot can be the same length or shorter than the one in Track 1.

❸ Expand Track 2 to view the Transparency line.

❹ Add a keyframe approximately a quarter of the way into the duration of the clip on Track 2.

❺ Add another keyframe approximately three quarters of the way into the duration of the clip on Track 2 (Figure 4-9).

❻ Drag the first keyframe down to the lowest level.

❼ Drag the last keyframe down to the lowest level (Figure 4-10).

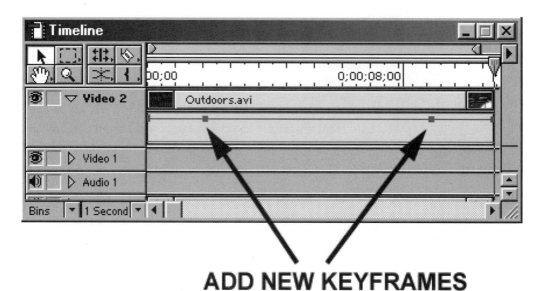

Figure 4-9 Add additional keyframes between the first and last keyframes.

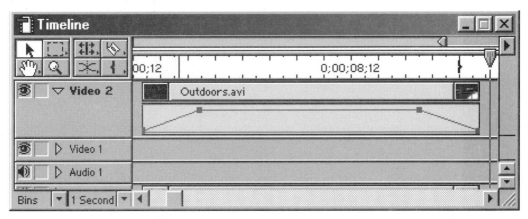

Figure 4-10 Dragging down the first and last keyframes creates a smooth fade-in and fade-out effect.

 Depending on your system, you will most likely have to render out that effect in order to see it during playback.

CONTROLLING THE SPEED AT WHICH THE WORLD MOVES

Life happens in real time. Wouldn't it be great if we could change the way we viewed events? Premiere gives you the ability to control the speed at which these video clips play back. Altering the rate of a clip is generally referred to as a Motion Effect. This means that changing the speed of a clip adjusts how fast or slow the clip you have selected plays back. Therefore, a clip set at 50 percent speed will take twice as long to play back the same material as it would at normal speed (from the same in point to the same out point). To create a motion effect:

❶ Select the clip in the timeline that you want to change its playback rate.

❷ Select Speed from the Clip menu.

❸ Enter a new percentage for the rate of playback in the Clip Speed window (Figure 4-11).

OR

If you know the duration you would like the clip to cover, enter the new duration time value. This feature will automatically calculate the rate of the clip (percentage of change) from the clip's original duration in the timeline to the new rate it takes to show the same portion of the clip over the new time period.

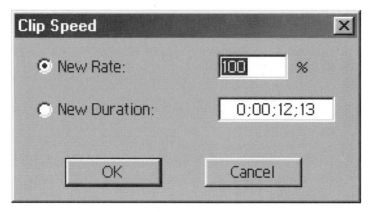

Figure 4-11 Use the Clip Speed window to alter the playback rate of a clip.

 Whichever field you choose to enter your new value, keep in mind they will both affect the overall duration of the clip in the timeline.

Once the rate has been set for that clip, you can then use the trimming tools to change the duration of the clip in the timeline without affecting the new rate, or its motion effect, set for that clip. For example, if you previously set a particular clip to play back at 40 percent of its original speed, trimming the shot in the timeline after the rate has been set does not alter the rate at which the clip will play back. Whatever footage you add to a clip during a trim will also play back at the adjusted rate.

 Type in a negative value to have the clip play in reverse.

An alternative method for changing the rate at which a clip plays back is to use the Rate Stretch Tool, located in the timeline window (Figure 4-12).

To use this feature:

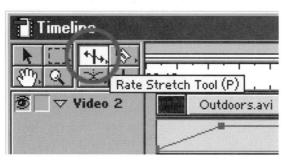

Figure 4-12 The Rate Stretch Tool.

❶ Edit the desired clip (original source material) into the timeline. This means specifying the correct In and Out points, without being concerned about the duration of the clip for now.

❷ Select the Rate Stretch Tool from the timeline window.

❸ Move your cursor to the Out point of the clip in the timeline. Notice that the cursor changes to the Rate Stretch icon.

❹ Drag the Out point to the new position on the timeline to change the rate of speed of the clip. Lengthening the clip will slow down the rate while shortening the clip will speed the rate of playback (Figure 4-13).

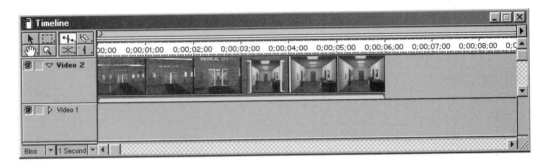

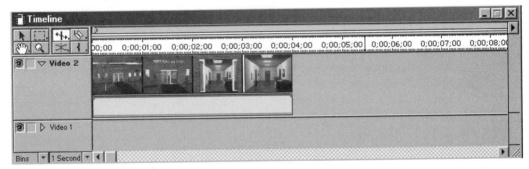

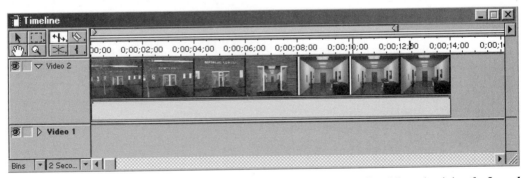

Figure 4-13 The Rate Stretch Tool varies the duration of a clip while maintaining the In and Out points.

The Rate Stretch Tool is not the same as trimming your clip. The Rate Stretch feature allows you to keep the same In and Out points as you initially had marked when you added the source material to your timeline. What it does change is the overall duration of the clip. In order to play the same amount of footage (In point to Out point) over different durations, Premiere must calculate the new percentage rate at which the clip must play.

CHANGING SPEEDS AT THE SOURCE

There is no reason you have to wait until you edit the clip into the timeline in order to change the speed of the clip. You can change the speed or rate at which the clip will play directly in any of the Project, Bin, or Library windows. To change the speed of any source clip:

❶ Select the clip in the Project, Bin, or Library window.

❷ Select Speed from the Clip menu.

❸ Enter the new percentage rate or duration of the clip.

❹ Click OK.

Entering a negative value makes the clip play in reverse.

This will now change the frame rate setting for your original source material. You can obviously keep going back to repeat the above process every time you need to switch rates, but that can be very time consuming and wasteful, especially if you are using the same shot at different rates several times throughout your project. My suggestion is to duplicate the clip, rename it, and change its speed accordingly.

❶ Select the clip in the Project, Bin, or Library window.

❷ Select Copy from the Edit menu or use Control-C (Windows) or Command-C (Macintosh).

❸ Paste the clip back in the same Project, Bin, or Library window. Select Paste from the Edit menu or use Control-V (Windows) or Command-V (Macintosh).

❹ Rename the clip appropriately to differentiate the new clip.

Rename duplicate clips to help identify what is different between the original and altered clips. If you change the rate of the new clip to 25 percent, you might consider naming the new clip by its same name with a 25 added to the end of it (i.e., original clip = car_race, altered clip = car_race25).

CAPTURE THE MOMENT WITH FREEZE FRAMES

The ability to create freeze frames easily not only comes in handy creatively, but can also get you out of a few jams when you are short on footage. A freeze frame is merely a way that Premiere creates a still image of whichever frame you select. You can choose to freeze the clip marked by either the selected clip's In Point, Out Point, or Marker Zero Point. To create a freeze frame:

❶ Select the clip in the timeline.

❷ Decide which frame you would like to freeze. You have three choices: The In Point, the Out Point, or the frame where you position the cursor, set as Marker Zero.

> **Tip** **In order for Premiere to recognize the marker as the defining point, you must set the marker beforehand. To set a marker, select Set Marker from the Clip menu. Select Zero from the pop-up menu.**

❸ Select Video from the Clip menu.

❹ Select Frame Hold from the pop-up menu. The Frame Hold Options window should appear (Figure 4-14).

❺ Click the Hold On check box.

❻ Choose from one of the three position selections in the pull-down menu.

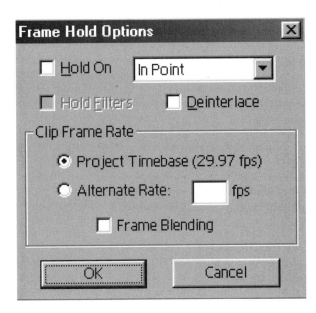

Figure 4-14 Use the Frame Hold Options window to create freeze frames.

❼   The following options are available from the Frame Hold Options window:

◆   Click the Hold Filters radio button to create the freeze frame while including any filters that may be applied to the clip in the timeline. This is important, especially if you are using the freeze frame directly before, during, or after the clip is playing in real time. The freeze frame would not match up if the same filters were not applied.

◆   You can choose to change the frame rate from the original source clip. The Frame Blending check box will interpolate, or blend, the missing frames that are associated with the new frame rate being selected. This creates a new intermediate frame combining the images from more than one frame (Figure 4-15).

◆   Click the Deinterlace radio button if the video clip was originally interlaced. This should reduce the amount of flicker in your freeze frame during playback.

Frame Blending

Figure 4-15 The Frame Hold Option can change the rate of a source clip without affecting the speed of the action by adding or deleting frames.

 Interlaced video is the process of displaying a single frame of video (1/30ᵗʰ of a second) using two scan lines (each at 1/60ᵗʰ of a second). Interlaced video draws out half of the image from top to bottom, and then goes back to fill in the remaining lines on the second pass (Figure 4-16). Progressive scan, used in computer monitors, draws the complete image, from top to bottom, in one pass (Figure 4-17).

 See Chapter 7 where I discuss how freeze frames can save the day when it comes to adding transitions.

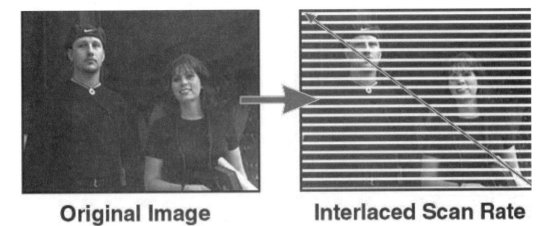

Figure 4-16 Interlaced video draws odd lines first and then goes back to fill in the even lines.

Figure 4-17 Progressive scan draws complete images in one pass from top to bottom.

FIX IT IN THE MIX

This title I must attribute to my assistant editor from way back when she worked with a producer who wasn't overly concerned with doing things correctly during the production phase and said that they would just "fix it in the mix." Well, it's not always that easy, but fortunately, computer-based editing systems have made it more feasible to correct a number of elements during the post-production phase of the project. The one that I seem to encounter most, especially when working with no-professional or amateur equipment is image correction. Image correction encompasses several areas, including adjusting image levels and color correction.

If you are going to edit any video (which, I'd assume is why you are working with Premiere), make sure you work with as many of the following as possible:

◆ Properly adjusted monitors

◆ Highest quality source footage (Beta SP, Mini DV, Hi-8, VHS at SP speed vs. SPL)

◆ Vectorscope

◆ Waveform Monitor

A Vectorscope and Waveform Monitor, for those of you who don't know, are test instruments more precisely measuring video signal levels (Figure 4-18). Professional external vectorscopes and waveform monitors do tend to be expensive. However, if you are planning to do any editing for broadcast or other high-end uses, these items are a necessity. Fortunately, several companies are coming out with third-party plug-ins that now bring the control and accuracy for adjusting video signals to your computer. If you're going to buy one plug-in product, I highly recommend you consider Video Finesse by Synthetic Aperture (Figure 4-19). They have created a software package that provides the ability to have precise control and complete customization of your video imagery, while working directly in Premiere. Not only do you have an easy-to-read waveform monitor and vectorscope on screen, but you also have full control to adjust just about every little parameter related to a video signal. Check out their Web site at www.synthetic-ap.com to get more information about their application or to download a free demo version.

Figure 4-18 Vectorscope and Waveform Monitor displays.

Whichever route you choose, having these test tools available will help ensure that you are working with, and more importantly, distributing the best quality video image possible. If you are editing for your own personal enjoyment, then you probably don't need test equipment, but it can make the difference between your footage looking amateurish and professional.

 Note: Networks and other broadcast stations will most likely reject your program if it is not set up with the proper levels.

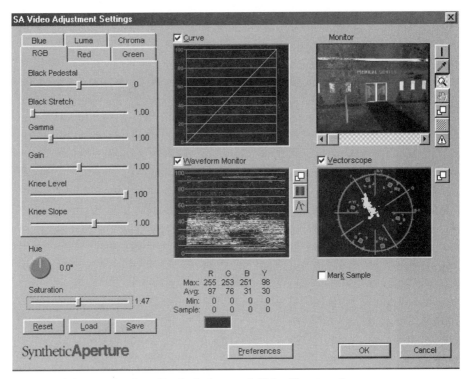

Figure 4-19 Screen shot from Synthetic Aperture's Video Finesse software.

VIDEO LEVELS 101

This section may be the most technical part of the book and is geared for people using a waveform monitor and vectorscope. Even if you do not have one, you will still probably benefit from reading the following sections. Video has certain basic properties that make it look the way it does. These standards help keep the images we see (especially being broadcast) look consistent and of the highest quality. There are a number of test patterns available to make sure your equipment is properly calibrated. These signals are used to "line up" all the various components and keep the signal quality and image consistent throughout the entire production process.

Many of the properties that are described below are controlled independently, yet can be affected by adjusting one or more of the other settings.

Since this book is focusing on how to work within Premiere, we are going to cover how to correct your image quality with the tools that come with Premiere. Once again, you can gain more control with some of these third-party applications, but you should be able to make the Premiere tools work for you.

The first characteristic is the video level itself, or brightness of the signal. This is referred to as the white level. For NTSC signals, using your waveform monitor, you should make sure that your signal does not surpass the 100 IRE level (Figure 4-20). If your image appears to be blown out, over-exposed, or so glaringly bright that it hurts your eyes, you can bet that your video level is probably set too high. If your image appears to be faded where, again, the image looks washed out and the blacks (or darkest parts of your image) do not appear to be black (or very rich), try adjusting the Contrast level of the signal to lower the black level of the image. On a waveform monitor, proper black levels should appear as 7.5 IRE.

To adjust the overall Brightness and Contrast of your clip:

❶ Select the clip in your timeline.

❷ Select Filters from the Clip menu or for keyboard shortcuts, hit Control-F (Windows) or Command-F (Macintosh).

❸ Select Brightness and Contrast from the list of Filters.

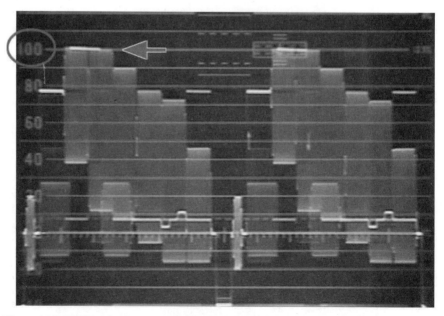

Figure 4-20 NTSC video levels should not exceed 100 IRE.

❹ Use the Brightness slider and Contrast slider to adjust the clip's level until you are able to get the brightest part of your signal to be just under 100 IRE and the darkest parts to be at 7.5 IRE on your waveform monitor (or appear more naturally if you do not have a waveform monitor).

❺ Click OK.

Tweaking the Contrast may affect the overall brightness of your image. You may need to bounce back and forth, making adjustments to one and then the other and back again to the first. With these parameters, your video signal should fall within (and as close to) the 7.5 IRE to 100 IRE range.

There are some video capture cards out there that have video signal analysis tools built in as standard features, such as the Perception PVR card.

WHAT YOU SEE MAY NOT BE WHAT YOU GET

This is an important section, so pay attention. I mentioned earlier the importance of having a waveform monitor and vectorscope to check the accuracy of your video signal. A vectorscope is predominantly used to ensure that the colors you are seeing are the same as the colors you will get in your final output media. To check the accuracy of your signal flow and monitor adjustments, you can use SMPTE color bars and a vectorscope to properly set up your system (Figure 4-21).

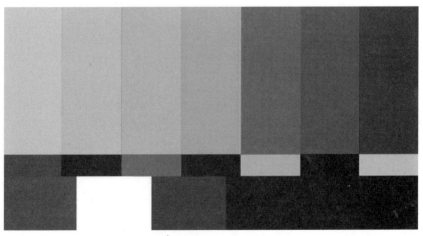

Figure 4-21 SMPTE Color Bars are the standard test pattern used to calibrate a video signal.

Do not use the hue and chroma adjustments on your monitor to "fix"
bad image color on your source footage if you have not properly set
up your system. Doing this only masks the problem until you output
incorrectly colored video.

Here's one quick method for setting up your system correctly:

❶ Use a color bar generator or other source of accurate color bars (from a test signal
generator, professional video camera, master tape of color bars, and so on.)

❷ Feed the color bar signal directly into the vectorscope to verify accuracy of signal.
Each color should appear in its respective box on the vectorscope screen. (Figure
4-22).

❸ Feed the signal into your monitor. Use the Loop Out feature to feed the signal into
the Vectorscope.

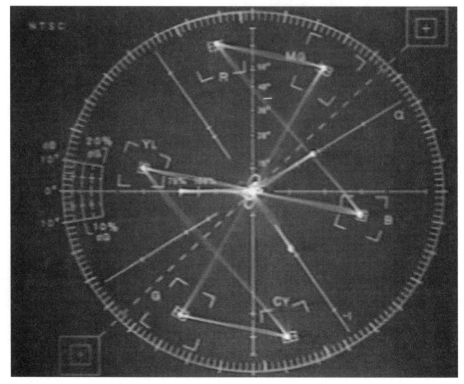

Figure 4-22 Properly adjusted colors should appear in their appropriate box.

❹ When the scope is properly displaying the test pattern signal, use the controls on your monitor to get the image on screen to display proper color bar colors.

❺ Now feed the color bars from the generator (or other source) through your editing system. If all controls with Premiere and your capture card are set properly, the color bars should appear correctly on your monitor.

❻ Digitize a few seconds of the color bars and output them to tape.

❼ Connect the vectorscope to the output of the video tape recorder. If all controls with each aspect of your system are set properly, the color bars should appear correctly on the vectorscope display.

If you are seeing color bars that are simply out of whack, you need to check all of the controls on your deck, capture card, and software to make sure that they are not altering the signal in any way.

GETTING JUST THE RIGHT COLOR (CORRECTION)

Ideally, you want color bars to be recorded on every source tape you use so that you can verify the signal levels, hues, color phases, and so on, and make any corrections necessary in order to reproduce the signal as accurately as possible. However, your footage may appear to be too red or too green. My recommendation is to use the controls on your deck or from your capture card (if available) during the initial digitizing portion of your project so that you digitize and work with footage at the proper video levels and hues. If you don't have all those fancy controls available to you, you can use Premiere's filters to color correct your image back to normal.

To adjust the color levels of your image:

❶ Select the clip in the timeline that you wish to fix.

❷ Select Filters from the Clip menu or Control-F (Windows) or Command-F (Macintosh).

❸ Select Color Balance from the Available Filters list (you may need to scroll down the list) (Figure 4-23).

❹ Click the Add button to add it to the Current Filters list. The Color Balance Settings window should appear (Figure 4-24).

❺ Use the sliders to adjust the color for each of the RGB values (red, green, and blue). The default for nonaltered video is 100 percent for each value.

❻ Click OK.

Refer to your vectorscope to ensure proper levels and settings.

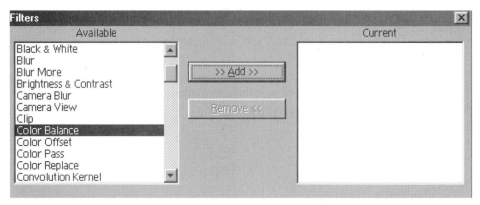

Figure 4-23 Premiere's default filters include tools to adjust the color levels of your clips.

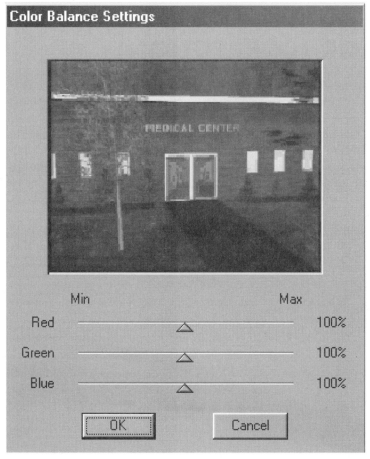

Figure 4-24 The Color Balance Settings window controls the red, green, and blue values independently for accurate color correction.

HUE AND SATURATION

I remember some of my first editing projects back when I didn't know a thing about properly calibrating my video decks. In the first project that I edited, every living creature seemed to be tinted purple. Little did I understand that the hue adjustment could have fixed this problem and returned the video signal colors back to normal.

If you do have the luxury of having a vectorscope, you will be able to adjust the Hue (or color phase) of an image more accurately. The Hue adjustment affects the color values for the entire scene globally, not just individual elements of that clip. If you look at your SMPTE color bar test pattern, as you adjust the Hue, you should see the display on the vectorscope rotating around depending on which direction you adjust the slider (Figure 4-25).

Saturation is the amount of color present in an image. Therefore, if we move the slider down to zero, we are in essence removing all of the color values, thus turning the image into a black and white scene (absent of all color). If you boost the Saturation value too high, you wind up getting an image that is so "over-saturated" with color, the colors begin to bleed out of the images and blend together, giving you a very bad attempt at a solarized image.

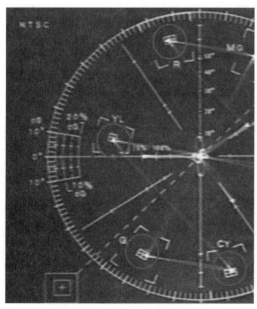
Proper Hue Position

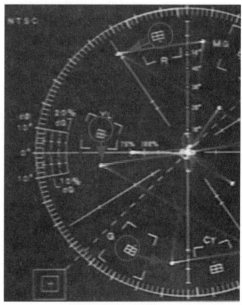
Hue Out Of Phase

Figure 4-25 The vectorescope is used to monitor the Hue or Phase of a video signal.

Keep in mind that over-saturated footage will look progressively worse for every generation you duplicate, especially on VHS tape.

To achieve a warmer feeling when trying to get a black and white image, do not drop the saturation level all the way to zero. Leave about 20 percent of the original color value to give it a nice warm look.

CHANGING THE COLOR BALANCE OVER TIME

What happens if the color begins to shift in a shot that you need? This can happen due to changes in lighting or circuitry going bad in a camera. Fortunately, Premiere's Color Balance Filter allows you to easily compensate for most shifts in color occurring over time. Or maybe you want the color to gradually change over time for some type of effect. The trick to having the color balance of an image change over time is to use keyframes.

To change the color value scheme over the duration of the clip:

❶ Select the Color Balance Filter for a clip in the timeline.

❷ Adjust any slider and click OK. A keyframe timeline should appear (Figure 4-26).

❸ Click on either triangle (keyframe) at the ends of the timeline to adjust the starting or ending frame's properties. The keyframe should be highlighted to indicate that it has been selected.

❹ Click the Edit button to open the Color Balance Settings window again.

❺ Adjust the sliders to the appropriate positions and click OK.

❻ Click anywhere on the timeline between the beginning and end keyframes to add additional keyframes (Figure 4-27).

❼ Click the Edit button to adjust any of the Color Balance Settings for any keyframe used within the duration of the video segment.

You can add as many keyframes as necessary throughout the duration of the clip. Premiere interpolates the changes that need to occur between the keyframes. This functionality is known as tweening (short for inbetweening). Tweening is the program's ability to calculate the percentage of change that needs to occur between each frame from the settings of one keyframe to the settings of the next keyframe. The further apart the keyframes are (depending on the variance of the settings), the more gradual the changes will be between keyframes. The closer the keyframes appear (assuming the same setting changes), the more radical each frame's changes will be as Premiere plays back the clip.

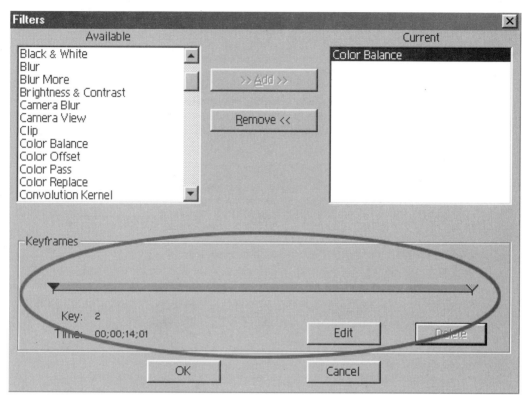

Figure 4-26 The keyframe timeline allows you to adjust your settings over the duration of the clip.

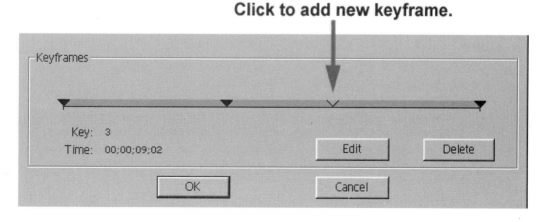

Figure 4-27 Customize filters by adding keyframes where necessary and making the proper adjustments.

HIGHLIGHTING A SINGLE COLOR

I love this effect. If you've ever wondered how they leave in a certain color in an image while turning the rest of the clip black and white, look no further. It's amazing how simple this is to do. For example, image a car commercial where you want the audience to focus on the car. Let's assume the car is red. You can drop out every color in the shot that does not contain any red in it. This means assuming your surrounding scenery does not have any red objects in it; everything but the red in the car will turn to black and white (Figure 4-28). How do you do this? Simple. Use the filter called Color Pass.

❶ Select the clip that you want to alter in the timeline.

❷ Select Filters from the Clip menu.

❸ Select Color Pass from the available filters list.

❹ Click the Add button. The Color Pass Settings window should appear (Figure 4-29).

❺ Click and hold on the color patch to choose the color you want to remain in the image.

❻ Drag the slide bar back and forth to adjust the clipping level of the selected color or enter a numeric value in the Similarity field. The further to the left (or the lower the similarity number value), the more precise the color needs to be in the clip. The further to the right (or the higher the similarity number value), the more tolerance of that color value Premiere allows to be visible. Moving the slider to the extreme left or extreme right either drops out all the color from the image or leaves all the color in the image respectively.

❼ Once you have set the desired value, click OK.

You can achieve the opposite effect (dropping out a selected color) by clicking on the Reverse check box.

Use the two monitors to compare the original image in the Clip Sample monitor on the left of the screen to the new image containing the Color Pass filter in the Output Sample monitor on the right. This filter works extremely well considering how much work it would take to use Photoshop (or some other paint program) and color correct each exported frame one frame at a time. The other option might have been to use a matte key with an alpha channel (see working with alpha channels below) and have the color car be visible through the mask. But if any objects appear between the car and the camera, they will wind up appearing in color as well. So the only real way (and relatively simple method) is to use the Color Pass Filter.

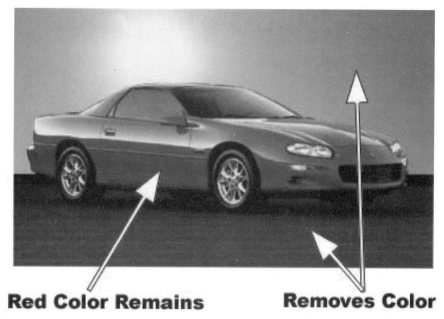

Red Color Remains   Removes Color

Figure 4-28 The Color Pass filter retains any single color value from an image while turning the rest black and white.

Figure 4-29 The Color Pass Settings window.

DO YOU HAVE IT IN ANOTHER COLOR

Let's continue with the example that we were working with in the previous section. (Now is a good time to read it if you haven't). Again, the red car is driving down the street. But what happens if you really want the car to be bright green or purple? What if you want the color to change while the car is moving down the road exactly in the same scene. Sure, if you have the budget (and an amazing, nearly unheard of talent), you could get multiple vehicles and shoot the same scene multiple times timing exactly the position of each car, etc. Obviously, this is extremely difficult, if not impossible, to execute. But with Premiere, you can achieve this effect with merely a few clicks of the mouse.

To swap image colors:

❶ Select the clip that you want to alter in the timeline.

❷ Select Filters from the Clip menu.

❸ Select Color Replace from the available filters list.

❹ Click the Add button. The Color Replace Settings window should appear (Figure 4-30).

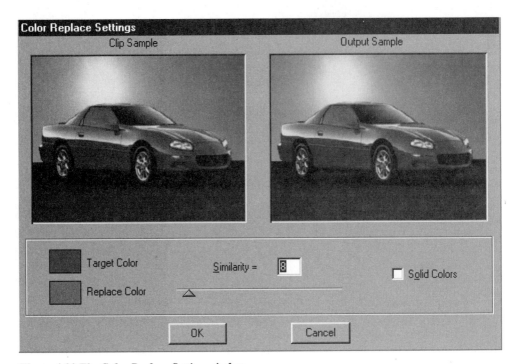

Figure 4-30 The Color Replace Setting window.

❺ Click and hold on the Target Color patch to choose the color you want to change in the image.

❻ Click and hold the Replace Color patch to choose the color that you want to substitute in place of the initial Target Color.

❼ Drag the slide bar back and forth to adjust the similarity level of the selected color or enter a numeric value in the Similarity field. The further to the left (or the lower the similarity number value), the more precise the color needs to be in the clip in order to swap colors. The further to the right (or the higher the similarity number value), the more tolerance of that color value Premiere allows to change color values (Figure 4-31).

❽ Once you have set the desired value, click OK.

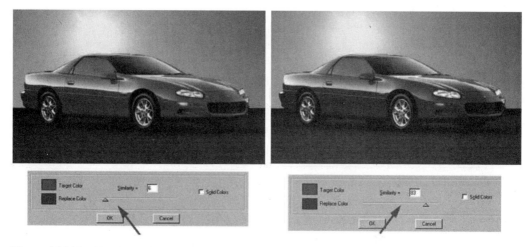

Figure 4-31 The Similarity slider adjusts the amount of tolerance for a color when replacing colors in an image.

Clicking the Solid Color check box disregards the contrast of the targeted colors and replaces anything within the targeted colors value with the Replace Color value in its entirety as a solid color. There are no gradient (more natural looking) variables.

Getting back to our car commercial, in order to keep the shot moving as one continuous image (including the tires rotating without skipping a beat), and yet having the color of the car change over time, set up your timeline as follows:

❶ Editing your original source footage into your timeline and add the Color Replace filter as described above.

❷ Once you hit OK, a keyframe timeline should appear in the Effect Edit window.

❸ Click anywhere in between the first and last keyframes to add more keyframes throughout the duration of the selected clip.

❹ Select the new keyframe and click the Edit button. This will reopen the Color Replace Settings window controls and allow you to set new values for that keyframe.

OR

❶ Edit your original source footage into your timeline on video Track 1A.

❷ Use the Razor Tool from the timeline window to cut the continuous shot into smaller segments (Figure 4-32).

❸ Move alternating segments down to video Track 1B.

❹ Apply the Color Replace filter for each new segment as described above in the Swapping Image Color section.

❺ Trim each shot's start and end frames to overlap each other between Tracks 1A and 1B.

❻ Add a dissolve into the Transition Track of video Track 1 (Figure 4-33). Now when you play your movie back, the video clip should appear to be one continuous shot with the selected image (and its colors) gradually changing from one color to another.

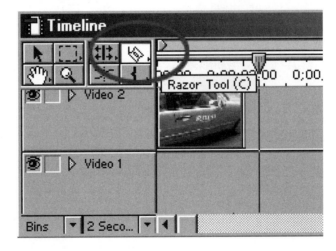

Figure 4-32 The Razor Tool allows you to slice a clip, adding new edit points.

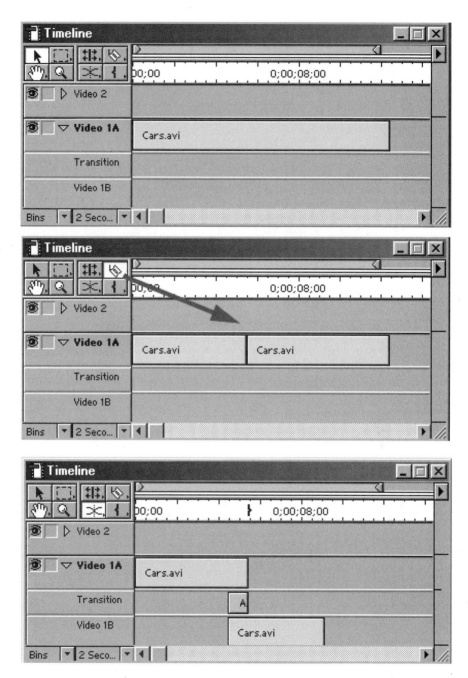

Figure 4-33 Adding dissolves to continuous clips allows you to slowly blend between different filter effects.

CREATING FUNKY
BACKGROUNDS WITH FILTERS

Here's a neat and simple trick I came across one night by messing around with some filters (which is a technique that I highly encourage). Playing around with the value settings on most of the filters may inspire you to come up with some wild and off-the-wall ideas. This effect worked well for a background:

❶ Take any piece of source footage and edit it into the timeline.

❷ Select Filters from the Clip menu.

❸ Select Crystallize.

❹ Click Add to apply the effect and open the setting controls.

❺ Increase the Cell Size to a very high value rendering the image virtually impossible to decipher what the image actually was and how it appeared before the effect.

❻ Click OK.

When you play the image back, you wind up with some very abstract images that seem to animate around. This type of effect seems to work well as a background for an upbeat movie or music video (or whatever you choose) (Figure 4-34). Obviously there are many other filters that can be applied to create useable background from standard source video clips, including Blur Filters.

Note: Images with motion work out much better than images with very little movement.

Crystallize

Figure 4-34 Using the Crystallize Filter makes for some interesting background images.

WORKING IN 3D SPACE

One of the great features of editing with Premiere is its ability to manipulate images in a three-dimensional work space. This feature is usually a very expensive upgrade on many other computer-based editing systems (I believe I spent close to $15,000 for that feature on my Avid system just a few years ago). Premiere uses a filter called Camera View to control the perspective of a video segment in your timeline (Figure 4-35). This allows you to more or less control how and from where your audience views your clips (where the camera lens is in relationship to where the shot or action took place). This is one filter that I recommend you become familiar with because I find I've used it on just about every type of project I've worked on.

Here are just a few examples of what can be done to an image while using this filter:

◆   Rotate on the X-, Y-, and Z-axis

◆   Reposition a clip on screen

◆   Zoom the clip In and Out

◆   Multiple combinations of these settings

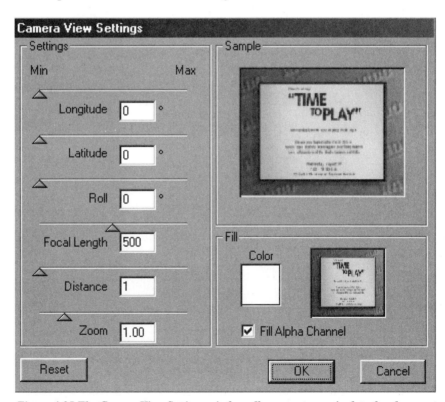

Figure 4-35 The Camera View Settings window allows you to manipulate the placement of the image in all directions.

You can use this filter to add some interesting perspectives to your images. Create a Picture-In-Picture effect in a snap. Have a shot come flying in from infinity. Tumble a shot in from anywhere within this three-dimensional world using the rotation controls.

◆   To rotate your image on the X-axis, adjust the Longitude slider (Figure 4-36).

◆   To rotate your image on the Y-axis, adjust the Latitude slider (Figure 4-37).

◆   To rotate your image on the Z-axis, adjust the Roll slider (Figure 4-38).

◆   Use a Combination of the Focal Length, Distance, and Zoom sliders to move the image along the Z-axis (bringing the image closer to the camera or sending it back into infinity) (Figure 4-39).

 See Chapter 5, Using Transitions Tastefully, to learn how to use segment effects as scene transitions.

Click the Reset button in the bottom left of the Camera View Settings window to return all of the sliders back to their normal (default) positions. You can also click on the color swatch in the bottom right of the window to fill any default background space that becomes visible while manipulating the image where portions of the clip do not cover the full screen view.

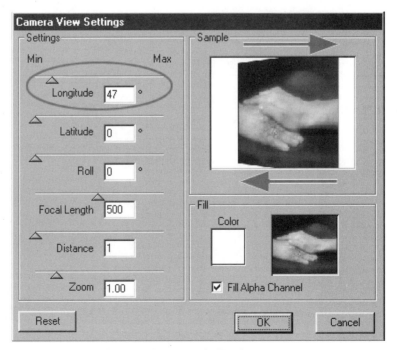

Figure 4-36 Reposition your image on the X-axis.

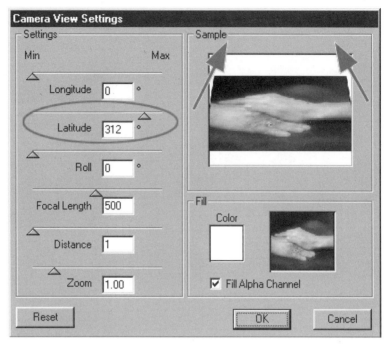

Figure 4-37 Reposition your image on the Y-axis.

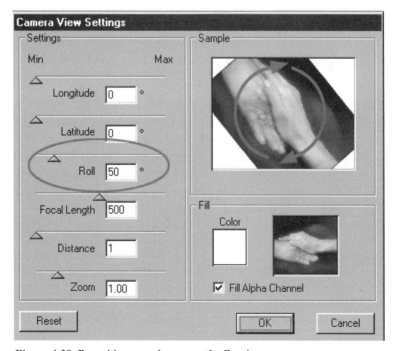

Figure 4-38 Reposition your image on the Z-axis.

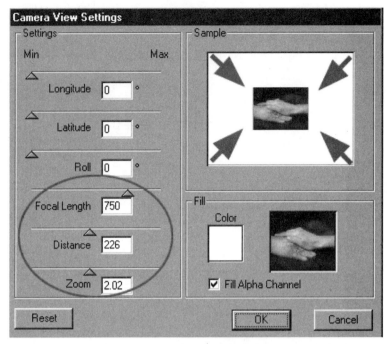

Figure 4-39 With the adjustment of a few sliders, you can set the keyframes so that your clip appears to come flying in from infinity.

Once you tweak your settings, click the OK button. This will bring you to the general Filters window. Here you have complete control to work with the image using keyframes. These keyframes allow you to adjust and manipulate your image anywhere, anytime in 3D space.

SUMMARY

As you can see from the variety of topics covered in this chapter (and this isn't close to being all of them), there are many image adjustments and special effects that you can utilize to either correct a bad image or transform a perfectly good shot into something out-of-this-world. The sky's the limit. I truly recommend starting with the best quality image to begin with so you don't have to spend half of your editing time fixing poor image quality. It's more fun to focus your efforts on being creative than assuming the role of a video janitor. With that in mind, the examples I used throughout this chapter barely touch on the type of segment image effects that are available. Play around as much as possible and create your own world of insane segment effects. You cannot spend enough time trying out all of the standard video filters and combining them to make some of the most outrageous image effects. I strongly encourage you to have some fun with filters. Feel free to send me your demo tape showing off all of the wild effects that you have created using Premiere.

chapter **5**

GETTING CREATIVE

WITH KEYS

I think I should explain what this chapter is going to cover before you get any further into it. Working with video layers allows you to create imagery that you cannot create with single-layer video clips. The question is how do you get those shots that are impossible to capture with a camera, yet build fairly easily and inexpensively during post-production? Shots like having an image over a background that wasn't really there or parts of an image in black and white while the main focus of your shot remain in color. The answer is simple: Use alpha channels and key effects.

Alpha channels can be thought of as a transparency layer within an image. This transparency layer is available in 32-bit images. If you take a standard 24-bit image, which is composed of your 8-bit Red channel, 8-bit Green channel, and 8-bit Blue channel (RGB) and add an additional transparency layer, you get your alpha channel or key channel (Figure 5-1). You may also hear this referred to as a mask or one of many different names. There are several different ways to achieve this effect and this chapter explains how to create them and discuss several applications where they might be useful.

TYPES OF ALPHA CHANNELS

There are several different ways to get the same end result of an alpha channel. There are fifteen different types of transparencies and keys listed in the Transparency Settings Window (including NONE) (Figure 5-2). In this chapter, we are going to take the four general categories and explain common useful methods of working with alpha channels in Premiere. They include:

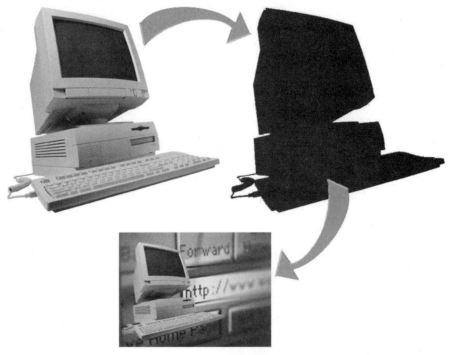

Figure 5-1 Alpha Channels are transparency channels found in 32-bit images.

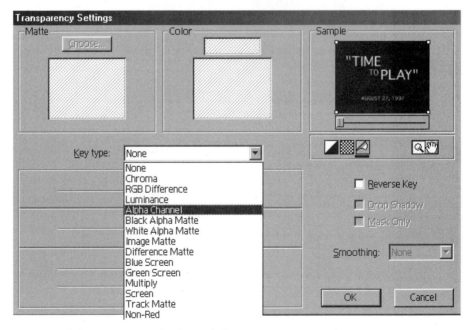

Figure 5-2 The Transparency Settings Window.

◆   Luminance Keys

◆   Chroma Keys

◆   Matte Keys

◆   Graphics Containing Alpha Channels

If each effect seems to give you a similar end result, how do you know which application to use? It's pretty easy to determine depending on what type of source material you have to work with and what your desired end result is.

EXTREME CONTRAST FOR IMAGE SEPARATION

One of the most common types of techniques for separating parts of an image to reveal only the desired portion is to use what is called a Luminance Key. A Luminance Key works with the difference in video level, or contrast of the clip's signal. You can set your key to either drop out the lightest or brightest portion of your clip or switch it to drop out the darkest portions of the clip first. For example, let's take this black and white logo (white image over a black background) and show you what happens when you key out different luminance values of that clip.

❶ Place any video clip (original source image) you want for the background on video Track 1.

❷ Place the logo/graphic clip on video Track 2 above the original source clip.

❸ Click on the clip in video Track 2 to select it.

❹ Select Video from the Clip menu.

❺ Select Transparency from the pop-up menu or Control-G (Windows) or Command-G (Macintosh). The Transparency Settings window should appear.

Or

❻ Right-click (Windows) or Option-click (Macintosh) on the clip to open a pop-up menu. Click Video from the menu and Transparency from the pop-up menu.

❼ Select the Luminance Key effect from the Key Effect pull-down menu in order to drop out the black background. Adjust the Threshold and Cutoff sliders to find the correct levels (Figure 5-3).

❽ Now reverse the values to drop out the white portion of the same images. You should now see a black image with the logo filled in with the image from the original source clip below (Figure 5-4).

There are three ways to view your Luminance Keyed effects in the Transparency Settings window (Figure 5-5):

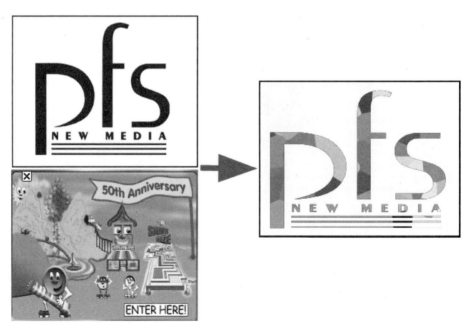

Key type: Luminance

Threshold = 86

Cutoff = 11

Figure 5-3 Use the Luminance Key filter to drop the black portions out of an image.

Figure 5-4 Reversing the key drops the white portion out of an image.

Figure 5-5 There are several ways to view keyed effects in the Transparency Settings window.

- ◆ The Black and White Box puts a black or white background in the place of the part of the image you are trying to key out.

- ◆ The Checkerboard Box puts a checkerboard pattern in the place of the part of the image you are trying to key out.

- ◆ The Image Display Box shows the portion of the video clip (from the footage placed in the video track below the keyed video clip in your timeline) through the keyed-out portion of the clip that contains the effect.

USING LUMINANCE KEYS WITH NON-BLACK AND WHITE IMAGES

If you are looking for some interesting video combinations and special effects, try playing around with luminance key effects on a variety of different types of source footage. What I mean is that you don't always have to use black and white images to get spectacular special effects. Here is an idea that I used on one of my projects. I hope it gets the ball rolling as far as some creative ideas:

❶ Use any moving video footage on video Track 1 (here I used a shot of horses galloping).

❷ To convey the strength and intensity of the horses, I placed a shot of fire on video Track 2.

❸ I applied the Luminance Key effect to the fire, dropping out the actual image of the flames and just keeping its shape and motion (Figure 5-6).

**High Contrast Source on Track 2
(Fire over Black)**

Video Source on Layer 1

*Figure 5-6 Create unusual effects by simply placing
Luminance Key over high-contrast moving video footage.*

> The advantage of using a Luminance Key was that I was able to use standard video of moving flames that constantly gave me a "moving" key, without having to create a key for each frame.

Luminance Keys do not work well if the image you are trying to drop out has the same brightness (or darkness) values that are in the image you are trying to keep. You wind up dropping out portions of your image that are usually less than desirable (Figure 5-7).

Original Source   **Luminance Key Applied**

Figure 5-7 Images with little contrast do not work well with Luminance Keys.

USING COLOR TO KEY IMAGES

Another type of keying effect that works in a similar way to the Luminance Key, but which offers more control by specifying a particular color value (or color range) to drop out is the Chroma Key effect. This effect allows you to take any image and begin to drop out, specific portions of a clip based on a color you select and control. Like the Luminance Key effect, the greater the separation in value the more control and accuracy you will have in creating a clean key. As you start adjusting the slider controls in the Transparency Settings window, you will notice that the key starts taking effect with the color value closest to the color that you have selected. The more you increase the slider settings, the more the color value starts to expand into colors that are closely related to the initial color you selected. If you continue to increase the slider values, you will eventually key out all of the colors, therefore dropping out the entire image.

The more distinct the color values are in your image, again, the more accurate your key will appear. For instance, if you are trying to key out the blue in the sky of a shot of a tree and a cliff (made up primarily of shades of green and brown), you should be able to get a fairly clean key (Figure 5-8). If you want to key out the sky in a shot of a boat on the ocean, the blue values in the water are probably too similar to the blue values in the sky. Therefore, you will wind up dropping out parts of the oceans as you adjust the key values for the sky (Figure 5-9).

Figure 5-8 Solid colors work well for clean Chroma Keys.

To create a Choma Key effect:

❶ Place a video clip in your timeline that will be used as the background image or image appearing through the key.

❷ Place the clip that you would like to use as your primary image on a video track directly above the clip you added in Step 1.

❸ Click on the clip in upper video track to select it.

❹ Select Video from the Clip menu.

❺ Select Transparency from the pop-up menu or Control-G (Windows) or Command-G (Macintosh). The Transparency Settings window should appear.

Too Similar

Figure 5-9 Similar shades of colors create undesirable Chroma Keys.

Or

Right-click (Windows) or Option-click (Macintosh) on the clip to open a pop-up menu. Click Video from the menu and Transparency from the pop-up menu.

❻ Select Chroma from the Key Type pull-down menu.

❼ Use the sliders to accurately adjust the key settings.

❽ Click on the color swatch to open the standard Color Picker window to select which color you want to use as the key color (any color similar to this value will become transparent, revealing those portions of the image below) (Figure 5-10).

You can use the eyedropper to select the exact color image from your video clip by simply rolling your mouse over the Color portion of the Transparency Settings window

How the Chroma Key sliders and pull-down menus work:

◆ The Similarity slider narrows or expands the range of colors that will make up the keyed portion of the clip.

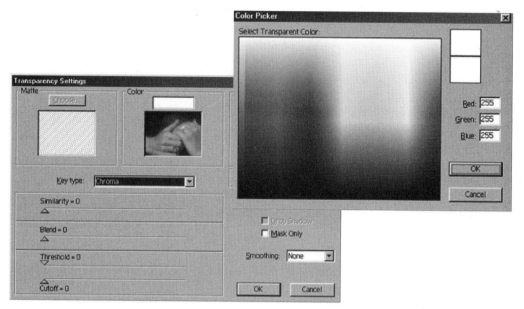

Figure 5-10 The Color Picker allows you to drop out any color value from an image.

◆ The Blend slider is used to make a softer, smoother blend between the keyed image and the one below.

◆ The Threshold slider is used to control the amount of shadows that appear in the color value of the selected key color or color range.

◆ The Cuttoff slider adjusts the lightness or darkness of the shadows. Do not drag the slider past the value set in the Threshold slider. This may invert gray and transparent pixels in your image, therefore, not giving you the desired key effect.

◆ The Smoothing pull-down menu on the right of the window controls the amount of anti-aliasing (stair-stepping vs. pixel-blending edges) that occurs between the portion of the image that is to remain visible and the portion that is being keyed out. Smoothing offers three degrees of blending: None, Low, and High.

HOLLYWOOD EFFECTS AND THE WEATHER REPORT

What do these two things have in common? More than you might think if you're not familiar with blue screen/green screen chroma key effects. From the big Hollywood studio lots to your local news station, blue screen and green screen backgrounds are commonly used to key out specific areas of a video clip.

The main reason these somewhat fluorescent blue and green colors are used for chroma keying is that these color values are least apparent in the human skin. Therefore, you can completely key out these values without altering the appearance of most human beings on screen.

Your local weather person is not actually standing in front of a giant computer screen that is displaying the maps and weather conditions. In reality, that person is standing in front of a wall that is painted with this bright "chroma" blue or green paint. They are usually looking at monitors of the final combined (broadcasted) image to see which maps and graphics are being displayed (Figure 5-11).

The process looks like this:

Figure 5-11 News weather anchors stand in front of a blue screen wall while the weather maps are digitally combined in the control room.

❶ The weather person stands in front of a blue or green wall. Evenly balanced lighting is always important for getting clean keys.

❷ The camera shoots the person so that all you see is the person over a blue or green background (completely filling up the remaining visible area). All other images should be kept out of frame.

❸ In the control room, the live camera feed is combined with the computer-generated graphics (weather maps, etc.). A Chroma Key effect is applied to this combined image.

❹ The result is a single image of the weather person displayed over the computer-generated maps.

This technology is used for many Hollywood-style effects found in many feature films. A good example occurs when you want an actor to be in a scene where it is too dangerous or virtually impossible to shoot a scene live. Think of any movie you've seen where an actor appears in a "virtual" world where amazing 3D effects occur around the person. If you created a scene consisting of a computer-generated room and you wanted to show your actor interacting with this scene as if he were really there, you would need to shoot and edit this using blue screen or green screen technology.

❶ The first step is to carefully plan, storyboard, and coordinate the scene before you shoot any footage or create any graphics.

❷ Set up a room (preferably a studio) where you can paint the entire shooting area chroma blue or green. Be aware of lighting to reduce the number of shadows and various shades of your key colors. The greater the variances in shade of key colors, the more difficult it will be to accurately separate the actor from the background.

❸ Shoot the actor doing his routine as if he were really in the virtual scene.

❹ Create the graphics and animations of the virtual scene.

❺ Digitize the video footage of the actor's scene into Premiere.

❻ Import the virtual animation scene into Premiere.

❼ Edit the animation footage onto Video Track 1.

❽ Edit the actor's footage onto Video Track 2.

❾ Apply the Chroma Key effect onto the actor's footage, keying out the blue/green background to display the animation scene behind the actor.

CLOTHING AND PROPS ARE "KEY"

You can get very creative with your props when shooting actors in a studio that will be used in conjunction with a 3D animated virtual world. If you want it to look like your actor was jumping on top of an object that was computer generated, have your actor really jump onto an object of the same proportions during the studio shooting. This means have the actor jump onto a box or crate of approximately equal size or proportion to create a realistic effect. The important part is to completely paint any props or objects that you do not want visible in your final scene the same color as the background chroma walls. If you choose to have a real object appear with the actor in that virtual world, then you would shoot the object as is during the filming of that scene.

Clothing is a very important factor when shooting scenes over a chroma wall. We solved (or minimized) the problem of not dropping out skin tones by shooting over chroma blue or green walls. These colors (or similar color values) must also not appear in the actor's clothes. If similar color values do exist, those portions of his clothes will become transparent or keyed out once the chroma key effect is applied to the video clip. Think back to the weather anchor person scenario described above. I saw the weather person on a small local station do the weather without even realizing that he had blue designs in his tie. When he walked in front of the blue "weather wall" (where the maps are digitally imposed), you saw portions of the maps appear in those blue portions of his tie. This looks pretty bad considering no one has transparent portions of his torso.

IMAGE MATTE KEYS FOR COOKIE CUTTER EFFECTS

Television is filled with so many complex images and effects these days, you might be wondering how they create some of them. The Image Matte Key effect allows you to use a still image to cut out any custom shape you design and fill that shape with video. Therefore, you can design a still black and white graphic (in any paint program) and use that shape to define the boarders of your image. No more plain, rectangular picture-in-picture windows (Figure 5-12). Black and white images work the best for clean, crisp-edged cuts. You can also use any shades of a grayscale image for matte keys. This will result in shadow or blend style effects. Gradients in your still image (fades from black to white) will produce a soft edge shadow effect. Image Matte Keys work with layers.

To use the Image Matte Key effect:

❶ Edit your background video clip onto any video track.

❷ Edit your foreground video clip onto the video track directly above the first clip.

❸ Select the upper clip by single-clicking on it. You should see the "marching ants" around the clip to signify that you have selected that clip.

❹ Select Video from the Clip menu.

❺ Select Transparency from the pop-up menu or use the keyboard shortcut Control-G (Windows) or Command-G (Macintosh). The Transparency Settings window should appear.

❻ Select Image Matte from the Key Type pull-down menu.

❼ Click on the "page peel" icon to view the actual keyed image (Figure 5-13).

❽ Click OK.

Key In Second Source

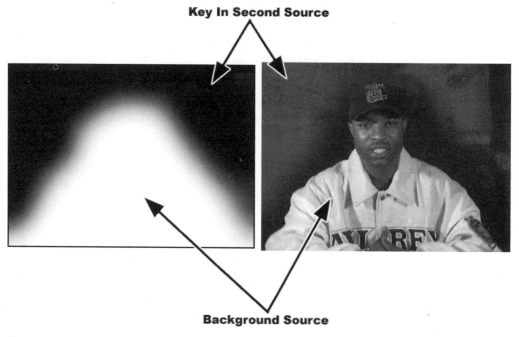

Background Source

Figure 5-12 Create custom matte keys using any grayscale image.

By default, Premiere uses the white portion of the matte graphic to display the clip selected and drops out the rest of the image indicated by the black portions of the still graphic. If you're not sure which area will remain and the matte key drops out the portion of the clip you wanted to keep, click on the Reverse Key check box in the Transparency Settings window to get the desired results (Figure 5-14).

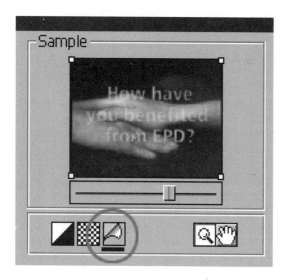

Figure 5-13 The "page peel" icon displays how an effect looks without leaving the Transparency Settings window.

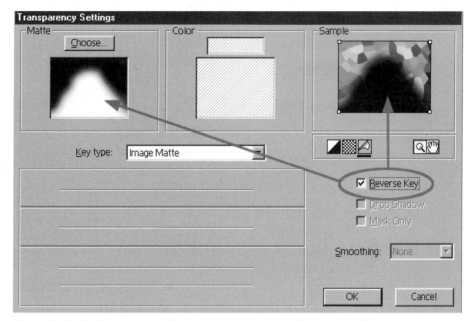

Figure 5-14 The Reverse check box drops the opposite of the normal default key value.

CREATING IMAGES FOR MATTE KEYS

Although this book is focused on Premiere, I find that you really need to have an arsenal of tools in order to use any application to its fullest. This goes for video editing programs as well. I think Photoshop is a very underrated tool for video editors. There are so many things you can use it for to improve your video projects, including touching up frames that have dirt marks or scratches, creating professional looking graphics and titles, and of course, creating images for matte keys.

This is going to be a brief description on how to create a graphic (in Photoshop or any paint program on the market) that can be used in Premiere as a matte key:

❶ Create a new graphic (preferably one that is the same size as your video image). If you are working with a final output size as 720 x 486, then make your graphic 720 pixels wide by 486 pixels high. This of course is only a general rule and can vary under different circumstances.

❷ Make sure the background of your image is entirely white.

❸ Select one of the painting tools (paintbrush, airbrush, etc.) and apply black to the areas that you want to make transparent.

❹ Save the image in one of the file formats listed below.

❺ Import the file into Premiere by selecting Import from the File menu.

❻ Select File from the pop-up menu.

❼ Find and select the file you just created.

❽ Click Open.

You can also choose to work with a black background and paint with white.

Premiere can import any one of the following still graphic formats:

◆ Adobe Illustrator (.AI)

◆ Adobe Photoshop (.PSD)

◆ Graphics Interchange Format (.GIF)

◆ Joint Photographers Experts Group or JPEG (.JPG)

◆ Macintosh Picture (.PICT)

◆ Targa (.TGA)

◆ Tag Image File Format (.TIFF)

And Windows version can also import:

◆ PCX (.PCX)

◆ Windows Bitmap (.BMP)

CREATING SOFT EDGE KEYS

Keeping with the Photoshop method for creating your custom matte key images, you can easily avoid the hard edge cutouts and add a touch of softness. To create the soft edge matte key cutouts:

❶ Select a soft edge brush in Photoshop when painting your matte key image (Figure 5-15).

❷ To select different brush sizes and edges, select Show Brushes from the Window menu.

❸ The gradient or feathered areas will appear as a soft edge image when you apply the Image Matte Key effect in Premiere (Figure 5-16).

You can make the soft edge very subtle by utilizing a small pixel spread. I recommend always using a very small amount of soft edge on my matte keys. It helps make the blend between the two images more natural without making the image look like it was cut out with a pair of those safety scissors that you used in first grade. To create a

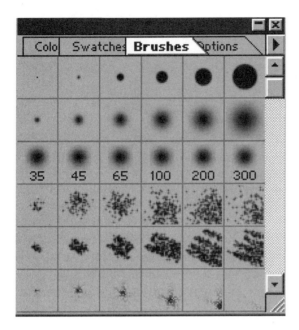

Figure 5-15 The Brush palette in Photoshop.

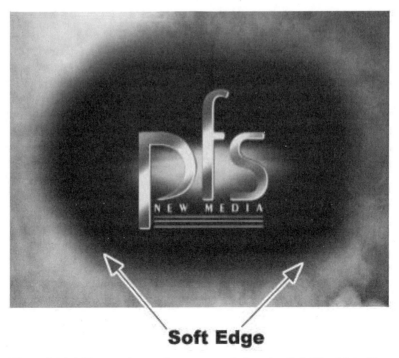

Figure 5-16 Add a creative touch to your movie by using Soft Edge Matte Keys.

larger, more extreme soft edge key, use a brush with a broad pixel spread. This will apply the "feathering" look over a wider area. This gives the image a very soothing, mild blend into the background image.

MATTE KEYS TO EMPHASIZE YOUR IMAGE

I personally like looking for books that go beyond the "how to use a certain feature" in the program and apply a more creative approach. This example should help spur some ideas that you can use in your everyday projects. For this particular example, I wanted the viewer to focus on the product in the center of the screen. The desired effect was to keep the product in its natural color while applying a dark-colored tint to the moving footage around the product. (Figure 5-17). Fortunately, the main image was not moving so applying a single still matte key would work.

To create this effect:

❶ Export a single frame from Premiere from the clip of the image you want to use.

❷ Import that still graphic (of the video clip) into Photoshop.

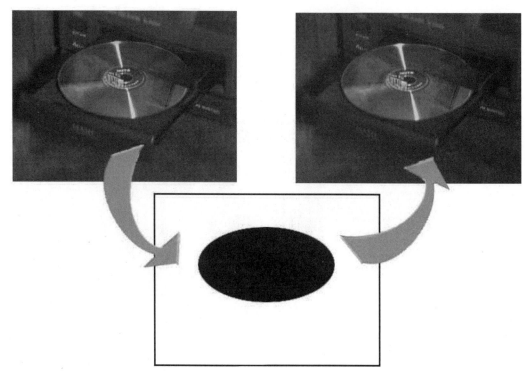

Figure 5-17 Use Matte Keys to make your main image stand out from the rest of the image.

❸ Paint the entire object white, paying very close attention to the edges for accuracy.

❹ Cover the rest of the image with black. (My tip from the previous section is to leave a slight soft edge around the object to help blend the images together more naturally).

❺ Save the new black and white image. I tend to name my files to describe the image. For Matte Key images, I'll put the word matte in the file name to help identify the appropriate file. (i.e., Original File Name: box.tga; New Matte Key Image: box-matte:tga).

❻ In Premiere, edit the video clip onto Video Track 1.

❼ Edit the same clip with the same exact starting point onto Video Track 2.

❽ Select the clip on Video Track 2 by clicking on it.

❾ Select Video from the Clip menu.

❿ Select Transparency from the pop-up menu or use the keyboard shortcut Control-G (Windows) or Command-G (Macintosh).

⓫ Select Image Matte from the Key Type pull-down menu.

⓬ Click Choose from the Matte section in the upper left portion of the Transparency Settings window

⓭ Find the file you just created for your matte key and select it in the Load Matte window. (Figure 5-18).

⓮ Click Open.

Now your matte key is in place, although it doesn't appear to be doing anything since the two layers of video are identical. Now you must alter the video clip on the first layer to get the desired results.

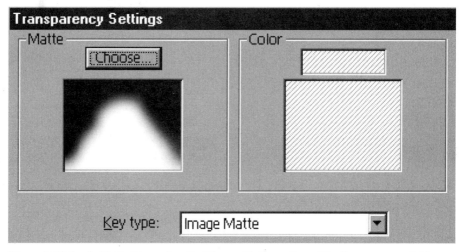

Figure 5-18 Apply Matte Keys using the Choose Matte section of the Transparency Settings window.

⑮   Select the clip on Video Track 1 by clicking on it.

⑯   Select Filters from the Clip menu.

⑰   Choose Color balance or any other filter you would like to apply.

⑱   Make the appropriate filter adjustments.

⑲   Click OK.

When you render the video segment out or drag through the clip holding the Alt key (Windows) or the Option key (Macintosh), you should see the image you selected remain in full color while the rest of the clip plays with which ever filtered effects you applied to Track 1. This technique can be used in so many different applications. I encourage you to experiment and come up with your own useful applications. (If you come up with something cool, let me know).

Tip

Add filters to background portions of Matte Key effects for more image distinction.

USING ANIMATED MATTES TO TRACK THE KEY

Once you get the feel for how still matte keys work, you can move on to more exciting matte key features such as animated matte keys. The basic idea is that you can now change the shape and/or position of the matte over time. In the past example, the image that you were focusing on was static (not moving). What happens if we want to use that same type of effect with an image that is moving? This process is much more involved. Depending upon what it is you are trying to highlight, there are several ways to approach this type of effect.

One situation may involve images or objects you created in a third-party animation program (Figure 5-19). The matte can be automatically generated by the animation software. This will save you a tremendous amount of time. If the image you would like to highlight was not created in an animation program or shot against a blue screen, you may have to export every single frame and paint each one individually to get the exact matte shape for each frame. The process is long and very time-consuming, but you can create some exciting effects. My personal favorite example using this technique is to take any person or object that you have shot, cut them out, and have them appear over some other type of background (including cartoons or other such animations). Once again, the ideal situation would be to have shot the scene in a studio using a blue screen chroma wall. Since this isn't always a perfect world, you need to be prepared for how to get that same result using any existing footage. The type of matte key we want to use is referred to as Track Matte (or Traveling matte). This process lets Premiere "track" the movement of your image frame by frame, providing you with a matte key that follows as your video clip plays.

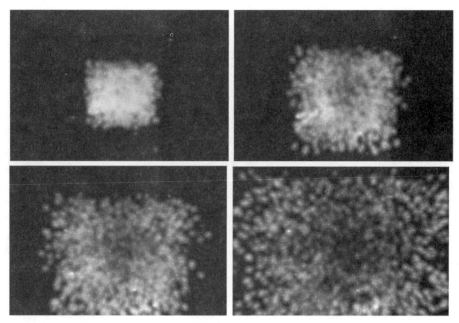

Figure 5-19 Animated Mattes are a series of individual matte keys being played back one frame at a time.

❶ Export each frame of the video from which you would like to keep a particular portion of the image.

❷ Import each frame individually into Photoshop.

❸ Paint the portion of each frame that you want to keep white and fill the remaining portions black,

❹ Re-import the frames individually or as a movie clip. (When edited together, you should see an animated version of your image silhouetted in black and white) (Figure 5-20).

❺ Edit the background video on Video Track 1.

❻ Edit the original clip of the video you want to key in Track 2.

❼ Edit the animated matte key clip (black and white) that you just imported onto Track 3. (Figure 5-21).

❽ Select the clip on Video Track 2 to highlight it.

❾ Select Video from the Clip menu.

❿ Select Transparency from the pop-up menu or use the keyboard shortcut keys Control-G (Windows) or Command-G (Macintosh). The Transparency Settings window should appear.

⓫ Select Track Matte from the Key Type pull-down menu.

⓬ Click OK.

Figure 5-20 With some hard work and a bit of time, you can create any moving image into an animated matte.

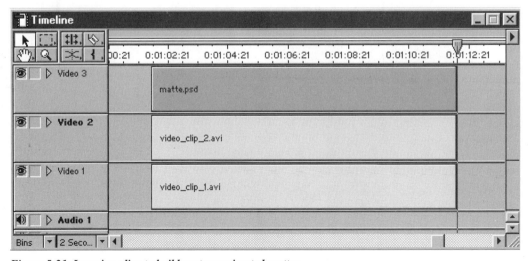

Figure 5-21 Layering clips to build custom animated mattes.

COLOR FIGURE 1
Premiere is being used in today's top nonlinear editing suites.

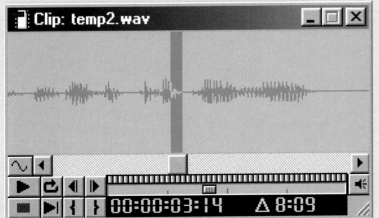

COLOR FIGURE 2
Waveform display of a digital audio sound file.

COLOR FIGURE 5
Pixilization of the image increases as greater compression ratios are applied while digitizing clips.

1:1 (Uncompressed)

4:1 Compression

50:1 Compression

Photoshop

Premiere

Skyline Graphic (Track 2)
Golden Sunset Video (Track 1)

Alpha Channel

COLOR FIGURE 6
Use layers of alpha channels and matte keys to get the desired results not always available in a single shot.

COLOR FIGURE 7
Create your own custom countdown screens.

COLOR FIGURE 8
Original camera angle.

COLOR FIGURE 9
Use segment effects to create a variety of camera angles and effects.

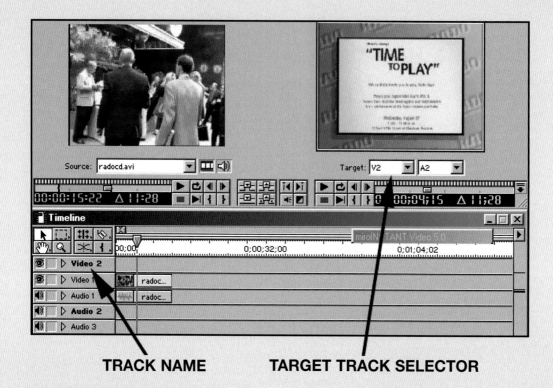

TRACK NAME　　　　**TARGET TRACK SELECTOR**

COLOR FIGURE 10
*Use the Target Track Selector to determine
which track you want to add source video
clips to your timeline.*

COLOR FIGURE 11
*Timelines can display multiple frame views of the clips
contained in that track.*

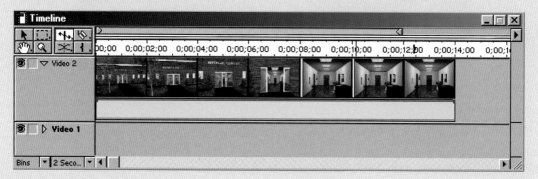

COLOR FIGURE 12
SMPTE color bars test pattern.

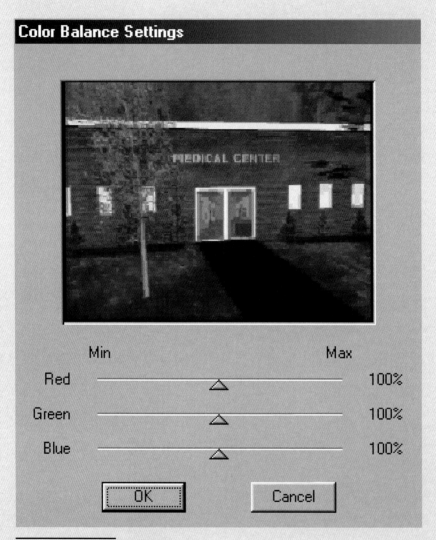

COLOR FIGURE 13
Individual RGB sliders can be used to color correct your footage.

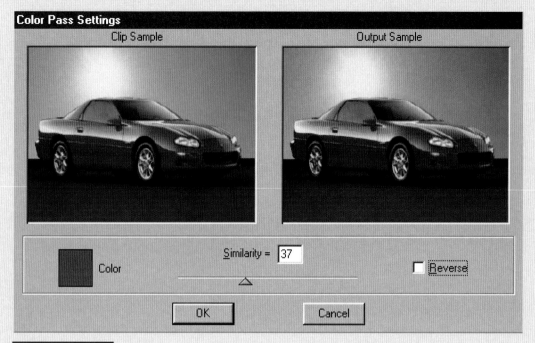

Color Pass Settings

Clip Sample

Output Sample

Color

$\underline{S}$imilarity = 37

☐ $\underline{R}$everse

OK

Cancel

COLOR FIGURE 14
Use the Color Pass Filter to drop out every color in an image except the one you wish to highlight.

COLOR FIGURE 15
You can easily alter the hue of any given shade of a color. Not sure if you want a red car? Try blue.

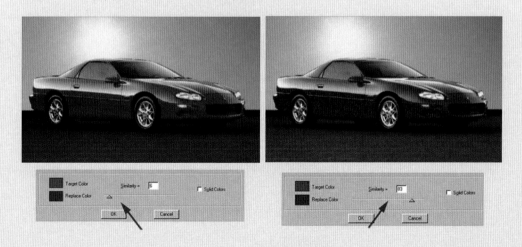

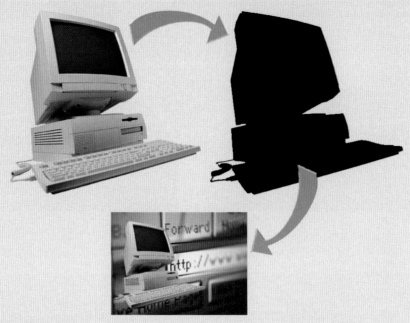

COLOR FIGURE 16

Alpha channels remove the areas outside the desire portions of an image, allowing you to place custom shaped images over other video clips.

COLOR FIGURE 17

Gradient black and white images make nice, soft edge effects when added to layered images in your timeline.

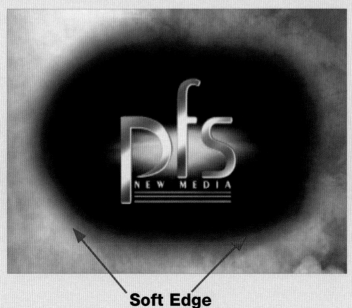

Soft Edge

COLOR FIGURE 18

Chroma Key effects work well for mixing live people with other source material.
This is how your local weather is reported on your favorite news station.

COLOR FIGURE 19

Luminance keys work well as "cookie cutters" when applied to high contrast images.

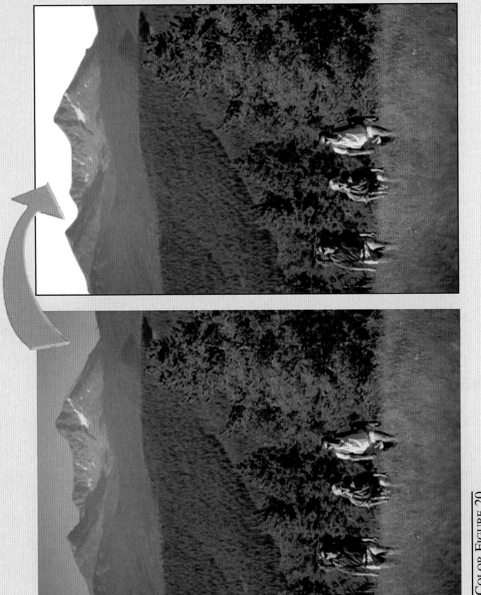

COLOR FIGURE 20
Solid color areas work well for clean Chroma Keys.

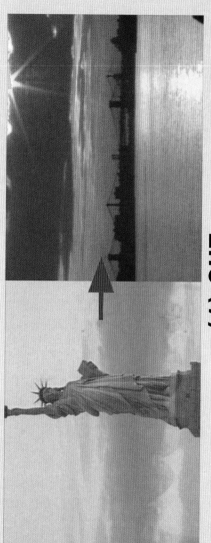

(1) CUT

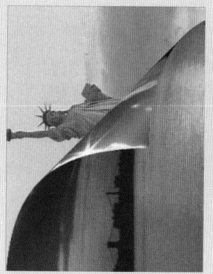

(3) DVE

(2) DISSOLVE

COLOR FIGURE 21
Premiere allows you to add any of the hundreds of customizable transitions.

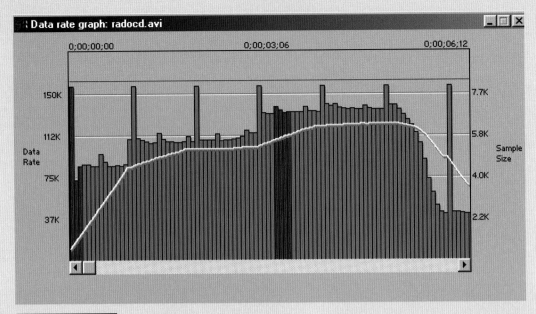

COLOR FIGURE 22
Monitor the data rate of your clips being digitized.

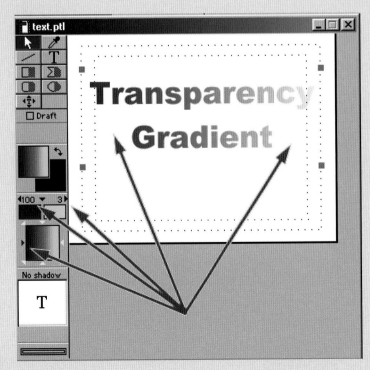

COLOR FIGURE 23
Use Color and Transparency Gradients for some interesting text effects.

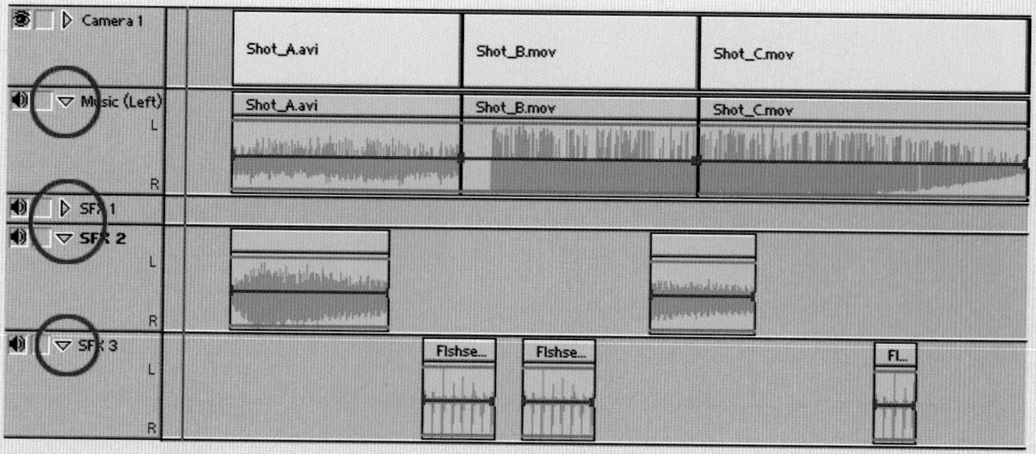

COLOR FIGURE 24

Expand audio tracks in your timeline to view the file's waveform display.

COLOR FIGURE 25

Using graphics, text, and animations to create lower thirds.

COLOR FIGURE 26
You can use third party 3D animation programs to create high-end text animations.

COLOR FIGURE 27
The standard color picker.

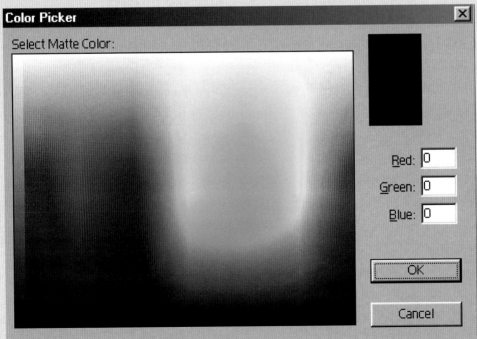

When you play your edited video segment back (after either rendering the segment or holding down the Alt key (Windows) or Option key (Macintosh) and dragging through your timeline), you should see the image that you masked (using the animated matte) over the background video clip. Once again, there are probably a million and one uses for this type of effect. I encourage you to try some different applications.

If you need a long segment with this type of effect, I strongly encourage shooting the scene over a chroma blue screen wall to save you the hassle of exporting and painting each individual frame.

USING ANY MOVING VIDEO AS YOUR MATTE KEY

The Track Matte Key effect works with just about any type of moving video clip you choose for your "matte" image. You can layer any three video clips (stills or moving video) and use the Track Matte key to generate an animated or traveling matte key effect.

To accomplish this technique:

❶ Edit the background video on Video Track 1.

❷ Edit a second clip of video on Video Track 2.

❸ Edit a third video clip that will act as your matte key onto Track 3.

Matte keys work best when there is a clear distinction in contrast of the image. To improve the keying capability of the video in Video Track 3, apply filters to adjust the contrast and brightness as well as turn it to grayscale).

❹ Select the clip on Video Track 2 to highlight it.

❺ Select Video from the Clip menu.

❻ Select Transparency from the pop-up menu or use the keyboard shortcut keys Control-G (Windows) or Command-G (Macintosh). The Transparency Settings window should appear.

❼ Select Track Matte from the Key Type pull-down menu.

❽ Click OK.

The result you get should show you the image that is in Video Track 2 where the white (or brighter) portions of the video in Video Track 3 (that shape). The areas that are black (or darker) portions of the video in Video Track 3 should hold the shape while displaying those portions of the video clip found in Track 1.

SUMMARY

There are many useful techniques that you can use to create some very interesting composites in your video projects. Each one just takes a bit of time and creativity to figure out which technique will work best depending on the circumstances you are working under and the type of footage you have available. Try playing around with the different type of keys and you'll be pleasantly surprised at some of the results you achieve. Good luck and be patient.

chapter 6

FINE TUNING USING TRIM MODE

For those of you who worked on linear tape-to-tape editing systems, you probably remember the frustrations of finding just the right frame and committing to an edit. If you wanted to lengthen or shorten a shot on your edited master tape, you would have to re-edit all of the shots that came after that revision. If you didn't have timecoded tapes and an EDL (Edit Decision List), you might as well have given up.

Today, Premiere and other computer-based nonlinear editing systems allow for these types of changes to be done in a few seconds instead of a few days. This chapter is going to look at how you can fine-tune your edits without affecting the rest of your timeline.

THE ART OF TRIMMING

Once your movie is put together, you have the ability to go back and tweak each edit point. Trimming is the feature that allows you to add or remove frames to either side of an edit point. The three basic methods of trimming involve adding or removing frames from the outgoing clip, from the incoming clip, or simultaneously working both sides of the edit point at the same time (Figure 6-1).

To understand how trimming works, I am going to use an analogy that I think will help you understand how editing with Premiere works. When you mark In and Out points in a source clip and edit that particular segment into your timeline, the remainder of the source footage that you initially digitized for that clip still exists. This remain-

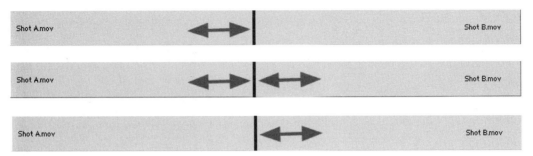

Figure 6-1 Three basic methods for trimming an edit point.

ing footage is referred to as handles. These handles are what are being referenced when you trim a segment in your timeline, without having to go back and find the source footage yourself. I tell people to imagine that all source clips are made up of two spools, similar to paper towel rolls or film reels. The portion of the source footage that is unwound is the portion displayed in your timeline. The handles, or unused source footage, is what is rolled up on each end of the clip, not being displayed in the timeline (Figure 6-2).

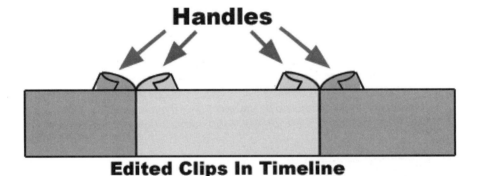

Figure 6-2 The portions of your source clips not used in your timeline are available for trimming, known as handles.

The only times where no source footage handles exist are when you use the entire length of the footage you digitized or when you select the option to delete unused footage from your project. This option allows you to permanently delete the portions of your digitized footage not used in your timeline.

The trimming of a clip, in a sense, is this rolling up or unrolling of the remaining portions of the source footage. Therefore, if the end of Shot A was being cut off, instead of having to actually go back to the source footage yourself and make a new edit

(Figure 6-3), you can simply enter into Trim Mode and extend the outgoing portion of Shot A. Like most features in Premiere, there are several different ways you can trim clips. The two most common ways are by entering Trim Mode or working directly in the timeline.

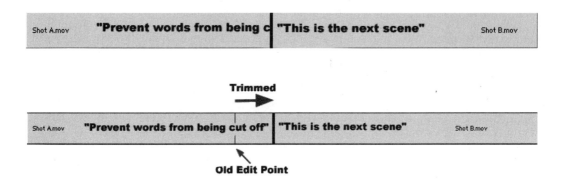

Figure 6-3 As long as the source material exists, you can use the trim feature to fix bad edit points.

ENTERING TRIM MODE

Use the Trim Mode to get the most accurate control over the edit point you are trimming. To switch from the normal mode that you spend most of your time working in, where the source clips are displayed in the left window and the edited timeline is viewed in the right window, to Trim Mode:

❶ Click the arrow in the upper right corner next to the edit monitor (Figure 6-4).

❷ Select Trim Mode from the pop-up menu.

❸ Notice the change in controls for the monitor window in Trim mode (Figure 6-5).

To enter Trim mode using keyboard shortcut keys, hold the Control key (Windows) or Command key (Macintosh) and hit the T key.

The monitor display will vary depending upon what you have selected in the Monitor Window Options. To open the Monitor Window Options screen:

❶ Click the arrow in the upper right corner next to the edit monitor.

❷ Select Monitor Window Options from the pop-up menu.

❸ Select from one of the different display views available (Figure 6-6).

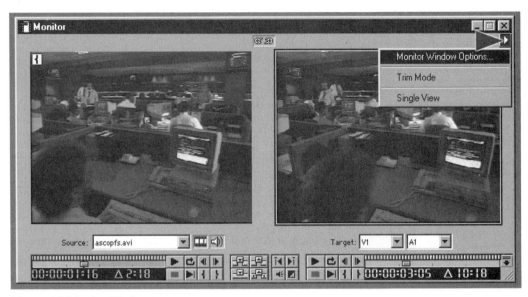

Figure 6-4 Monitor Display pop-up menu.

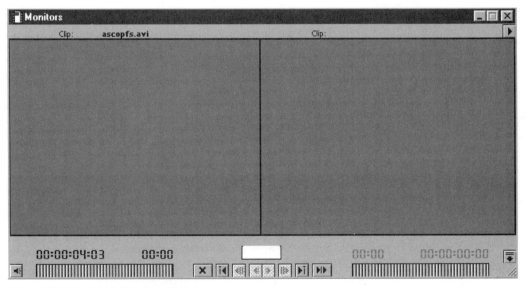

Figure 6-5 Trim Mode Monitor Display.

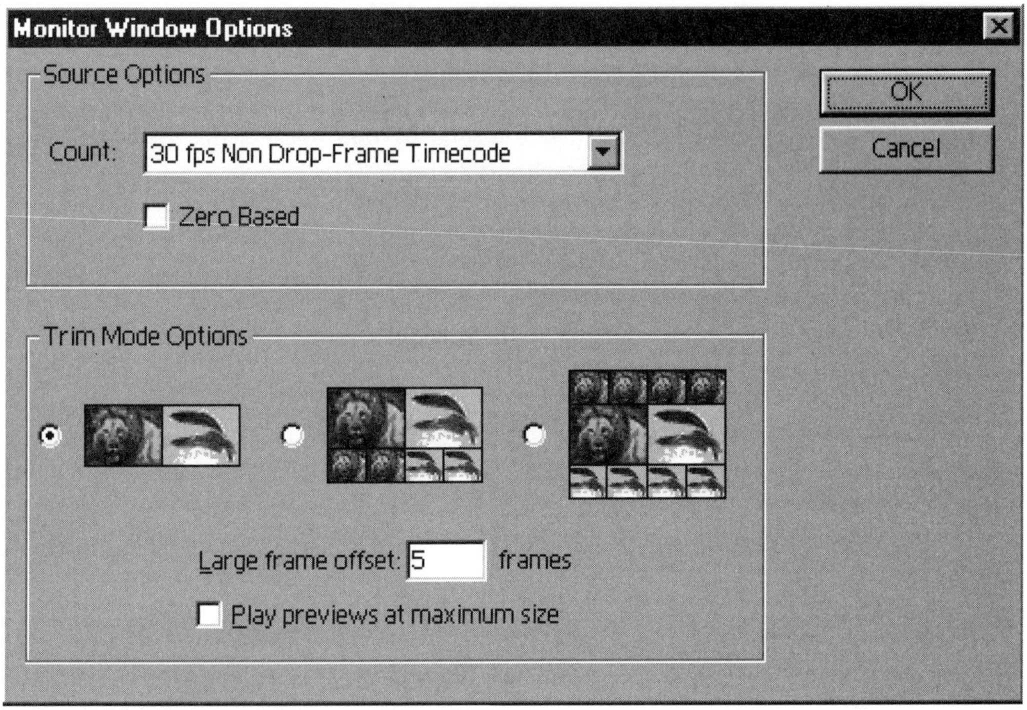

Figure 6-6 Monitor Window Options screen.

OR

❶ Click anywhere in the Monitor window to select it.

❷ Click the right mouse button (Windows) or Alt-click the mouse button (Macintosh).

❸ Select Monitor Window Options from the pop-up menu.

❹ Select from one of the different display views available.

For trimming the beginning or ending frames of a straight cut edit, I recommend working with the default two-screen display. These screens represent the last frame of the outgoing clip on the left and the first frame of the incoming clip on the right. Keep it simple to avoid confusion.

HOW TRIM MODE WORKS

Once you have edited at least two clips into your timeline, enter into Trim Mode. Using the default setting, you should see two monitors. These monitors are not displaying the usual source footage on the left and edited clips from your timeline on the right anymore. Instead, the left monitor is displaying the last frame of outgoing shot (Shot A), and the right monitor is displaying the first frame of the incoming shot (Shot B) (Figure 6-7). In Trim Mode, you have the choice to trim an edit in one of three ways:

◆   Trim only the end of Shot A.

◆   Trim both Shot A and Shot B at the same time.

◆   Trim only the beginning of Shot B.

To trim only the end frame of the outgoing shot, simply click on the left monitor. The timecode numbers below that monitor should become highlighted, indicating that your actions will be altering only that side of the edit point. To trim only the start frame of the incoming shot, click on the right monitor. The timecode numbers below that

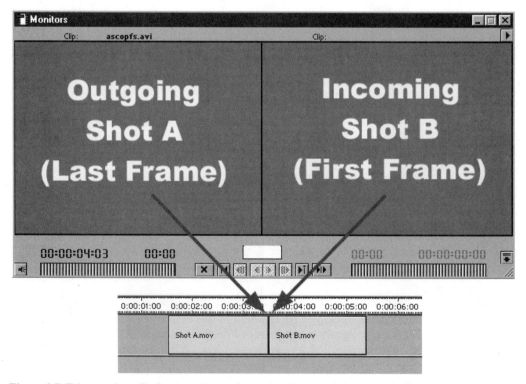

Figure 6-7 Trim monitors display incoming and outgoing frames of the selected edit point.

monitor should become highlighted, indicating that your actions will only be altering that side of the edit point. To trim both sides of the edit point, simultaneously affecting the end frame of the outgoing shot while changing the start frame of the incoming shot, click on (or very close to) the dividing line separating the two monitor views. The cursor should change icons to indicate that you will be trimming both sides of the edit (Figure 6-8). The timecode numbers below both monitors should become highlighted.

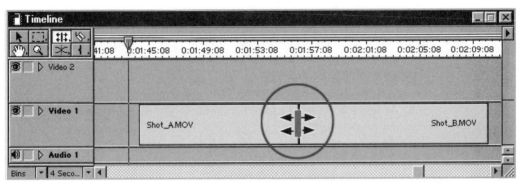

Figure 6-8 The cursor icon changes to signify you're in Trim Mode.

 When entering into Trim mode, your timeline marker does not need to be exactly on an edit point. Premiere will select the closest available edit point, so the timeline marker just needs to be close enough to the desired edit point.

TRIMMING ONE SIDE OF AN EDIT

There are a few points to be aware of when trimming on one side of an edit point. Thinking of trimming in "time-values" may help you understand the outcome of a trim more than thinking in positive and negative values. The outcome of a trim is dependent upon the value of that trim (positive or negative) and which side of the edit you are working on. Think about it in relation to when an event took place in time. If you trim ahead on an outgoing clip, you will see what happened at a later point in time. If you trim in the opposite direction, you will see what took place at an earlier point in time. This principle also works the same for the incoming side of an edit, rather than trying to think in positive and negative values. Here are a few points to explain what happens during a single side trim:

◆ The opposite side of the edit point should not change.

◆ If you are extending the length of the outgoing clip, or trim with a positive value (i.e., +4 frames), you will add to the duration of that clip as well as the overall duration of your sequence. This will change the last frame, displaying frames that occur later in the clip.

◆ If you are shortening the length of the outgoing clip, or trim with a negative value (i.e., –4 frames), you will reduce the duration of that clip as well as the overall duration of your sequence. This will change the last frame, displaying frames that occurred earlier in the clip.

◆ If you are changing the length of the incoming clip, or trim with a positive value (i.e., +4 frames), you will reduce the duration of that clip as well as the overall duration of your sequence.

◆ If you are changing the length of the incoming clip, or trim with a negative value (i.e., –4 frames), you will add to the duration of that clip as well as the overall duration of your sequence.

Notice the opposite effect going on here. Adding time (increasing the duration) of a clip does not always mean that you work with a positive trim value. You must pay attention to which side of the edit you are working on (Figure 6-9).

 Trimming one side of an edit can affect audio and video sync if all tracks are not selected. See Chapter 8 for more details on working with synced tracks.

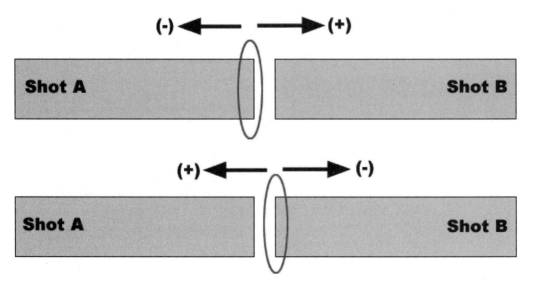

Figure 6-9 Think of Trimming an edit point in terms of displaying a frame "earlier in time" or "later in time."

TRIMMING BOTH SIDES OF AN EDIT

When you select both sides of an edit for trimming, you change a few things at once. Depending on which direction you are trimming, moving earlier or later in time, you are ultimately using a combination of two of the steps outlined for trimming one side of an edit. Using a two-sided trim allows you to combine these steps into one process and see the outcome right away.

◆ If you are trimming later in time (using a positive trim value), you are extending the length of the outgoing shot (changing the last frame to a frame that occurred later in the clip) while reducing the duration of the incoming shot (changing the starting frame to a frame that occurred later in time).

◆ If you are trimming earlier in time (using a negative trim value), you are decreasing the length of the outgoing shot (changing the last frame to a frame that occurred earlier in the clip) while increasing the length of the incoming shot (changing the starting frame to a frame that occurred earlier in time).

When trimming both sides of an edit at the same time, you add the same number of frames to one side of an edit while you remove an equal amount of frame to the other side. Therefore, trimming both sides of an edit at the same time does not change the overall duration of your sequence.

CONTROLS IN TRIM MODE

The first thing you will notice when entering Trim Mode is a whole new set of control buttons located along the bottom of the window between the two monitor displays. These controls allow you to precisely control the number of frames you are trimming (Figure 6-10).

❶ Cancel Edit—this button works similarly to an undo feature. It reverts back to the original position before the trim was made. You can also use the keyboard shortcut keys Control-Z (Windows) or Command-Z (Macintosh) to undo the step you made.

Figure 6-10 Trim Mode buttons allow you to fine-tune edit points.

❷ Previous Edit—this button allows you to jump back one edit point at a time without leaving Trim Mode. The keyboard shortcut is Control+Shift+Left Arrow Button (Windows) or Command+Shift+Left Arrow Button (Macintosh).

❸ Trim Left 5 Frames—this button allows you to trim either side or both sides of the edit point (depending on what you have selected) 5 frames earlier in time (visually to the "left" looking at the timeline). This means that if you have the outgoing shot selected, each click of the button will move your edit point in intervals of 5 frames back in time, shortening the overall length of the clip. If you have the incoming shot selected, each click of the button still moves your edit point back in intervals of 5 frames at a time, revealing portions of the clip that occurred earlier in relative time to the portion of the clip that was previously displayed. This approach increases the overall duration of the clip in the timeline. A combination of these steps occurs if you select both sides of the edit point. The keyboard shortcut is Shift+Left Arrow Button.

❹ Trim Left—this button performs the same feature as described above in the Trim Left 5 Frames function, only in intervals of a single frame at a time. The Left Arrow Button performs the same function in Trim mode.

❺ Trim Right—this button allows you to trim either side or both sides of the edit point (depending on what you have selected) forward in time (visually to the "right" looking at the timeline) in intervals of a single frame at a time. This means that if you have the outgoing shot selected, each click of the button will advance your edit point 1 frame forward in time, revealing portions of the clip that occurred later in time, extending the overall length of the clip. If you have the incoming shot selected, each click of the button still moves your edit point forward 1 frame at a time. This approach, however, decreases the overall duration of the clip in the timeline. A combination of these steps occurs if you select both sides of the edit point. The Right Arrow Button performs the same function in Trim mode.

❻ Trim Right 5 Frames—this button performs the same feature as described above in the Trim Right function, only in intervals of 5 frames at a time. The keyboard shortcut is the Shift+Right Arrow Button.

❼ Next Edit—this button allows you to jump forward one edit point at a time without leaving Trim Mode. The keyboard shortcut is Control+Shift+Right Arrow Key (Windows) or Command+Shift+Right Arrow Key (Macintosh).

❽ Play Edit—this button allows you to preview the edit, playing the movie a few seconds before the edit point, continuing a few seconds past the edit point, and then stopping. Use the keyboard shortcut [`] to play the edit.

Another way you can trim an edit point is to enter a numeric value for the number of frames you want to trim. To trim using numeric input:

❶ Select which side(s) of the edit you want to trim.

❷ Click in the numeric value field located above the trim control buttons (Figure 6-11). If you roll your mouse over this area, you should notice the cursor changing into an I-bar, indicating a user entry field.

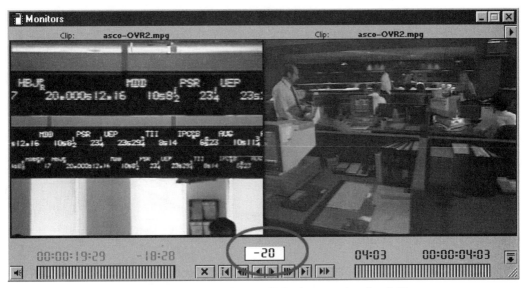

Figure 6-11 Enter the number of frames to trim an edit in the numeric value field.

❸ Enter the value (number of frames) you want to trim the edit point. Enter only positive or negative whole numbers.

❹ Click Enter (Windows) or Return (Macintosh).

OR

❶ Select which side(s) of the edit you want to trim.

❷ Use the keypad on your keyboard to enter the value (number of frames) you want to trim the edit point. Enter only positive or negative whole numbers.

❸ Click Enter on the keypad.

Using the keypad saves you the time of having to click in the entry field every time to perform a trim. The keypad automatically places the numeric entry in that field, allowing you to quickly tweak your edit points.

The last method for trimming your edit points inside of Trim Mode is to interactively trim your edit points on the fly. To do this, manually drag the jog tread located below each edit point monitor for trimming one side of the edit point at a time (Figure 6-12). To trim both sides of the edit point at the same time, click and hold your mouse in between both monitors. While still holding the mouse button down, drag the mouse to the right or the left (depending which direction you want to trim) to quickly trim your edit points on the fly. The numbers will indicate the number of frames you have trimmed your shot since entering Trim Mode. A negative number indicates that you have trimmed your clip earlier in time (to the left) from the original edit point and a positive number indicates that you have trimmed your clip later in time (to the right) from the original edit point. Keep in mind that once you close out of Trim Mode and return, the number indicating the amount of frames trimmed will be reset to 00:00.

Jog Tread

Figure 6-12 Manually Trim each clip using the jog tread.

Even if you have both sides of the edit point highlighted, dragging the jog tread will affect only the side of the incoming or outgoing clip you are moving.

TRIMMING WITHOUT TRIM MODE

Once you have become familiar with the concept of trimming and how Trim Mode works, you will probably be ready to save yourself time by trimming your shots without entering into Trim Mode. (After all, isn't this book designed to teach you how to improve your projects and save you time?) Premiere allows you to trim directly in the timeline for fast, easy editing.

When performing any kind of edit directly in the timeline, especially trimming, expand or enlarge your view of the timeline. Which timeline view makes more sense to you to perform precise trimming and editing (Figure 6-13)?

Trimming complex sequences and multi-layered timelines can be difficult no matter whether trimming directly in the timeline or trimming in Trim Mode. It becomes very easy to knock segments that occur later in the timeline out of sync. I recommend creating multiple sequences at first, until you get the hang of trimming. This way, you can always go back to an older version that is in sync with little hassle.

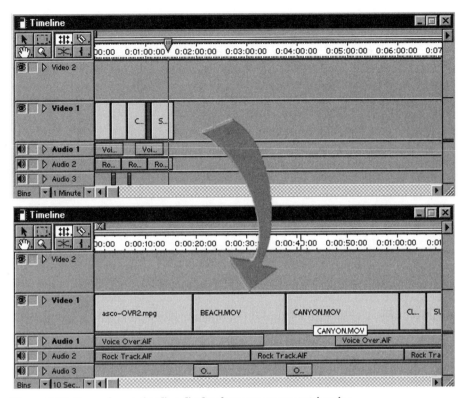

Figure 6-13 Expand your timeline display for more accurate trimming.

Once you have edited a few clips together, you can fine-tune your edit points by trimming these clips directly in the timeline. There are several different types of trim features available when trimming in the timeline window (Figure 6-14):

◆ Rolling Edit—trims both sides of an edit point equally. Whatever number of frames is added to one side is equally reduced on the other side of the edit. This type of edit does not affect the overall duration of your movie, yet it does alter the duration of each of the individual segments being affected (Figure 6-15). Notice how when you trim (to the right) the edit point between Shots B and C using the

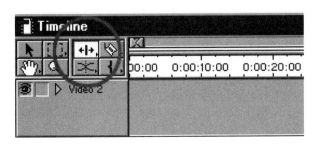

Figure 6-14 Trimming Tools available directly in the timeline.

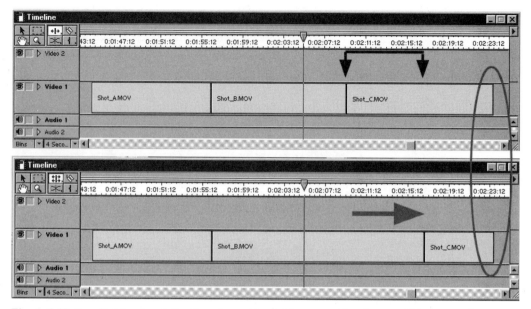

Figure 6-15 *Equally trimming both sides of an edit point does not affect the overall duration of your timeline.*

rolling edit technique, the length of Shot B increased (displaying an Out point that occurred later in time from the original source clip) while the length of Shot C decreased (changing the starting frame of the clip to one that occurred later in time in the original source clip).

To use the Rolling Edit feature:

❶ Select Rolling Edit in the Timeline window (Figure 6-16).

❷ Place the cursor over the edit point that you wish to trim. The cursor should change to the rolling edit icon.

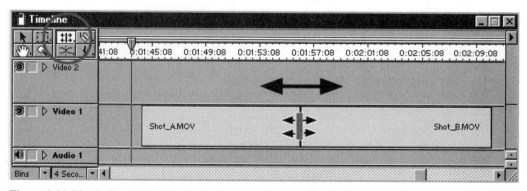

Figure 6-16 *The Rolling Edit Tool trims both sides of an edit equally.*

❸ Click and drag the cursor to the new desired trimmed edit point. Notice the change in duration for the two affected clips, yet the overall movie duration did not change.

◆ Ripple Edit—trims the selected clip but does not alter the duration of any other clips in the timeline. This technique will alter where in time any clips placed on the same track after the segment being trimmed occur (Figure 6-17). Notice how each clip in the timeline in Figure 6-17 is exactly 10 seconds long. If you used the Ripple Edit feature to extend Shot B, notice its duration has changed to 13 seconds. Each of the other shots are still 10 seconds in length with their original starting and ending frames, but they appear later in time in the overall sequence of the timeline, thus altering the duration of your entire movie.

To use the Ripple Edit feature:

❶ Select Ripple Edits in the Timeline window (Figure 6-18).
❷ Place the cursor over the edit point that you wish to trim. The cursor should change to the ripple edit icon.
❸ Click and drag the cursor to the new desired trimmed edit point.

Open the Info palette to display the timecodes of the starting and ending frames. This will help make trimming in the timeline more precise.

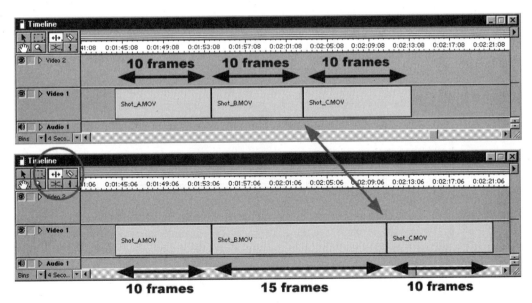

Figure 6-17 Ripple Edit trims the selected clip without changing the duration of other clips in your timeline.

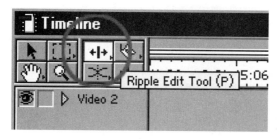

Figure 6-18 The Ripple Edit Tool.

◆   Slip Edit—is a unique, but extremely handy way of trimming a single clip inside of a timeline without affecting anything about the clips next to it in the timeline. What is taking place in a slip edit is essentially trimming the starting frame or In point of the selected clip and at the same time trimming the last frame or end point of that clip for the same relative value. This feature works extremely well when:

   ❶   You are satisfied with the placement and duration of the clip in the timeline that the edit occurs (the actual time when that shot comes in and ends).

   ❷   You don't want to change the overall duration of your movie.

   ❸   You don't want to change the edit points of the following clips (when the next clip starts in your timeline).

   ❹   You DO want to adjust either the starting frame (In point) or ending frame (Out point).

   Therefore, based on the above scenarios, if you slip Shot B (Figure 6-19) to have an earlier start frame (because you chopped off the beginning portion of the scene in your rough edit), the In point will now be adjusted back by the number of frames you choose. Accordingly, the end frame is adjusted the same number of frames earlier in the clip than its original out point.

   Think of my roller analogy when imaging how slipping a shot works. Picture a roller on the inside portions of clip you are adjusting, with nothing affecting the clips on either side of it in the timeline (Figure 6-20). As you trim the In point of the clip (either releasing some of the handles from the original source material to show earlier portions of the clip or reeling up the footage to show a later portion of the clip as the new start frame), the opposite trim effect is taking place at the other end of the clip in the timeline. Therefore, if you go back earlier in time (to the left) at the starting frame using slip, the system automatically tightens up the rollers at the other end, going back in time the same number of frames. If these two techniques did not function properly at the same time, there would be extra "slack" in the line (which in Premiere terms means extending the duration of the clip—something we do not want happening).

   You can only trim, slip, or slide footage for a maximum duration of the handles that exist for the clip from the original source footage. If no handles exist, then you will not be able to adjust the clip at all.

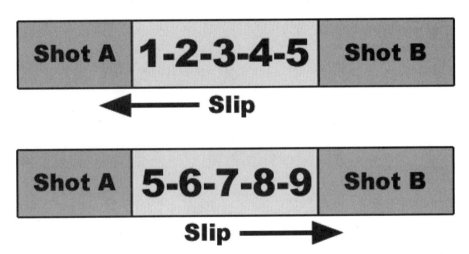

Figure 6-19 "Slipping" a clip trims the beginning and end frame by the same number of frames.

Figure 6-20 Slipping is a technique of trimming both ends of a single clip.

Try this as an example: A great way to visualize what is happening when slipping a shot in your timeline is to set up three videotapes (Figure 6-21). Imagine the front two tapes as the shots on each side of the clip you are slipping, with the back tape the shot that is being altered. As you move the tape in the back side to side, you'll notice that the theoretic "In point" and "Out point" are changing without affecting the other clips in your timeline (Figure 6-22).

◆ Slide Edit—is a variation of the slip edit techniqu:, this function allows you to move a clip around in your timeline, or "slide" it along top of other clips in the sequence. The slide technique of trimming a shot works by trimming the shots on both sides of the selected shot, changing the position of the selected shot in the timeline without altering its in and out points or its duration. This feature works well when:

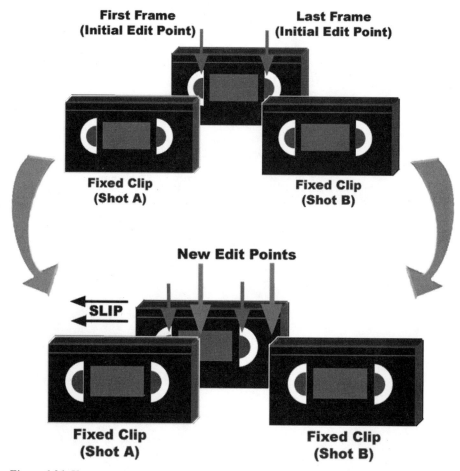

Figure 6-21 Use props (such as video tapes) to help visualize what is happening while trimming and slipping shots.

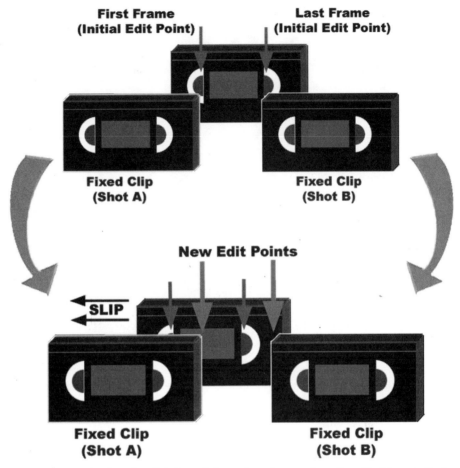

Figure 6-22 Notice how the clip's In and Out points change when slipped but do not affect the rest of the timeline.

❶ You are satisfied with the duration of the selected clip.

❷ You are satisfied with its In and Out points.

❸ You are satisfied with the overall duration of your sequence.

❹ You do not like where the selected clip is placed in the timeline.

Let's use the roller theory again. This time imagine the rollers on the outside of your selected clip. This means the rollers are actually affecting the end frame of the outgoing clip and the starting frame of the next incoming clip (Figure 6-23). What essentially happens when you slide a shot in your timeline is that the selected clip winds up covering a portion of the clip in the direction you are sliding, decreasing the duration of that particular shot. If you simply moved the selected clip in the timeline with the arrow

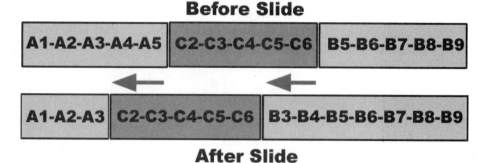

Figure 6-23 *Sliding a clip affects the position of the selected clip by changing the incoming and outgoing frames of the clips around it.*

tool instead of sliding, you would wind up moving portions of the clip in the direction that you are shifting (the same as with sliding) but you would wind up with a hole in your timeline (Figure 6-24). What's so unique about the slide feature is that it fills in the gap from where the selected clip was originally positioned. The "roller" on the outside of the selected clip unravels footage from that shot's original source footage.

If you slide Shot B forward in your timeline 20 frames, two trims take place simultaneously to Shots A and C (Figure 6-25). The starting frame of Shot C is trimmed ahead in time by 20 frames, shortening the duration of the clip. The last frame of Shot A is trimmed ahead in time, extending the length of that shot by revealing portions of the original source clip (also referred to as handles) that were beyond the initial out point. If Shot A did not have any extra "handle" frames then you would not have been able to slide Shot B forward in the timeline.

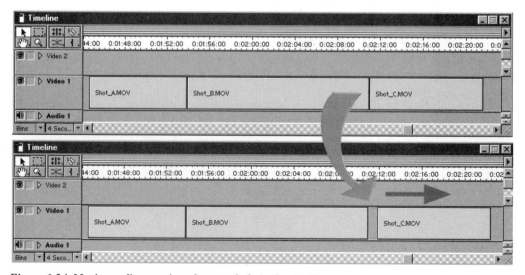

Figure 6-24 *Moving a clip sometimes leaves a hole in the timeline.*

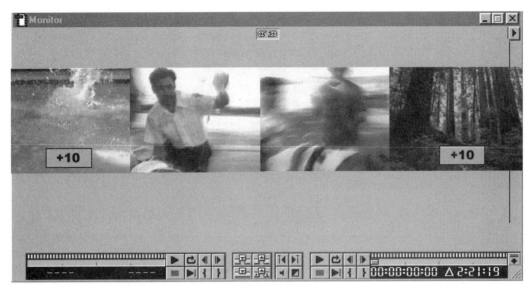

Figure 6-25 Sliding adjusts both edit points at the same time.

Let's use our three videotapes example to help visualize how slipping and sliding are different. (If you have not read the above example for slipping a shot, read it now). To understand what happens when you slide a shot, set up the three tapes as shown in Figure 6-26. The two back tapes represent the outgoing clip prior to the shot you will be sliding (Shot A) and the incoming clip after the selected shot (Shot C). Shot B in the front represents the clip you will be sliding in your timeline. Shot B will always main-

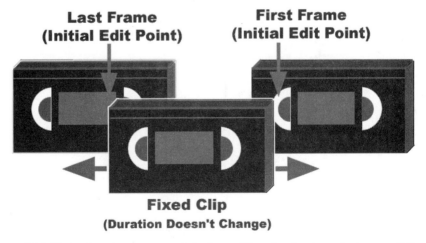

Figure 6-26 Notice that the center tape is in front of the other two tapes during our sliding example.

tain the same In and Out points as well as its duration. The only aspect that will change for Shot B is its position in the timeline (at which point in time the shot becomes visible). As you slide Shot B to the left or to the right in your timeline, notice what happens to Shots A and C. If you slide Shot B to the left, Shot A becomes much shorter while revealing earlier portions of Shot C. Sliding Shot B to the right reveals more source footage at the end of Shot A while changing the in point and shortening the duration for Shot C (Figure 6-27).

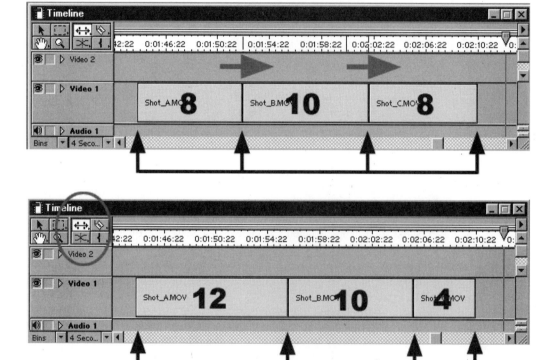

Figure 6-27 *Sliding a clip repositions the placement in your timeline without changing the clip's duration, starting frame, or ending frame.*

TRIMMING DOWN TIMELINE CLIPS FROM THE SOURCE MONITOR

As you can see from the previous section, there are many ways to trim the clips in your edited sequence. Even though you will choose to use certain techniques over others, it's good to be familiar with the various methods because you never know when a situation will arise when one method of trimming (or other aspect of editing) will be better suited for that particular situation. To be quite honest, the technique I'm about to discuss I have not found to be very effective myself. The only time I think it may come in handy is if you want to view the source footage to make a better determination where and when to trim a shot from your rough cut. (If in the course of your editing you come across a situation where this technique is the best method to use, please let me know. You can e-mail me at dennis@pfsnewmedia.com).

To use the original digitized footage in the Source Monitor to trim a clip:

❶ Double-click the clip you want to trim in your timeline. The selected clip should load up into the Source Monitor with the first frame of the timeline clip visible in the monitor.

❷ Use the controls under the Source Monitor to mark a new In point, Out point, or both.

❸ Once you have made the corrections, click the Apply button above the Source Monitor to readjust the clip in the timeline.

The clip that is loaded into the Source Monitor is not the original full-length source clip, but more of a subclip—the portion of the clip that was edited into the timeline. Therefore, all of your trims will shorten the duration of the clip in the timeline. Premiere automatically uses these new in and out points and changes the duration of the clip directly in the timeline. Since the new duration will be less than the clip's original duration, an empty space will be left in the timeline for the difference of its original duration.

❹ Select the Track Selection Tool in the Timeline window to move the rest of the clips on that track and close any gaps left by any clip adjusted to have a shorter duration (Figure 6-28).

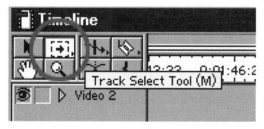

Figure 6-28 The Track Selection Tool.

LOCKING TRACKS TO AVOID SYNC PROBLEMS

Trimming clips in your timeline is one of many ways to knock shot out of sync (either with its natural sound or with other clips that you have already lined up during previous editing). One way to avoid knocking clips or entire tracks out of sync (messing up their timing and positioning) is to lock your tracks (Figure 6-29). Locking tracks can be beneficial if you want to protect the work you've done while you continue your edit on other tracks in the timeline. If you started your project by completely editing and finalizing an audio mix, you may consider locking the audio tracks before going on to edit your video tracks as a precaution.

Figure 6-29 Track locks protect from accidentally ruining your edited timeline.

 If you want to lock video clips that contain synced audio, you must select each track and lock it separately.

To lock timeline tracks:

❶ Click in the empty box next to the eye icon (video tracks) or the speaker icon (audio tracks) on the appropriate track in the timeline that you want to lock.

❷ An icon of a pencil with a red arrow through it should appear indicating that track has been locked.

❸ Click on that icon again to unlock that particular track.

With a track locked, you will be unable to add any clips to that track or trim any shots within that track. Premiere will not let you select a locked track in the Target field, located under the Edit Monitor (Figure 6-30). For example, if you lock Video Track 1, you will not be able to add or remove any clips already edited into that track. You can make changes, however, to any of the unlocked track. This is where you can wind up knocking your unprotected clips out of sync in your timeline.

When a track is locked, not only is it protected from insert or over-write editing from source clips, but each segment is locked so that you can't accidentally drag a clip even slightly out of position in the timeline. The cursor changes to a black arrow with a padlock when you roll your mouse over a locked track, indicating that you cannot move any clips in that particular track (Figure 6-31).

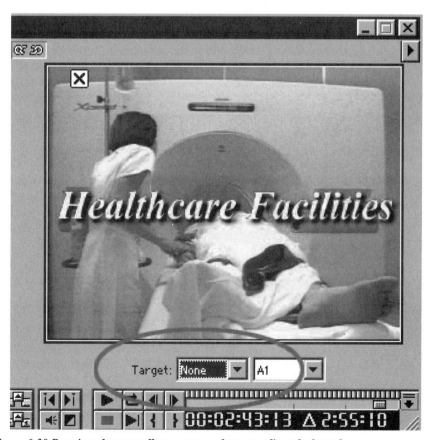

Figure 6-30 Premiere does not allow you to perform an edit on lock tracks.

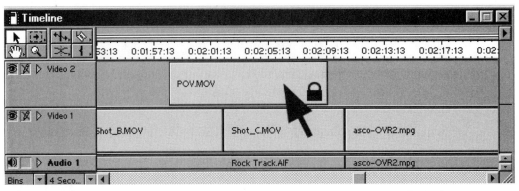

Figure 6-31 On locked tracks, the cursor changes to a solid black cursor with a padlock when the track is rolled over.

HOLD THAT CLIP IN PLACE

What if locking an entire track is too much? Completely locking an entire track can hinder your adding footage later in the timeline or just making slight adjustments to your existing edits. Premiere allows you to go in and select individual clips in your timeline and lock them in place. To lock individual clips in place in your timeline:

❶ Select the clip you want to lock.

❷ Choose Locked from the Clip menu.

When you lock a clip, a striped or "hatched" pattern appears on the clip in the timeline (Figure 6-32). This does not alter the way the clip is viewed during playback. Once the clip is locked, you will not be able to move it around in the timeline or trim it in any manner. If you try to add a shot to the timeline or move a clip already there that would normally affect a clip, but is now locked, Premiere will make an error sound indicating that you cannot perform that edit.

GETTING CREATIVE WITH SPLIT EDITS

Split edits are also commonly referred to as "L-cuts" since they visually look like an L-shaped edit in a timeline. There are many situations where using a Split Edit improves the flow of your movie. This generally works very well when cutting straight dialog shots between two people together or when going from an action shot with natural audio to a talking head (on-camera interview). You can make these scenes flow better by extending either the audio track or the video track over (or under) the next

Locked

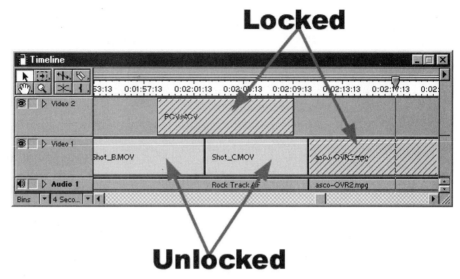

Unlocked

Figure 6-32 Premiere displays a striped pattern on individual clips indicating lock clips.

clip. This avoids the "ping pong" effect that many beginning editors tend to develop. This means that when Person 1 is speaking, you cut to him or her on-camera and when Person 2 begins to speak, you cut to that person on-screen. This technique of rapid editing makes the viewer feel like they're watching a Ping Pong game. Talented editors know when to use the original source video with its synced sound and when to use a reaction shot while continuing the other clips audio.

 There are many different areas when Split Edits or L-Cuts can be used. They are not only used for dialog scenes.

Being able to use split edits during dialog scenes goes back to careful preparation during the actual shooting of the scenes. If you have more than one camera available for a shoot, use one for each person that is speaking (and possibly a wide shot as well). This way you wind up having synced audio and timing and can easily cut back and forth between cameras without any timing issues. If you have only one camera, always have the other people read their script as if they were being recorded to help the talent that is on-camera with the timing and feel of their lines. This way you get a chance to record the person's reaction shot to the lines that are being read off-camera. Try to avoid constantly changing the talent's lines, the speed at which each person reads, or reactions when not on-camera. Playing it smart during the actual production (shooting) time will allow you more freedom and fewer headaches when trying to be creative with Split Edits during your post-production session. Let's take a look at how to build a Split Edit:

❶ Rough-cut the scenes you want to use in the proper order.

❷ Trim the shots to clean up any unnecessary footage in your timeline (still leaving it as straight cuts).

❸ After deciding which clip you want to extend, select the appropriate track that you will be altering. (For this example, we want to see Person 2's reaction shot as Person 1 continues to speak).

❹ Select the Rolling Edit Tool from the Timeline window.

❺ Click on the video tracks for the appropriate edit point and drag it back trimming back the on-camera portion of Person 1 and revealing the reaction shot of Person 2 before he or she begins to speak (Figure 6-33).

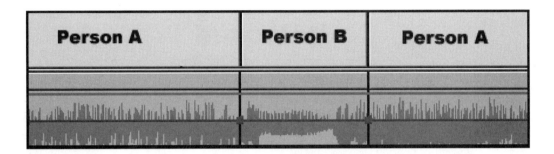

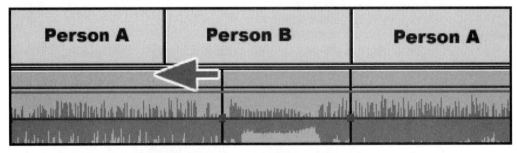

Figure 6-33 Trimming just the video track (both sides of the edit) just to create a more natural "L-cut".

  Tip: You may want to have the audio waveform visible to help make the timing of the Split Edit more effective and flow better. See Chapter 8 for more details on working with audio.

QUICKLY EDIT MULTI-CAMERA SHOOTS

Nonlinear editing systems have made editing multi-camera production shoots a breeze. Producing the ultimate video still requires well-planned scripting and coordination between all members of the production crew; however, much of it can now be mastered during the post-production phase. In an ideal world, each camera would be synced together using some type of GenLoc, or sync generator, and also be fed a timecode signal from a timecode generator. This would make each camera have the same exact timecode address for any given moment. Therefore, if you wanted to check how a certain scene looked from another camera angle, you can scan the tape to the same timecode number on the other tapes (Figure 6-34).

Unfortunately, every project will not have the budget to provide all this professional equipment. You must learn to make do with what you have. Before you decide to just

Camera Angle #1

Camera Angle #2

Camera Angle #3

Figure 6-34 Ideal multi-camera setup involves synced timecodes for tracking and matching scenes.

set up and shoot, there are a few tips that you can do in the production phase that will make editing flow more smoothly:

◆ Coordinate when cameras are running. Do not allow camera people to start and stop on their own. You will never be sure whether each angle was properly captured until it's too late.

◆ If you don't have timecode-synced cameras, use some type of sync point so that you can sync tapes during editing. Use a camera with a flash. The actual flash generally appears for one frame, or 1/30 of a second. This allows you to use that "flash" frame as your sync point.

◆ Use headsets to communicate with each camera operator. This way, if one camera operator is zooming in or fixing the focus, the other camera(s) know to hold steady so you don't lose the shot. Nothing is more heartwrenching than realizing all of your cameras missed a shot because of improper communication.

With this said, it's time to edit. I started this section by stating that multi-camera editing can be quick and painless. Here's what I recommend to do:

❶ Digitize the footage for each camera angle and properly label each clip.

❷ Edit camera 1 onto Video Track 1.

❸ Edit camera 2 onto Video Track 2. Repeat this process for each camera, placing each angle onto its own track (Figure 6-35).

❹ Use the "flash" frame to sync each video track. Line that flash frame up at the same point on each track in your timeline.

❺ Begin by playing through your timeline. When you come to a point where you want to compare other angles, you can simply view the other tracks, knowing your shots are already in sync.

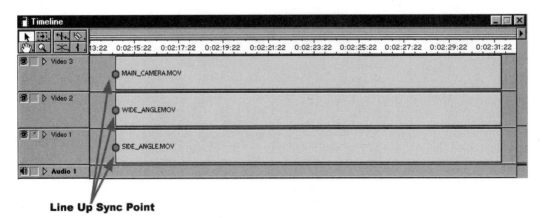

Figure 6-35 *Line up each camera angle on multiple tracks using a photographic flash or easily identifiable image.*

> Due to the way the layering of video tracks work in Premiere, if you have a main camera angle (one being used for the majority of the selected shots), place that on your highest video track. This will reduce the amount of cutting or lifting you will have to do in the timeline.

❻ Use In and Out Markers and the Lift feature to take away the portions of shots from the timeline that you do not want to use, leaving a staggered pattern of selected takes (Figure 6-36).

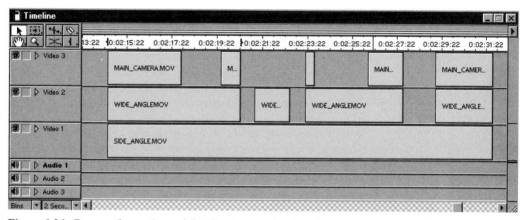

Figure 6-36 Remove the portions of the clips in your timeline that you don't want visible.

Once the selected shots are in place in your timeline, you can simply use the Trim feature (discussed earlier in this chapter) to fine-tune your sequence. This technique takes a little time to get used to, but if you become familiar with your footage and have some idea of which shots you want to use, you'll be amazed at how fast you can fly through editing an entire project using this multi-camera editing technique.

> If you are working with timecoded tapes and have deck control through Premiere, digitize all of the raw footage in low resolution. Once your show is cut and you've selected the best angles, let Premiere redigitize just the footage for the shots used in your timeline in high resolution.

SUMMARY

Computers are every video editor's dream-come-true. They allow you to go back at any point of the project and fine-tune your edits. A tweak here. Trim a few frames there. The Undo feature allows you to try an adjustment, seeing if trimming a few frames improves your edit point. If not, simply go back to the way you had it. Practice using all of the edit and trim feature so that you'll know which tool is the right choice when creating your masterpiece project. Premiere makes cleaning up your edit points fast, easy, and, most importantly, extremely accurate.

chapter 7

ADDING
THE RIGHT
TRANSITION

Look at any feature film and count how many scene changes occur. Probably thousands. Now count how many page peels and warp effects you see. My guess is none. Now turn on MTV, Nickelodeon, or your local cable station running the local mom- and pop-store commercials. I bet you see more twist, turns, and fly-in transitions in one hour than you care to see for the rest of your life. The point is that you can't just pick any transition from the list and plunk it down wherever you feel like. You need to gauge the type of project you are working on, who your audience is, and a number of other factors that we will cover throughout this chapter before you add random transitions to your video masterpiece.

There are basically three types of transitions: the cut, the dissolve, and the Digital Video Effects (Figure 7-1).

The point with my first comment is that feature films that are winning Academy Awards and other top honors consist of 90 percent or more cuts and dissolves. Do not feel obligated that just because all of these amazing computer-generated transitions exist, you have to incorporate every single one into your edit session. As you can probably guess, I am one for clean, simple transitions when appropriate. There are many situations where you are going to have to use a transition to fix an inconsistency with the continuity of an edit. Producers and directors are not always perfect and we the editors need to fix their mistakes. Unless you are cutting one of those cheesy used-car commercials, people should pay attention to the content of your program and not the tran-

(1) CUT

(2) DISSOLVE

(3) DVE

Figure 7-1 The Cut, Dissolve, and Digital Video Effect (DVE).

sition. If they are more intrigued by the special effects that occur in between each shot, they probably cannot focus on the message of your program. But keep one general rule in mind when working with transitions: Transitions should help make the program flow without distracting the viewer.

THE SIMPLE ART OF THE CUT

Believe it or not, it takes a good editor to make a program flow very smoothly when only working with cuts. A cut is nothing more than the last frame of the outgoing video clip being placed right next to the first frame of the incoming video clip. That's about it. There's not much more to say other than it is the simplest transition to use, the most common type, and arguably one of the most powerful transitions in any type of project if used correctly.

Tip: If you want to use cuts but do not want to create that ping-pong effect for whoever is speaking is on camera, check out the section on split cuts or L-cuts in Chapter 6. This technique can really improve the flow of your program.

SMOOTHING OUT EDIT POINTS WITH DISSOLVES

Besides the Cut, the dissolve is the most commonly applied transition covering all types of industries. The dissolve, also called a cross fade, is used to blend one image into another, avoiding the harshness of a scene change that sometimes comes with cuts at the edit points. A dissolve is nothing more than a progression of frames that, over the course of the transition, equally changes the percentage of opacity between the outgoing shot and the incoming shot. Therefore, in the first frame of the dissolve, the outgoing shot is 100 percent opaque while the incoming shot is completely transparent. Halfway through the duration of the dissolve, each clip is displayed at 50 percent, an equal blend of each image. The last frame of the dissolve is where the cross fade completes its transition, making the outgoing shot 100 percent transparent and the incoming shot 100 percent opaque (Figure 7-2).

Figure 7-2 A dissolve is a gradual blend between two clips.

The length or duration of the dissolve is completely dependent on the mood you are trying to create as well as the amount of source footage available. You cannot obviously hold a dissolve longer than the duration of the source footage for the clip you digitized.

If a dissolve does not appear to play back very smoothly, with an almost flash-frame effect, do not panic. This is a common mistake that is easily correctable. This may occur if the clip you have digitized has a natural camera cut in it. What is most likely happening is that the camera cut is being played back during the dissolve transition. If this is occurring towards the end of the transition, just as the scene becomes transparent, the scene change in the faded frame(s) is enough to cause a jarring visual effect that your eye catches but probably flew by too quickly to realize what happened the first time around. Your eye can generally catch something visually wrong (Figure 7-3).

Camera Cut Before Transition Ends

Figure 7-3 If you are not careful, a frame or two may appear in transitions of source material that contains natural camera cuts.

To add a dissolve in Premiere:

❶ Spin the triangle icon next to the Video 1 Track in the timeline window (if you haven't done so already) (Figure 7-4).

❷ Edit the first video clip you want to see on Video Track 1A.

❸ Edit the second video clip you want to see on Video Track 1B as shown in Figure 7-5. You need to overlap your video clips in order for Premiere to implement the transition. This is commonly referred to as checker boarding the clips in your timeline based on the alternating pattern of tracks.

❹ Select Show Transitions from the Window menu.

❺ Drag the icon for the Additive Dissolve onto the transition track of the timeline located in between Video Tracks 1A and 1B (Figure 7-6).

❻ Play back your video or drag the playback head in your timeline while holding the Alt key (Windows) or Option key (Macintosh) to view the dissolve transition.

Remember, you can only place a dissolve or any type of transition in between Video Tracks 1A and 1B. If the shots do not overlap with a transition in place, the edit points will play back as a simple cut. You may need to play around and try different length dissolve transitions to get the right look and feel you're after.

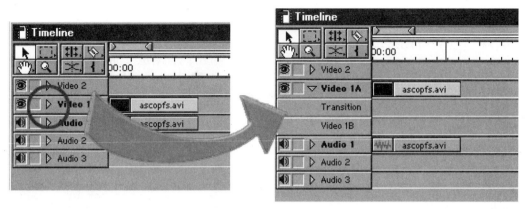

Figure 7-4 Expanding video tracks in Premiere.

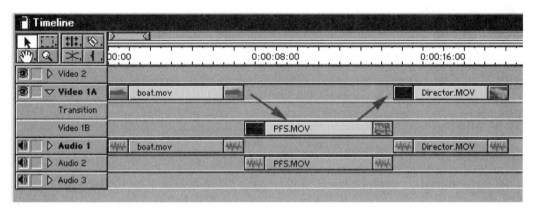

Figure 7-5 Checkerboard your clips on Video Track 1A and 1B to add dissolves or other transitions.

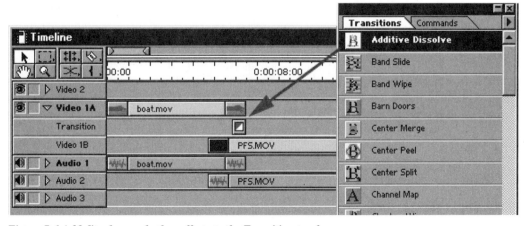

Figure 7-6 Add dissolves and other effects to the Transition track.

You can alter the length of the transition (trimming the effect similar to trimming any video clip) by moving your mouse over either end of the effect. The cursor should change into a red trim icon similar to the Rolling Edit Tool icon (Figure 7-7). Click the right mouse button to drag the edit point to change the duration and speed of the dissolve transition.

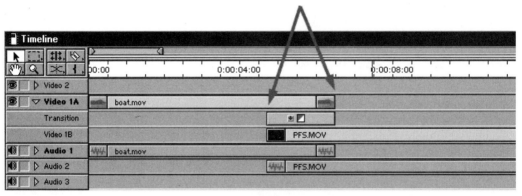

Figure 7-7 Trim dissolve transitions to set a desired length of the effect.

Lengthening the duration of the dissolve makes the transition occur over a longer period of time. This creates a slow, gradual fade from one scene into the other. This is a good approach when you are trying to create an emotional effect or show the passage of time. A short, quick dissolve may be used to soften the effects of a scene that does not cut together well (Figure 7-8).

One other tip for getting the right look sometimes requires a bit more accuracy than just plopping two shots in the timeline haphazardly. You may be trying to work with definitive starting frames or ending points that are not hidden by the dissolve. I would recommend cutting your clips for the proper edit points and then trimming each edit point to get the desired results. Therefore, if you know precisely where you want a scene to end and what must be visible in the next incoming shot, and you know you want a 1-second (30 frame) dissolve between the two shot:

❶ Edit the first video clip into the timeline (on Video Track 1A) with an additional 30 frames on the end after the desired Out point.

❷ Edit the second video clip into the timeline (on Video Track 1B) with the first necessary shot starting at the cut point that comes directly after the last frame of the clip on Track 1A.

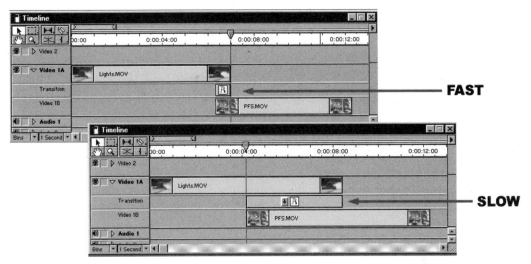

Figure 7-8 *Slow dissolves can create an emotional effect or the passage of a long period of time.*

❸ Trim the beginning of frame of the clip in Track 1B back 30 frames (Figure 7-9).

❹ Add the dissolve into the Transition track so that it begins where the clip in track 1B begins and ends where the clip in Track 1A ends.

Changing the duration of a transition in the timeline automatically changes the duration of one of the two clips that the transition falls between. Depending upon which

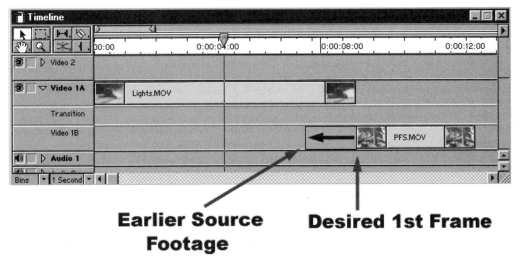

Figure 7-9 *Trim clips to allow for the transition to be finished in time for the desired first frame of the incoming clip to be visible.*

direction you are trimming, the transition will determine whether the clip in Video
Track 1A or 1B gets trimmed.

**If you want to change the duration of the transition and not affect
the edit points of the clips, hold the Control key (Windows) or the
Command key (Macintosh) while adjusting the end points of the
transition.**

ADDING THE DEFAULT TRANSITION

The Transitions Palette can take up a good amount of space on your desktop. It's also
a pain to constantly open and close the Transitions Palette window every time just to
add a dissolve to your timeline. Premiere gives you a feature on your regular interface
that allows you to add the default transition (initially set up as the dissolve transition)
to your timeline with one click of the mouse. You can customize this to make the
default transition any transition you use most often.

To use this feature:

❶ Select the transition you want to set as the default in the Transitions Palette window.

❷ Click on the triangle to bring up the Transitions Palette menu.

❸ Select Set Selected As Default.

❹ Enter the length or duration of the default transition (in number of frames) in the
Default Effect Duration window.

❺ Click OK.

**Note: You can always adjust the duration of the transition in the
timeline regardless of the default duration previously set.**

Figure 7-10 The Add Default Transition adds a dissolve or whichever transition you preselect.

Then, when you are editing in your timeline, simply click the Add Default Transition button located in the Monitor window or use the keyboard shortcut Control-D (Windows) or Command-D (Macintosh) to add the transition you selected to your timeline (Figure 7-10).

AUTOMATIC CHECKER BOARDING

One thing that I find to be a huge waste of time is trying to edit video clips onto either Video Track 1A or Video Track 1B so that I can prepare for adding transitions down the road. I find it very difficult to make these decisions early on while I'm editing my rough-cut. Premiere allows you to edit all of your clips on Video Track 1 in collapsed mode, adding one shot after the next. When you finish fine-tuning your edited sequence and it's time to add transitions, you can simply apply them to the edit points. Premiere automatically checkerboards your timeline for you.

❶ Cut a series of clips together on Video Track 1 (keep the track collapsed, making Video Track 1B not visible).

❷ Add transitions to the desired edit points.

❸ Click to expand Video Track 1. Premiere will automatically place the necessary clips on an alternating Video Track (Video Track 1B) when there is a transition applied to the edit point (Figure 7-11).

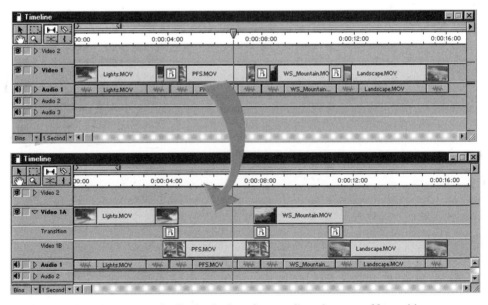

Figure 7-11 Premiere automatically checkerboards your clips when you add transitions to an unexpanded Video Track 1.

Premiere automatically places clips that have transitions applied in alternating tracks. It also automatically trims each edit to display the proper overlap of frames in order for the transition to take place properly. This feature works only if there are enough extra frames available from the original digitized clip to perform this function.

If there is not enough footage in the handles of the clip to cover the duration time of the transition, an error prompt will appear indicating that the transition could not be applied to this edit point (Figure 7-12).

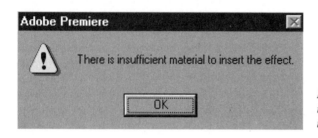

Figure 7-12 An Error Prompt will indicate if there is not enough source footage for the transition.

CUSTOMIZING THE TRANSITIONS PALETTE

Speed and efficiency are key with any video editing project. When putting your finishing touches on your edited rough-cut, you will probably spend a great deal of time adding effects and transitions. Premiere offers you a way to reduce your time and increase efficiency by allowing you to customize the Transitions Palette. One feature allows you to see a cycling animation of how the transition looks once edited into your timeline. Another feature allows you to remove transition icons that you are not using for this project so that you can quickly and easily work with the transitions that you will need for the current project. There are many different ways you can group and display the transition icons:

Animate the Icons:

❶ Select Show Transitions from the Window menu (if not already open).

❷ Click on the triangle in the Transitions Palette window to display the pop-up menu (Figure 7-13).

❸ Select Animate. The icons will begin to animate, showing a representative version of how each particular transition will look.

To stop the icons from animating, simply click on the Animate menu choice to deselect it.

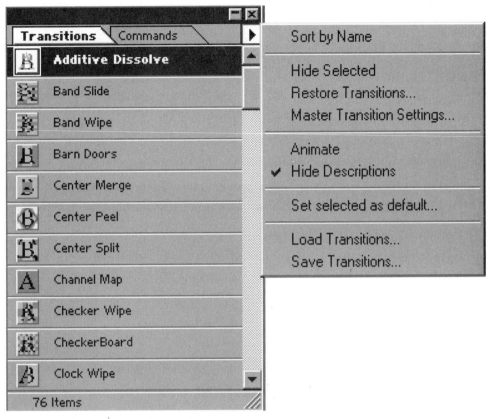

Figure 7-13 The Transitions Palette window pop-up menu.

Display Description:

❶ Select Show Transitions from the Window menu (if not already open).

❷ Click on the triangle in the Transitions Palette window to display the pop-up menu.

❸ Deselect Hide Description to display a brief overview of how the transition works.

To hide the description and return to the smaller icons, click on the Hide Selection menu choice a second time.

Display Only Selected Icons:

❶ Select Show Transitions from the Window menu (if not already open).

❷ Select one or more of the transitions you would like to hide.

❸ Click on the triangle in the Transitions Palette window to display the pop-up menu.

❹ Select Hide Selected. Only the icons that you did not select should remain.

To restore the hidden icons individually or the entire hidden group:

❶ Click on Restore Transitions from the pop-up menu. The Restore Transitions window should appear (Figure 7-14).

❷ Click on one or more of the icons that you would like to return to the main Transitions Palette.

❸ Click Show.

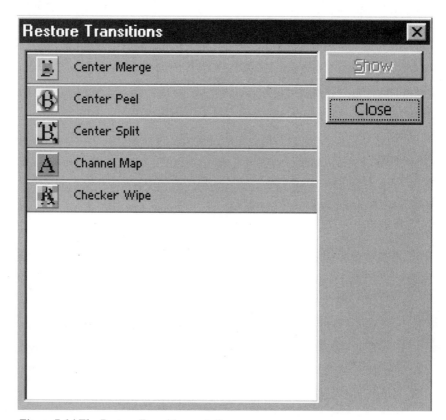

Figure 7-14 The Restore Transitions window.

Hold the shift key down while clicking to select a contiguous group of icons. Hold the Control key (Windows) or Option key (Macintosh) to select multiple icons not in a contiguous order (Figure 7-15).

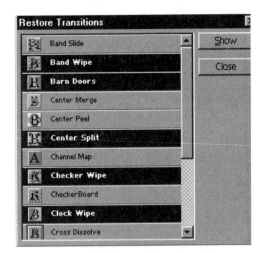

Contiguous   Random

Figure 7-15 Use modifier keys to select different groupings.

To rearrange the order of the icons in the Transitions Palette:

❶ Click and drag an icon to any other location in the palette. This allows you to group the ones you are most often using together. This saves a great deal of time and avoids scrolling through the list.

❷ To restore the default (alphabetical) order, click on the triangle in the transition palette window to display the pop-up menu and select Sort by Name.

SAVING AND RESTORING CUSTOMIZED TRANSITION PALETTES

This is a great idea if certain projects dictate certain types of transitions. You can create specialized palettes for each type of client. I have one client who uses every zany, crazy, wild and wacky transition known. On the other hand, when I'm working on corporate communications videos, I work with a completely different set of transitions. The nice thing about Premiere is that you can create many different versions and bring any one into any project. This is because the Transitions palettes are saved outside of Premiere, in any location on your hard drive you choose. To save a custom palette:

❶ Select Show Transitions from the Window menu (if not already open).

❷ Select one or more of the transitions you would like to hide.

❸ Click on the triangle in the Transitions Palette window to display the pop-up menu.

❹ Choose Hide Selected. Only the icons that you did not select should remain.

❺ Click on the triangle again and select Save Transitions.

❻ Enter a file name and location in the Save Effects Set window (Figure 7-16).

❼ Click Save.

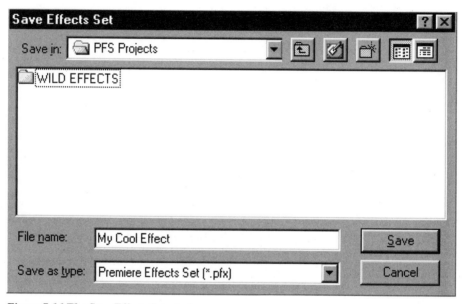

Figure 7-16 The Save Effects Set window.

  Make sure to include the .PFX extension after filename for Windows systems.

To restore a previously saved transitions palette:

❶ Select Load Transitions from the Transitions Palette menu.

❷ Find the location where you have saved the palette.

❸ Double-click on the desired file.

You can open any Transitions Palette in your current Premiere project, even if it was created and saved under a different project.

Create a folder on your hard drive to store all of your Transitions Palettes, such as "Custom Transitions." Keep the folder in a place that is easy to find and identify.

ADJUSTING TRANSITION SETTINGS

The majority of projects you do are going to require customized transitions, more than the default Premiere settings. Fortunately, it's very easy to adjust the settings of Premiere's transitions. Each setting has its own variables, but overall you can set the transition's direction, start and end values, add a border and adjust its thickness, and smooth out the edges with anti-aliasing.

♦ To adjust the basic transition settings for a single use that is already edited into your timeline, either double-click on the transition or click on the transition to select it and choose Transitions Settings from the Clip menu. The Transitions Settings window should appear for that particular transition (Figure 7-17).

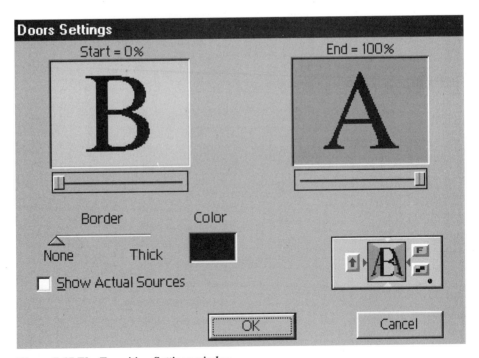

Figure 7-17 The Transition Settings window.

◆ To change the default settings of the duration in the Transitions Palette, either double-click on the transition icon in the Transitions Palette or select the icon and choose Master Transition Settings from the palette menu. The Transition Settings window should appear for that particular transition.

Inside the Transition Settings window, you can adjust each variable for the given transition. The following describe the variables for the basic transitions:

◆ Select Show Actual Source to view the image of the clips rather than the A and B windows.

◆ Adjust the sliders under the source windows to change the starting and ending display of the transition. You can choose to start a transition already in progress or end a transition earlier than the default setting. Personally, I haven't come across too many situations where you might use this feature. I think a transition should complete the transition all the way through, from one source clip to another.

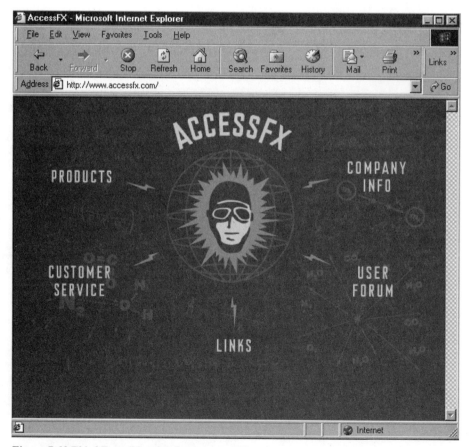

Figure 7-18 Third Party Plug-Ins from AccessFX.

◆ Adjust the Border Slider to add a border to the edges of a transition. You can also pick a custom color for the border by clicking on the color swatch to open a standard color picker window.

◆ Click the Track Selector (arrow button) to toggle between which track starts the transition, either the source in Video Track 1A or Video Track 1B. This icon is also found on the actual transition icon once placed in your timeline.

◆ Click the Edge Selector to set which direction the transition comes from. The Edge Selector is indicated by little red and white triangles pointing to the edge of the transition's thumbnail display. Red indicates the desired direction. The Edge Selector option is available only on certain transitions. •

◆ Click the Forward/Reverse (F/R) button to change the direction of how the transition plays. This means that for a transition that comes zooming up from infinity to fill the screen, clicking the reverse button would send the full-framed image back into infinity.

◆ Click the Anti-alias button to smooth out the edges of a transition. This button toggles you through different levels of aliasing, blurring the edges of the pixels to give you softer edges between the transition.

Many of the standard transitions that come with Premiere also have more customizable features. Click the Custom button to open the custom settings window for that particular transition.

INCORPORATING THIRD-PARTY TRANSITIONS

Over the years, many software developers have opened up their architecture and allowed third-party companies to develop software applications that can be used to enhance the basic program package. This is very true for Adobe Premiere. Throughout this book I have mentioned a number of third-party vendors, what features they offer, and how their software works. Probably the most common third-party plug-in for Premiere is the transitions. Probably the most popular out there today is Boris Effects. One of my personal favorites is a company called AccessFX in Phoenix, Arizona. They have released two major transition effects plug-ins for Premiere called TransLux and Lord of the Wipes (Figure 7-18). Check out their Web site for more information at www.accessfx.com. Their software has some wild pre-fabricated transitions as well as completely customizable settings to create your own radical transitions. There are many plug-in packages out there for you to choose from. Adobe lists a number of third-party developers for Premiere on their Web site (www.adobe.com). This page gives you a brief description of the company and what types of plug-ins they have created for use with Premiere.

WHEN THERE'S NOT ENOUGH SOURCE FOOTAGE

What tends to happen with people new to the business is that they tend to cut the recording of the camera just after the on-camera talent finishes speaking. This creates a problem in post-production because you have very little footage to work with to create a pause or to breathe before going into the next scene. Generally, when I'm on location or in a studio shooting a scene, I try to let the camera roll a few extra seconds to make sure that I have enough footage to use in case I want to add a transition. If the footage is cut too tightly, you'll be faced with one of two situations: Choose a very simple, very quick transition or begin the transition earlier into the end of the outgoing scene. This can look very strange if a person is speaking and the transition is taking place over his or her last few words.

One trick is to add a freeze frame of the last frame and apply the transition to that freeze frame. This works out well if you do not leave the freeze frame up there too long. My suggestion is to edit only the portion of the freeze frame for the time that you plan to have your transition take effect. By that I mean, if you are using a standard 30-frame (one second) transition, edit in exactly 30 frames of the freeze frame and have the transition start at the first frame of the freeze frame and end on the last frame (Figure 7-19). This will disguise the freeze frame as much as possible without forcing you to cut the edit point too tightly to the end of the clip.

For example:

❶ Edit in the footage into Video Track 1A (the footage that cuts very close to the end of the speaker's words).

❷ Create a freeze frame that matches the last frame of your out-going clip.

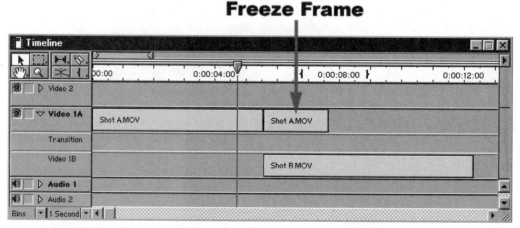

Figure 7-19 Use dissolves the same length as the freeze frame to extend a transition.

❸ Edit the freeze frame into your sequence right after the original clip.

❹ Trim the duration (if necessary) of that freeze frame to the exact duration of the transition you are going to add.

❺ Edit the new clip (the incoming clip) into your timeline on the opposite Video Track 1. If the first clip was placed in Video Track 1A, then place the second shot in Video Track 1B and vice versa.

❻ Trim the starting frame for the incoming clip to align with the first frame of the freeze frame.

❼ Add the desired transition to the transition track. If necessary, trim the start and end frames of the transition to coincide with the start and end frames of the freeze frame (Figure 7-20).

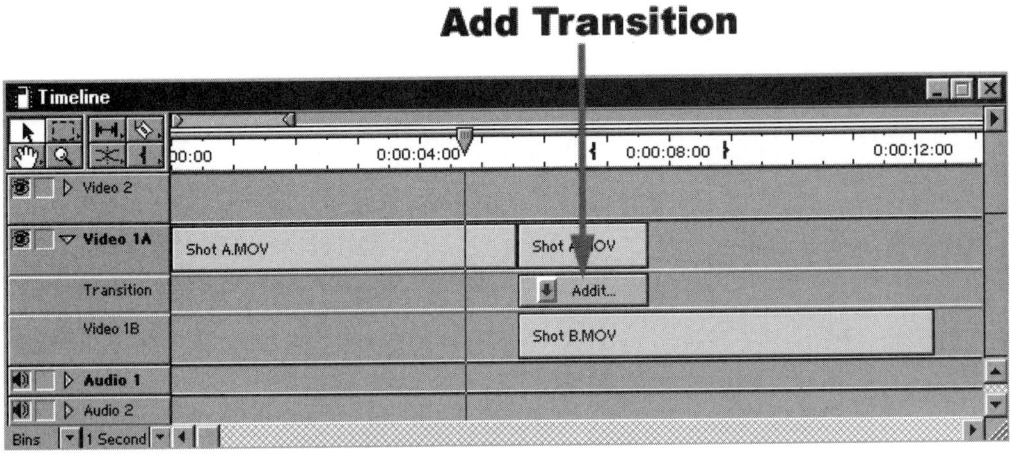

Add Transition

Figure 7-20 Add and trim the dissolve to match the duration of the freeze frame.

This should give you a nice clean transition without starting the transition too early, cutting off the end of the outgoing scene and not having to put it up against the start of the incoming frames. Using the freeze frame as the buffer really creates a nice touch that is extremely helpful in any tight editing area.

USING GRADIENT WIPE TRANSITIONS

One of my favorite transitions is the Gradient Wipe transition. You can use the default gradient transition or create your own using any grayscale image. Premiere will then animate that image into a transition for you. The default wipe consists of a grayscale gradient blend from black to white (Figure 7-21). From this image, Premiere creates a

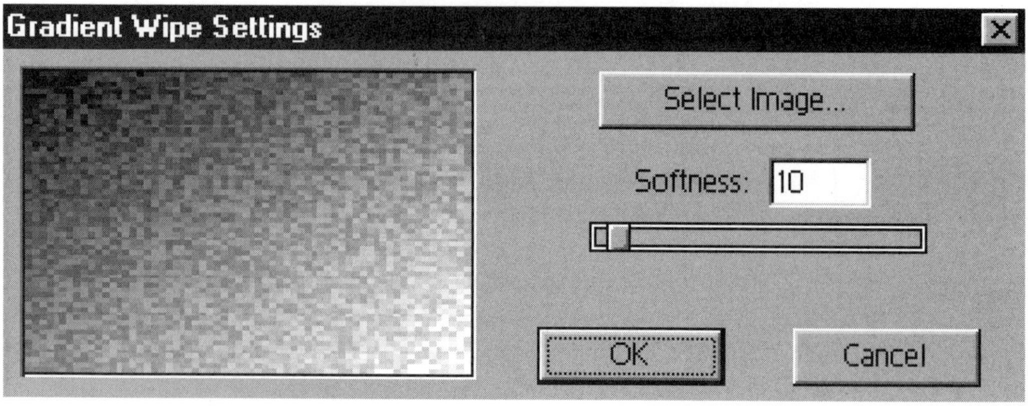

Figure 7-21 Default image pattern for Gradient Wipe.

Figure 7-22 The Gradient Wipe transition in effect.

transition over whatever duration you specify and blends the outgoing scene into the incoming clip (Figure 7-22).

It is extremely easy to create your own custom gradient wipes. Create a grayscale still image in Photoshop or any paint program you prefer. Then follow the same process as you would for applying any standard transition. When prompted, open the grayscale image that you had just created. Premiere does the rest. To set the custom shape wipe before you add it to your edited timeline:

❶ Open up the Transitions Palette (if not already open).

❷ Select Gradient Wipe in the palette.

❸ Double-click on it to open up the Gradient Wipe Settings window (Figure 7-23).

❹ Click the Custom button. A smaller Gradient Wipe Settings window should appear.

❺ Click Select Image.

❻ Locate and select the grayscale image you created to use as a transition.

❼ Click Open.

Figure 7-23 Create your own custom images to use as gradient wipes.

Figure 7-24 Custom Images animating as a wipe.

Premiere now takes that shape and creates a gradient transition based on the pattern of the grayscale image you just applied to the transition (Figure 7-24). Once that is set, add the Gradient Transition to your timeline and take advantage of the custom transition you created with a single grayscale image.

USING MOVING VIDEO CLIPS TO DISGUISE EDIT POINT

Let's face it. Sometimes the standard transitions get boring and you're looking for something new to use as a transition in your video project. Have you thought of using another video source as the transition? It's simple. Use the basic principles of layering Video Tracks with a combination of animating that clip and you have yourself a creative new way to transition edit points with either a still video image or a moving video clip. Here's how to set this example up:

❶ Edit your outgoing and incoming video sources onto Video Track 1. These shots will cut from one to another when played.

❷ Add a third video clip (that you plan to use as the transitional shot) onto Video Track 2. This video source can be any still graphic image that you have imported into Premiere or other type of digitized video footage.

 Make sure that the video on Video Track 2 is centered over the edit point on Video Track 1. Otherwise, you will wind up seeing the video cut behind the moving clip and the transition will not be effective.

❸ Select the clip on Video Track 2.

❹ Select Video from the Clip menu or Right-Click (Windows) or Option-Click (Macintosh) and select Video from the pop-up menu.

❺ Select Motion from the submenu.

❻ The Default motion of the video clip sliding from left to right will work perfectly. Click OK.

The object of this effect is to have the video on Layer 2 be centered and full frame, covering over the cut that is taking place on the layer below. As this clip continues to move past the center point mark and off to the right out of frame, you are then viewing the second portion of the two clips edited together on Video Track 1. If you position the clip correctly on Video Track 2, you should not see the cut take place and wind up with a nice smooth transition (Figure 7-25).

Figure 7-25 Use full screen moving video as a transition.

USING GRAPHIC IMAGES FOR TRANSITIONS

The last topic discussed is using a full frame video source as a transition. What happens if you want to use a smaller image that does not cover the entire screen? This applies basically the same principles as above with only a few more steps. Let's use the example that you see so often on television. You may see a product (beer can, laundry detergent, automobile, or whatever you choose) come wiping across the screen and that is what is providing the transition. How that works is that there is a standard wipe-taking effect with a graphic image sitting on a layer above that follows the same wipe pattern. What you're left with is the effect that this image is really wiping your video clips from one scene to another (Figure 7-26). To set this effect up:

Figure 7-26 Use any image to create the illusion of a transition.

❶ Edit your outgoing video source on Video Track 1A.

❷ Edit your incoming video source on Video Track 1B.

❸ Add a standard wipe transition to the transition track (the Wipe transition works very well for this example) (Figure 7-27).

❹ Play your movie to see if you get the desired results, a basic wipe transition moving across the screen.

Figure 7-27 Use a standard wipe transition as the basis for more elaborate transitions.

Note: You may need to render your transition to see it take effect depending on your system and how it is configured.

❺ Edit a graphic image that contains an alpha channel (that you created in Photoshop) to Video Track 2. (See the section in this book covering working with alpha channels if you are unfamiliar with working with images that contain alpha channel).

❻ Select the Clip to highlight it.

❼ Select Video from the Clip menu.

❽ Select Motion from the pop-up menu. The standard animation from left to right should work with relatively little tweaking.

❾ Click OK.

The object of the effect is to use the graphic to cover up the standard transition taking place behind the graphic giving you a high-class transitional effect. Try to incorporate other graphics with other transitions. Another great one is for circular logos. Apply a standard circle wipe to an edit and have a round log on top of that layer that enhances the transition. Be creative and try different approaches. Not everything will work but you'll be surprised out how much of an improvement the ones that do work will add to the quality of your video productions.

DECIDING WHICH TRANSITION TO USE

One problem that I find with some novice editors is implementing the wrong transition. What I mean is not so much the wrong transition but that there are better transitions to choose from depending on what's happening with the video. For instance, if in the incoming shot, the camera is panning from left to right, you would not want to have the transition start from the right and move left. This creates tension with the movement and tends to look awkward. Granted this may be the effect you're looking for. There really are no rules, but instead see what looks right and feels comfortable. There may also be situations where you want to break up the flow of a transition because everything is constantly moving in one direction and needs a break so that the video doesn't get boring. You decide.

SUMMARY

The ideas discussed in this chapter are only the tip of the iceberg. I probably could have written an entire book on creative ways to use transitions. The point is that there are many different options available when it comes to adding transitions to your edited sequence. I would say the four basic principles to keep in mind when thinking about transitions are:

❶ Do you need a transition in the first place or does a cut work just as well?

❷ Do you need a fancy transition or does a dissolve work (again one of the most commonly used transitions)?

❸ Does the transition you apply fit the style and direction of your video?

❹ Can you get more creative than the standard prepackaged transitions that come with Premiere (such as using your own custom transitions)? Good luck with your finishing touches and keep me posted on any cool transition you develop.

chapter 8

AUDIO
SWEETENING
FOR PERFECTION

What is it that makes people sit on the edge of their seats when watching an action thriller? Or curl up into a ball during a horror film? Or shed a tear during a true-love drama movie? As much as it requires good acting, these emotions are usually carried out through the music. Don't believe me? Watch the same movie with the volume turned off and see if it has the same effect on you.

Music and sound can have a very powerful hold on people. They can be translated into every video project you edit. Imagine working on a corporate communications piece and the president of a major corporation sounds fuzzy and distorted. Would your client be pleased? On the other hand, if you added just the right motivational music to a sales video, complete with the proper voice over and sound effects and mixed to perfection, I bet that would inspire your viewers. I've seen many producers spend days setting up the right scenes to shoot and countless hours in the editing suites generating the most amazing visual effects and then drop the ball when it comes to enhancing the audio. The point is that no matter what type of project you are working on, audio is going to be a crucial part of your project and not something that should be overlooked.

In Chapter 2, I covered digitizing audio from your source decks, whether on video tape or from a CD. This chapter covers working with these audio files in more detail, including:

◆ What you can do once the sound is in Premiere

◆ What tools to use to get the best mix

◆ How to apply these techniques to real projects

UNDERSTANDING DIGITAL AUDIO QUALITY

There are so many variables that can affect the quality of a sound file that I think it's important if we touch on what digital audio files are comprised of and how these variables affect the quality and size of a sound file. If you are going to be working with audio files that have been digitized and compressed for other multimedia purposes, you will need to check their quality and make sure they are suitable for working in Premiere.

The quality or clarity of a digital audio file is the result of the sampling rate and bit depth. The higher the sample rate, or more samples taken per given second, the better chance the computer has at reproducing the sound accurately. Recreating CD-quality sound requires that 44,100 samples or "snapshots" of that sound source be taken for every second that the computer is capturing the sound. This is represented as 44.1 kHz. If you start working with sound files that were captured or compressed to a lower sample rate (22.05 or 11.025 kHz), you are talking about working with audio files that are going to be of lower quality. High-end frequencies are generally dropped when capturing audio at lower sample rates. The lower you drop with sample rates, the thinner the audio quality is going to sound and you will lose that full-bodied feel. There are other factors that are going to affect the quality of compressed audio files. The bit depth also plays a role in the clarity of your file. Sixteen-bit audio files are of much higher quality than an 8-bit sound file. Stereo sound files affect the file size of the clip, as much as even doubling the size if two tracks are used compared to one track with mono.

 There are many books on the market that go into further detail than the scope of this book and that cover all of the details of digital audio files.

WORKING WITH AUDIO FILES

Before you can begin mixing audio, you need to understand what types of files you can use with Premiere. Most likely your audio will come from various sources:

- Video tape (synchronized audio)
- Audio Cassette
- DAT
- Compact Disc
- MiniDisc

There are three basic rules to live by:

Rule #1: Always start with the best quality source material.
Rule #2: Always start with the best quality source material.
Rule #3: Always start with the best quality source material.

I'm sure you've heard these rules before (and multiple times), but the concept is critical for providing the best quality finish piece you can produce. Obviously, ideal situations do not always exist. That's why it is so important that you always pay attention and try to mix your audio to the best of your abilities.

Do not create lower quality audio samples than you need. You can not resample audio at a higher quality.

DISPLAYING AUDIO PROPERTIES

One of the hardest things to develop is a good ear for sound. It's not something you're necessarily born with, and it can take a long time. When listening for audio quality, especially when formatting files for multimedia, it can become difficult to distinguish what settings affect the overall sound quality. One thing in Premiere that I find very useful is to check the audio file's properties. This tells you information on the clip's name, source path, duration, compression formats, and quality settings. This information can come in handy while editing your projects. Most people are better at distinguishing the quality of video clips (because it is a visual format) whereas audio really requires you to listen closely for the little details and nuances that differentiate a sound file. To view the Audio Properties window:

➊ Click on the audio clip (in the timeline) or the audio icon (in the project bin) to select it.

➋ Click the right mouse button (Windows) or Alt-Click (Macintosh) to bring up the pop-up menu.

➌ Select Get Properties. The Audio Properties window should appear (Figure 8-1).
   OR

➍ Select Get Properties For in the File menu.

➎ Select File from the pop-up menu.

➏ Select the file you want to display the properties for using the Analyze File window.

➐ Click OK.

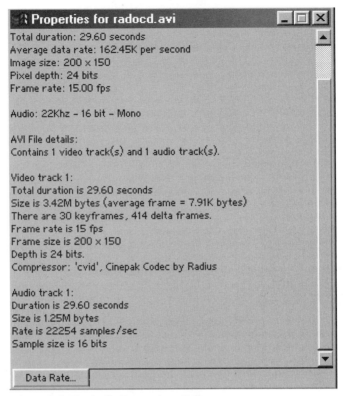

Figure 8-1 The Audio Properties window.

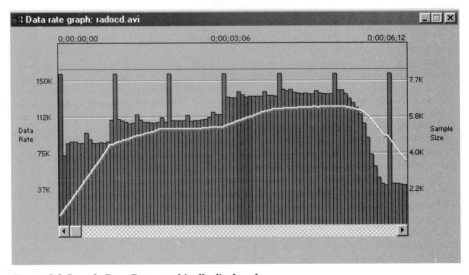

Figure 8-2 Sample Data Rate graphically displayed.

Click on the Data Rate button in the lower left portion of the Audio Properties window to view a graphical display of the Sample Data Rate throughout the duration of the clip (Figure 8-2)

LAYERING AUDIO TRACKS

Premiere handles audio clips the same way it does with video clips. Once you import or digitize your sound files into a bin, you can then add your In and Out marks and edit the clip into your timeline. You can add up to 99 different audio tracks. To add new audio tracks:

❶ Click the triangle on the right side of the Timeline window (Figure 8-3).

❷ Select Track Options from the Timeline window menu. The Track Options window should appear (Figure 8-4).

❸ Click Add. The Add Tracks window appears (Figure 8-5).

❹ Enter a value for the number of tracks you want to add.

❺ Click OK.

To delete a track:

❶ Click the triangle on the right side of the Timeline window.

❷ Select Track Options from the Timeline window menu. The Track Options window should appear.

❸ Select the track you would like to delete. The Delete button should be available once you select a valid track to delete.

❹ Click OK.

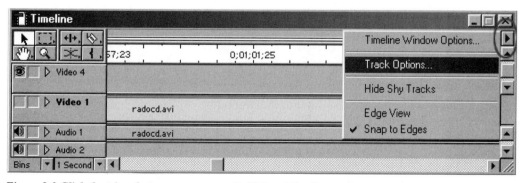

Figure 8-3 Click the triangle to open a menu of additional timeline options.

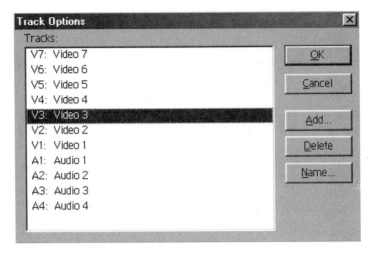

Figure 8-4 The Track Options window.

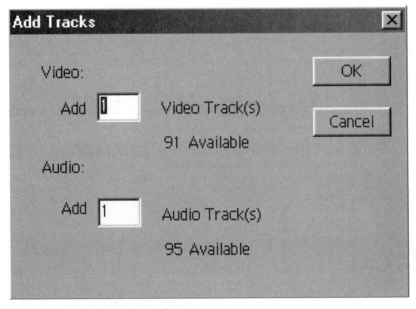

Figure 8-5 The Add Tracks window.

 You cannot delete Video Track 1 or Audio Tracks 1,2, and 3.

LABELING TRACKS FOR CLARITY

Viewing multiple tracks can get quite confusing, especially if you are dealing with ten, twenty, or even more. One means of clarifying which track to focus on when dealing with many layers of tracks is to rename the tracks appropriately to differentiate between narrator tracks, sound effect tracks, music tracks, and natural sound (synced audio from the video source tape). It might be helpful to put various elements of distinct tracks so that you can remove one without affecting the others, mute a track, or simply locate a particular clip more quickly (Figure 8-6). To rename your tracks:

❶ Click the triangle on the right side of the Timeline window.

❷ Select Track Options from the Timeline window menu. The Track Options window should appear.

❸ Select the track you would like to rename. The Name button should become active.

❹ Click the name button.

❺ Enter the new name in the Name Track window for the selected track.

❻ Click OK.

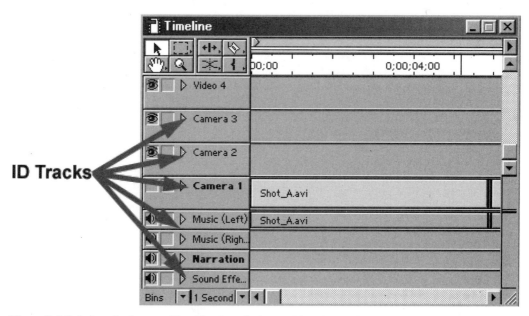

Figure 8-6 Label tracks for easy identification of what each track contains.

RAISING THE ROOF WITH GAIN CONTROL

If you had only one audio feature on any sound device, it would probably be the volume or gain control. You can independently control the gain for each audio clip or segment that you edit into the timeline. The gain changes the entire audio level for the entire portion of the clip in the timeline. If you want to make adjustments to the gain or volume within the clip, see the section on Rubber Banding below. To change the gain of the entire portion of the clip uniformly:

❶ Select the audio clip that you want to alter.

❷ Select Audio from the Clip menu.

❸ Select Gain from the pop-up menu.

❹ Enter in a numeric value in the Level Control Gain window to set the amount (in percent) that you want to adjust the level from the original 100 percent starting point (Figure 8-7).

❺ Click OK.

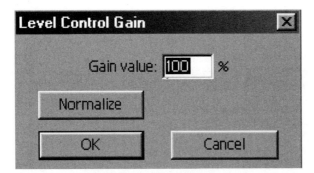

Figure 8-7 The Level Control Gain window.

OR

❶ Select the audio clip you want to alter.

❷ Right-mouse Click (Windows) or Option-Click (Macintosh) to open the timeline pop-up menu.

❸ Select Gain Control.

❹ Adjust levels as described above.

Entering a value higher than 100 percent increases the volume of the clip, where as a value lower than 100 percent decreases the volume of the selected clip.

ADJUSTING AUDIO GAIN
USING RUBBER BANDING

When you bring in a clip into Premiere, you may need to make more adjustments than just raising or lowering the volume for the entire duration of the clip. The ability to go inside a clip and make micro adjustments to the volume frame by frame is known as Rubber Banding. Basically, rubber banding gets its name from its graphical display on screen. Audio level rubber banding is indicated by a red line (Figure 8-8).

The audio starts off as one long string at the same level from beginning to end. If you want to make adjustments to a certain portion of that clip, you can add keyframe handles, or anchor points, which can be used to raise or lower your audio level. Adding these points to your audio clip and then adjusting their position will create a ramping effect. Raising the position of the keyframe vertically will increase the volume of your clip, while lowering the position decreases the volume. Premiere automatically calculates the changes to the volume frame by frame between two keyframe handles. For example, you would hear the audio gradually become lower in Figure 8-9. In Figure 8-10, the volume of the audio would change very quickly, simulating the effect of your turning the volume knob on your radio up and down very rapidly.

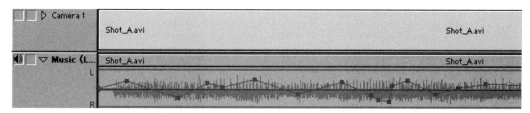

Figure 8-8 Adjust audio levels using rubber banding.

Figure 8-9 Gradual audio fades.

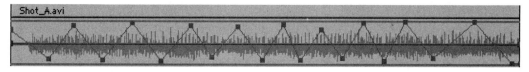

Figure 8-10 Radical audio adjustments.

Every audio clip must have a minimum of two keyframe handles, one at the first frame and one at the last frame. These handles cannot be deleted.

Ignore the Left/Right (L/R) indicators on the side of the audio track. They are used when working with audio Panning. This is indicated by a blue line.

To work with audio keyframe handles:

❶ Edit your audio clip into the timeline.

❷ Click the triangle next to the audio track to expand the track view.

❸ Roll your mouse over one of the keyframe handles. The cursor should change to the pointing finger icon, allowing you to drag the keyframe handle up or down.

To add keyframe handles to your audio timeline:

❶ Position the cursor over the audio track in the timeline.

❷ Click to add a keyframe handle.

❸ Raise or lower the position to increase or decrease the volume at that position.

To delete a keyframe handle, click and hold it while dragging it out of the range (above or below) of the audio track.

Select the Fade Adjustment Tool and hold the Shift key while raising or lowering a keyframe handle to change the level in 1-percent increments (Figure 8-11). Holding the shift key should also allow you to move the fader line above or below the boundaries of the audio track while still adjusting the track's level, without removing it.

You can even change two keyframe handles at the same time. This is helpful when you need to change their level by the same amount. To change two keyframe handles at the same time:

❶ Select the Fade Adjustment Tool.

❷ Click the triangle next to the desired audio track to expand it (if not already expanded).

❸ Move your cursor between two keyframe handles (Figure 8-12).

❹ Click on the fader line and adjust up or down (as necessary). The closest keyframe handles on each side of the Fade Adjustment cursor should move accordingly.

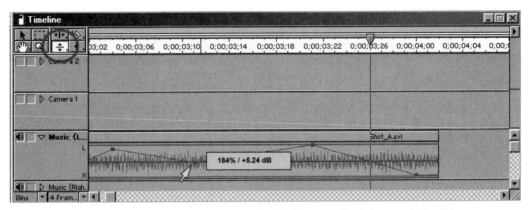

Figure 8-11 Holding the Shift key while using the Fade Adjustment Tool changes the level in 1 percent increments.

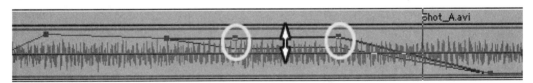

Figure 8-12 Click and drag between two keyframes to adjust both simultaneously.

PANNING AUDIO TO ENHANCE STEREO EFFECT

Panning audio allows you to adjust which speaker the audio plays back during preview and on your final output. Panning works regardless of whether you digitized your audio as a mono signal or a stereo signal. If you want a particular sound clip or portion of a sound clip to play back starting from the left speaker and gradually change over to the right speaker, panning is the technique you would use. Being creative with audio pans really adds depth to your mix and brings it to life. If you have a motorcycle enter the frame from the right, go driving across the screen, and end by going out of frame on the left, you would want to pan your audio to follow the motion of your visual. This would give the viewer a realistic sensation that the motorcycle came whizzing by them (on screen) from right to left. You can add as many keyframe handles as necessary to customize the direction of your sound clips.

Use the blue line in the audio track to adjust panning. The red line adjusts the volume or gain of that clip.

To add keyframe handles for audio panning:

❶ Edit your audio clip into the timeline.

❷ Click the triangle next to the audio track to expand the track view.

❸ Position the cursor over the audio track in the timeline.

❹ Hold the ALT key (Windows) or the Option key (Macintosh) and click to add a keyframe handle.

❺ Holding the ALT or Option key, raise or lower the position to change which speaker you want the audio clip to be played from.

Panning a clip 100 percent in either direction plays that clip out of that speaker only. You can also set pans at any percentage between centered (50 percent balance or equal amounts being played out of each speaker) and 100 percent to either direction.

 Open the Info palette before adjusting the gain or pan to see the exact amount of the values you are changing for that clip.

CROSS FADING AUDIO

As I mentioned in Chapter 7 on Transitions, the dissolve is the most common video transition (barring a straight cut). The same holds true for audio. Premiere allows you to add simple audio fades between two independent audio clips very easily. Keep in mind that when cross fading between audio clips, you need to have them on separate audio tracks and they must overlap in order to create the blend (Figure 8-13). The duration of the overlapping portions determines the duration of the cross fade. Longer overlapping portions create a slow, gradual fade. Shorter overlapping portions create a quick, more abrupt fade.
To create an audio cross fade:

❶ Edit one audio clip into your timeline.

❷ Edit a second audio clip on a different audio track, making sure that a portion overlaps.

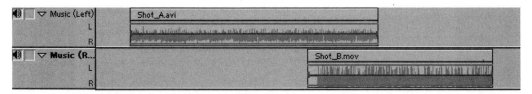

Figure 8-13 Overlap audio tracks to have them fade between each other.

❸   Select the Cross Fade Tool (Figure 8-14).

❹   Click on the clip you want to fade out.

❺   Click on the clip you want to fade in.

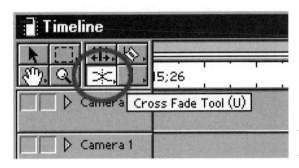

Figure 8-14 The Cross Fade Tool.

Premiere automatically creates the cross fade, calculating the number of frames for the fade based on the number of frames that your two audio clips overlap. This technique works well when working with independent audio clips. A few more steps are required when working with audio clips that are linked to video clips. See the section on creating audio cross fades when dealing with linked video clips below.

SPLIT EDITS—AUDIO CROSS FADES WITH LINKED VIDEO CLIPS

I covered creating split edits, or L-cuts in the chapter on Transitions, but I think it also pertains here as well. Besides using split edits as an editing technique for transitions, they are also necessary for creating audio cross fades when you have two sources to which the video and audio are linked. Linked files occur as you digitize audio and video source material at the same time.

Using standard editing techniques, most likely your video clips will be placed one after another, cut together with the outgoing frame of one clip edited up against the incoming frame of the next clip, with no spaces in between the edits (Figure 8-15). As discussed in the previous section, you need to overlap audio clips in order to create a smooth fade between them. With linked audio/video files, there are a few steps that need to be taken in order to create the split edit that's necessary for creating an audio cross fade. Separating the audio onto different tracks is the first step, but is not enough when trying to trim linked audio/video clips. You will not be able to drag the starting or ending frame of an audio clip to get the clips to overlap if they are linked with video.

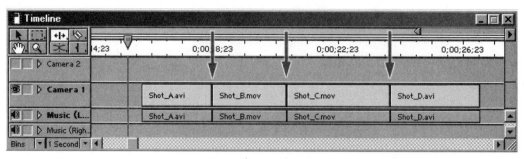

Figure 8-15 Standard editing with one cut placed right up against the next can make for a boring program.

To override the link between audio and video portions of a clip, to create the necessary split edit or overlap:

❶   Edit two clips together that contain linked audio and video.

❷   Move one clip's audio to a different track.

❸   Hold the Control key (Windows) or Command key (Macintosh) and drag one of the audio edit points to overlap the other.

Holding the Control key (Windows) or Command key (Macintosh) allows you to drag the audio track(s) independently of its linked video. Otherwise, you would not be able to drag the audio because the linked video clips are edited next to each other, without any room to move.

Performing this type of edit requires that the clip you are adjusting has enough handles from its original digitized source material in order to extend the In or Out point of the clip.

MONITORING AUDIO TRACKS

When you start working with multiple layers of audio clips, you will find it very important to start isolating tracks so that you can accurately hear what is going on. It becomes very difficult to hear how something sounds or check the timing of a clip if it is being disguised by a number of other audio clips. You may want to leave them exactly where you have edited them into your timeline, so deleting them is not the answer. The best solution is to mute tracks that you do not want to hear. This is very simple, but a technique that many beginning editors overlook as a means to making their life simple.

As I mentioned earlier, a good technique is to edit various audio clips onto different tracks. This means you might want to edit your narration onto Tracks 1 and 2 (or as many tracks as necessary). I would even recommend keeping different narrators on their own track(s) for easy identification and making changes. Then put your music on another set of available tracks. Sound effects might take up several tracks just for themselves. Keep them separate and spaced out so you have room to work with them (Figure 8-16). Now that you've set up your timeline this way, you now have complete control over monitoring your tracks. You can select which tracks you want to hear and which tracks you want to mute without changing any characteristics.

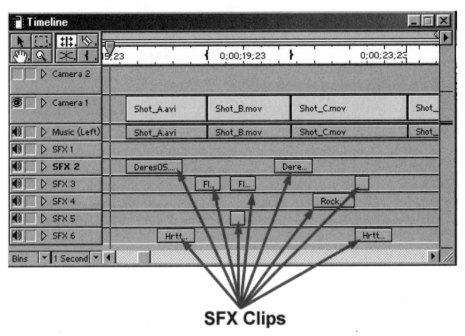

SFX Clips

Figure 8-16 Keep Audio Sound Effects spaced out in your timeline for easy manipulation (rather than all on top of each other).

To toggle the audio monitors on and off, click the audio speaker icon next to the audio track you have selected (Figure 8-17). A speaker icon indicates that the audio will play and be heard. A blank box indicates that that particular track has been muted. You can mute as many tracks as desired without affecting any of the clips or their attributes that you have set in the timeline.

Smooth, uninterrupted audio and video playback is dependent on the speed of your computer and amount of RAM. Shutting off all of the tracks but the ones you are working with allows the computer to play back your media with less difficulty, avoiding many pauses or glitches that may occur if too many files are being played at once.

Muted Tracks

Figure 8-17 *Toggle audio monitors on and off in the timeline to mute the selected tracks.*

EDITING WITH THE HELP OF AUDIO WAVEFORM DISPLAY

A common method for editing is to cut to the beats of the music or when a person says a new sentence. You can sit there and play the audio in real time with your trigger finger on the stop button or mark in key, ready to tag the position where you want to edit. An easy way to find your marks might be to just "look" at the audio. I know you think I've been typing too long when I start saying things like "seeing audio". Actually, by clicking on the triangle next to each audio track to expand it, Premiere displays the waveform for the audio clips in that track (Figure 8-18).

The stronger the audio signal, the larger the vertical, graphical display. The weaker the signal, the flatter the line will appear. You can visually follow when a person is speaking or when the downbeats of a music piece occur. This comes in handy for many editing situations:

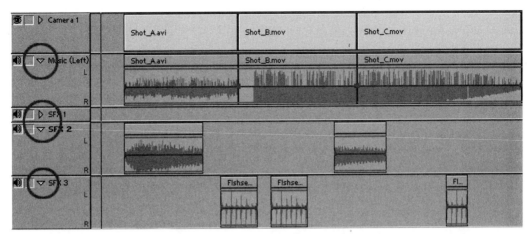

Figure 8-18 Click the triangle next to any audio track to view a waveform display of the audio in that track.

◆ You can easily find where musical sections occur very accurately. If you need to remove a portion of a piece of music, you can find the beats accurately, remove the desired section, and create a shorter version seamlessly.

◆ You can find where people begin and end their words, so now you'll never cut off part of a person's sentence again.

◆ If your audio contained some undesirable sound (an audio pop, a person coughing during someone's speech, etc.) you can now find it very quickly and remove it (as long as it does not occur at the same time as the person's words).

◆ If you are laying in a narration under some visuals, you can tighten (mark and cut) any pauses in between words or sentences that occurred during the recording session.

◆ You can easily identify the audio beats when cutting a music video (if cutting to the beats of the music) and mark your starting frame for your visuals.

There are many aspects where viewing the audio waveform becomes a necessary tool. I think once you become comfortable with how the waveform looks and understand what it represents, you will find it very valuable as well.

AUDIO TIP OF THE DAY— ROOM TONE

Here is a piece of advice that someone taught me that may help improve your audio editing. Have you ever had to space out a clip or remove a portion due to some undesirable sound? If you have, you've probably noticed something unnatural sounding about the clip when you removed the bad portion. You'd think it would sound better, but it might still sound funny. This may happen because (depending upon what type of audio you're working with) it's not natural to hear complete silence in the middle of your playback. Unless your recording took place in a soundproofed sound booth, your audio probably has some type of background noise. You might not even realize it or pay any attention to it unless it is suddenly gone. This is what I am referring to if you suddenly remove that unwanted sound (Figure 8-19).

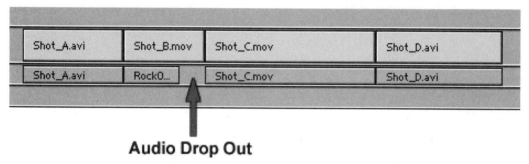

Audio Drop Out

Figure 8-19 Spaces left in audio tracks may sound very awkward if there is no other sound filling in that area. Audio dropping to complete silence is extremely noticeable in many cases.

This background sound is often referred to as room tone or natural sound. My advice to you is whenever possible (which should be a routine that you always keep), record at least half a minute of room tone. Keep the camera or recording device rolling while no one is speaking. This piece of audio becomes a great filler for those situations that you need to remove a bit of audio without removing any video (so you don't lose sync or create an unnecessary jump cut). Simply mark the portion that contains the hole and edit in the room tone. This will help remove any undesirable sounds, fill that portion with "natural sound" to smooth the edit, and not draw any unwanted attention to an otherwise silent section of audio. I hope this helps you.

KEEPING SYNC

Working with synced audio and video can make editing more complex if you are not paying attention to what you are doing. It can become very easy to knock your synced clip out of sync without even realizing it.
How your sequence can become out of sync:

◆   Inserting video or audio only before a piece that is already in sync (Figure 8-20).

◆   Trimming only one side of either video or audio clip of an already synced sequence in your timeline (Figure 8-21).

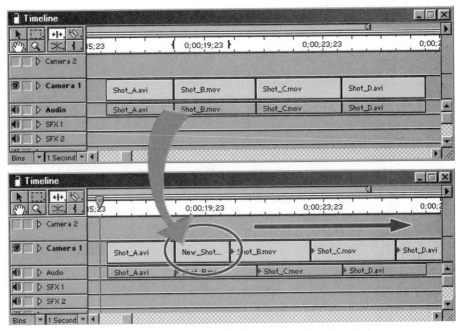

Figure 8-20   Inserting only video or only audio before synced tracks will throw your sequence out of sync.

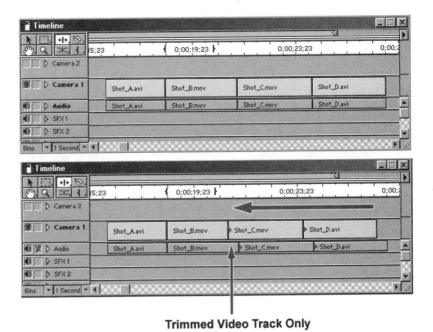

Trimmed Video Track Only

Figure 8-21 Trimming only one side of only video or only audio clips that are already synced together will knock the tracks out of sync.

◆ Removing any video or audio only that comes before a piece that is already in sync (Figure 8-22).

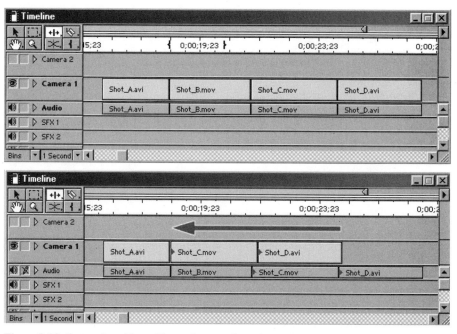

Figure 8-22 Extracting either video only or audio only portions of already synced tracks will knock the tracks out of sync.

Premiere indicates that linked clips are out of sync by displaying red triangles in the clip tracks in the timeline. If you click your cursor on any one of the triangles, you will be able to see the number of frames in which the clips are out of sync (Figure 8-23). Click and slightly drag a red triangle in the direction to re-match the clip. This resynchronizes the video and audio.

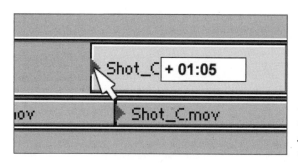

Figure 8-23 Click the cursor on any triangle to see the number of frames in which the clip is out of sync.

Note If the audio begins to play in sync and then falls out of sync at various times during different playbacks, the data rate might be too high for the computer.

WORKING WITH SYNC LOCKS

Premiere has the ability to help you keep you audio and video tracks in sync. If you have edited a track to perfection and don't want to make any adjustments to it, you can lock that track. Locking the track will keep you from adding or removing any portions of the locked tracks.

◆ To lock a track, click on the gray box next to the speaker icon of the desired audio track.

◆ To unlock a track, click again on the gray box next to the speaker icon of the desired audio track.

This is a great way to work with tracks one at a time. For instance, you might cut your voiceover tracks and master them to the final visual program. If you go and add music and sound effects afterwards, having the sync locks on for the voiceover tracks will take the worry out of accidentally knocking any of those tracks out of sync or deleting one of the clips. Locking any of the audio tracks (or video tracks for that matter) prevents you from adding, moving, deleting, or making any sort of changes to any of the clips in the locked tracks. The sync locks even override the target track selection if you are trying to edit a clip into a locked track.

AUDIO FILTERS FOR MASTERING YOUR SOUND

This is one of those topics that I can discuss forever. I believe audio filters, when used properly, can make an average production become spectacular. If you overuse them, you can wind up actually hurting your sound mix, ultimately diminishing the overall quality of your movie. I highly recommend playing around to familiarize yourself with each filter and to see what type of effect it has on your original source footage.

Tip I was taught that unless you're trying to create some type of funky sounds, if you can clearly hear the audio effect, then you've probably overdone it. A good sound mix uses filters to enhance the quality without drawing attention to the effects that you've used.

To apply audio filters:

❶ Edit an audio clip into your timeline.

❷ Click on the clip to select it.

❸ Select Filters from the Clip menu. The Audio Filters window should appear (Figure 8-24).

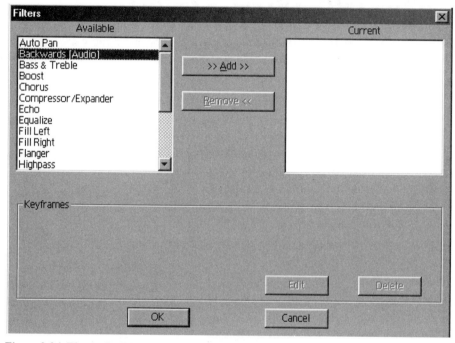

Figure 8-24 The Audio Filters window.

Or

Right-click (Windows) or Option-Click (Macintosh) to bring up a pop-up menu (Figure 8-25). Select Filters to open the Audio Filters window.

❹ Select from the default filters from the Available list of filters.

❺ Click the Add button to apply the filter.

❻ Make any adjustments to the settings as desired (if applicable).

The following are only some of the filters that come with Premiere and an explanation of how and when to use them. This, of course, is only a brief list. You can really do a great deal with them. I encourage you to mix and match, layering various filters to create some truly unique sound enhancements for your projects.

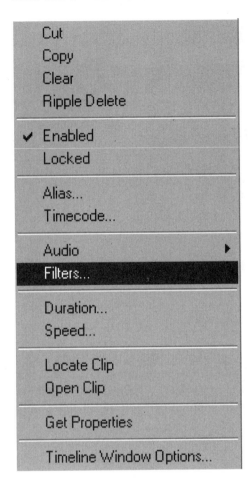

Figure 8-25 Use the Timeline shortcut pop-up menu.

◆ Backwards—This filter does what it says it does. This can come in handy if you are playing any video clips in reverse or if you want to get the sound of rewinding a tape.

◆ Bass and Treble—This is your basic EQ controls (Figure 8-26). Just like your home stereo system, you're probably pretty familiar with bass and treble adjustments. With the bass slider, you can cut (reduce) or boost (increase) the amount of low frequencies in your audio clip. The treble slider allows you to cut or boost the amount of high frequencies in your audio clip. If your audio sounds real thin and weak, try boosting the bass. If your audio sounds real "hissy" or has a lot of noise, try reducing the treble. If a voice sounds muffled and not cutting through your music, try boosting the treble a bit. If your audio sounds real "muddy" or "boomy," try cutting some of the bass. Click the Flat button to reset the sliders to the default zero position.

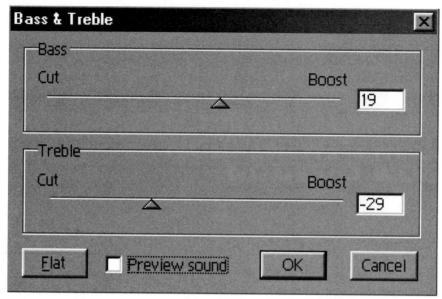

Figure 8-26 The Bass and Treble settings window.

All of the filters and adjustments require practice and slight tweaking of the sliders to find just the right amount, but the Bass/Treble filter alone can make huge improvements to your audio quality.

◆ Chorus—This is one of those "creative" filters that requires a great deal of practice to get a good sound but can really add a harmonious, slightly fluttering effect to the overall sound quality of the clip. Increasing the Mix will play more of the filtered effect sound than the natural sound. The Depth slider will determine how much fluctuation will occur (Figure 8-27).

◆ Compressor/Expander—This effect actually doesn't apply any sound-altering special effects (Figure 8-28). Instead, what it does is clean up your existing audio to make it sound more even in volume. Unless you had someone monitoring your audio and riding the input levels throughout the entire recording process, the dynamic levels may change dramatically throughout the course of the recorded segments. The Compressor filter actually keeps the dynamic levels unaffected up until it reaches a certain threshold (that you set). Any audio levels that exceed this threshold are diminished in order to keep the signal more even. This helps make your sound better balanced without those real loud unexpected "pops" that knock you off your chair. The Expander works from the opposite end, helping balance low level signals. Applying these filters really makes your audio productions sound professional. Be careful not to process your sound too much, or it will sound unnatural. Remember, real life sounds are not 100 percent even and do have some dynamic differences in range and level.

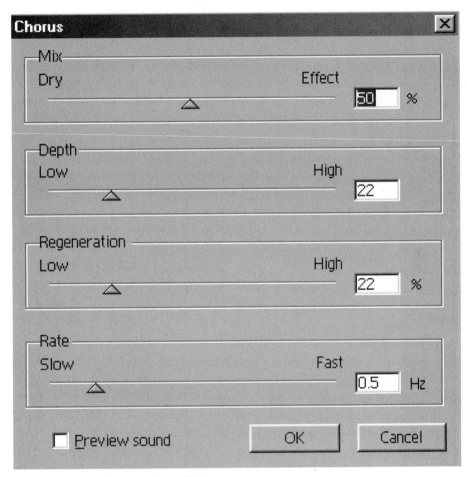

Figure 8-27 The Chorus settings window.

◆ Equalize—This filter offers more advanced control of your sound quality just like the Bass and Treble (Figure 8-29). Here you can control seven different frequency ranges to really customize the properties of your sound. See Bass and Treble above for some general tips on how to clean up your sound clips.

◆ Notch / Hum Filter—This filter is very simple to use and has a specific purpose (Figure 8-30). If you hear a "hum" in your audio, it could be that the frequency from your electrical current was recorded in with your signal. If your signal was recorded very low, you might also get this hum from the recording device or overhead lights. To reduce this hum, apply this filter and enter the frequency of your electrical current. The United States uses 60 cycles per second or 60 Hertz.

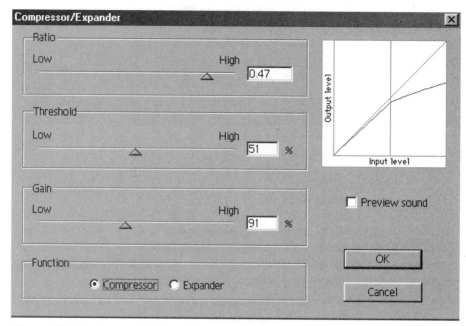

Figure 8-28 The Compressor / Expander settings window.

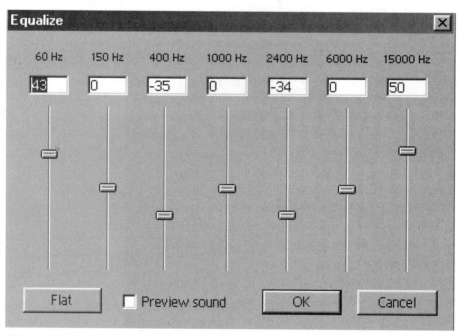

Figure 8-29 The Equalize settings window.

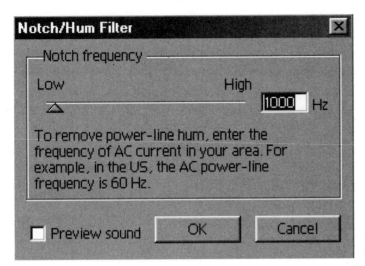

Figure 8-30 The Notch/Hum Filter settings window.

◆ Pan—This filter works the same way that you can set your pan settings directly in the timeline (using the blue fader line) (Figure 8-31). The filter setting is a global setting for the entire clip that you have selected. Working in the timeline offers you more control of your pan settings (frame by frame).

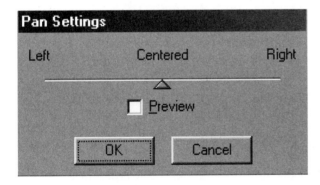

Figure 8-31 The Pan settings window.

◆ Parametric Equalization—This filter is for the ones who really understand audio frequencies and have a good ear (Figure 8-32). Describing how these controls work goes beyond the scope of this book, but I highly recommend that you find out more about how to use Parametric EQ's. This filter is the most advanced way to control the sound quality of an audio clip. You can dial in a specific frequency or frequency range and customize its properties. With this type of control and flexibility, you can take the time to make each sound clip sound perfect. Give it a shot.

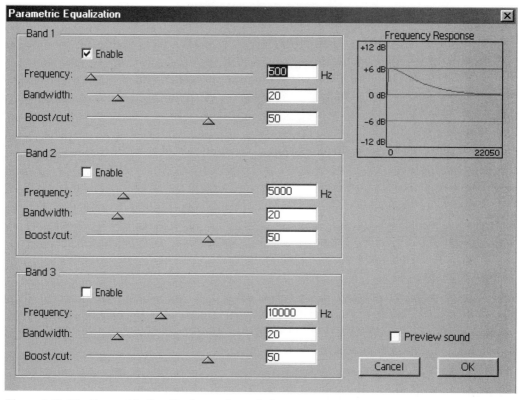

Figure 8-32 The Parametric Equalization settings window.

◆ Reverb—The best way to describe this filter is to say that it holds each sound longer than it is in its original format (Figure 8-33). That is, it works like a simple echo that doesn't repeat itself but sustains the original sounds. This is the effect that is occurring when you sing in the shower (that's why people think they can sing well in the shower). If you went into an empty gymnasium and bounced a basketball, the thunderous sound you hear is the reverb. Therefore, this effect should be used sparingly so as not to drown out your sound, but it can enhance and fill in some audio that sounds short or weak.

My advice is to take a number of different sound clips (music, narration, etc.) and apply these filters to each. This way you'll be able to see how each filter has different effects on different types of audio clips.

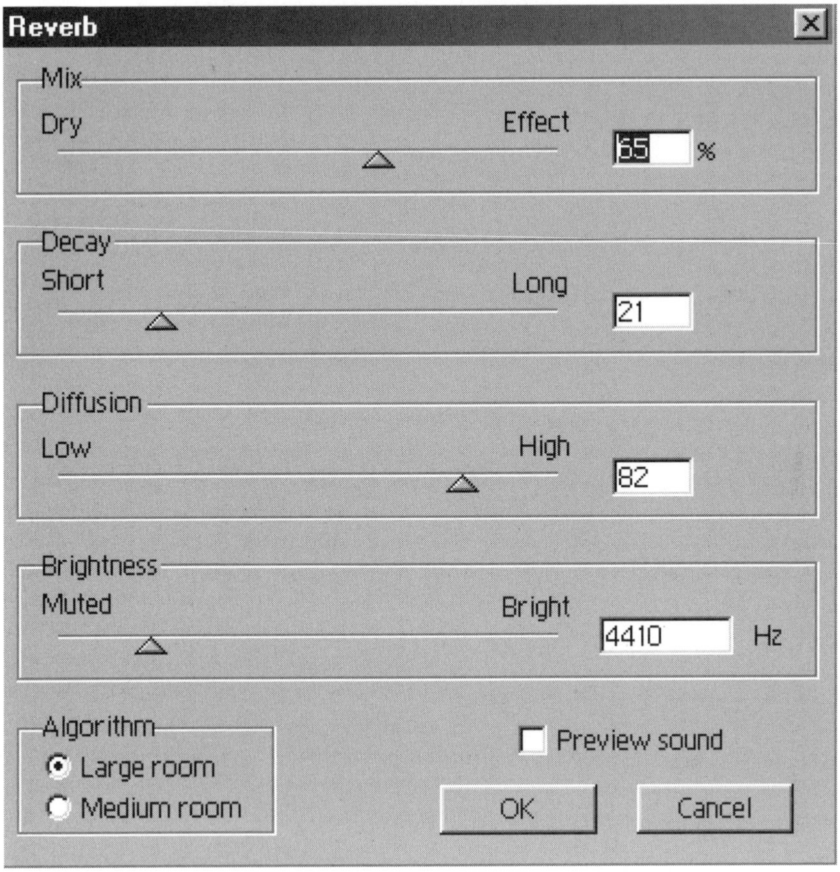

Figure 8-33 The Reverb settings window.

SUMMARY

I started off this chapter explaining how important audio is for your video projects. It can make or break your movie. You can see by the number of features and controls that you have with audio in Premiere that focusing as much time on your audio is just as important as creating the highest quality video for your project. Don't be afraid to experiment. There's always the undo command to change what you did if you don't like the way something sounds. You'll never know what it can sound like unless you try. Whatever you do, make sure it improves the overall sound mix. Your audience may not notice all the time and effort you've put into it, but they will appreciate a great audio performance.

chapter 9

THE MANY ATTRIBUTES OF THE TITLE TOOL

No video production would be complete without its fair share of titles and graphic elements. That's not to say that every project is going to be filled with text and still graphic images. You may only have an opening title screen or closing credits. Whatever the case, there are things you can do to make your titles look professional. There's nothing that makes a movie look amateurish than poorly created titles and graphics. Take a look at other people's work in the same style or category that you are working in (hopefully high-quality projects) to get a sense of what works and what doesn't. Documentaries may use simple, plain white Helvetica fonts. This looks simple, clean, and professional. A corporate sales video may require a bit more flare. Color, style, and layout all come into play to determine what you can do and what will look good. Keep in mind that there are no rules, but your viewers will be the judge of whether your titles and graphics work for the piece you've just produced. Some of them can even be pretty harsh.

HOW TO CREATE A NEW TITLE

The great thing about Premiere is that it is a complete program. By that I mean it contains everything you need to complete a project. All you need to supply is the source materials. Premiere even includes a title tool, allowing you to continue working without opening a completely new program. Creating titles in Premiere is easy:

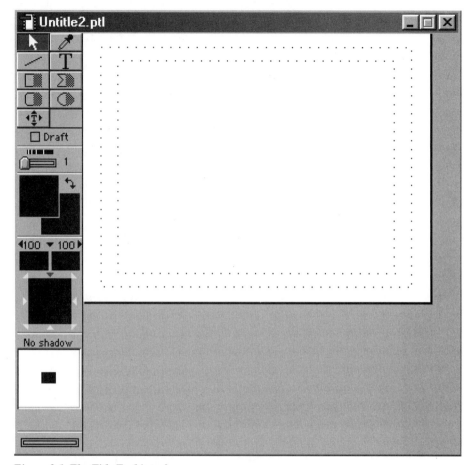

Figure 9-1 The Title Tool interface.

❶ Select New from the File menu.

❷ Select Title from the pop-up menu. The title tool should appear (Figure 9-1).

A new menu choice, Title, should appear across the top of your menu selections.

Once you have opened the title tool, you can begin typing. Premiere starts with a blank page for you to begin typing words or drawing images. To begin typing:

❶ With the Title tool window open, click on the Type Tool or hit Shift-T on the keyboard. The cursor should change to an I-bar.

❷ Click anywhere on the screen where you would like to start typing.

The dashed lines around the title tool typing area indicate Action Safe and Title Safe areas (Figure 9-2). The Title Safe area indicates the maximum area in which you should place text. Typing outside of these lines means that your text may wind up being placed at the edge of your viewing screen or even cut off by regular television monitors. Proper text position should have a little breathing room from the edges of your television screen. You can type anywhere on the screen you'd like, but unless you're going for some type of stylistic effect, keep your text within the boundaries of the Title Safe area.

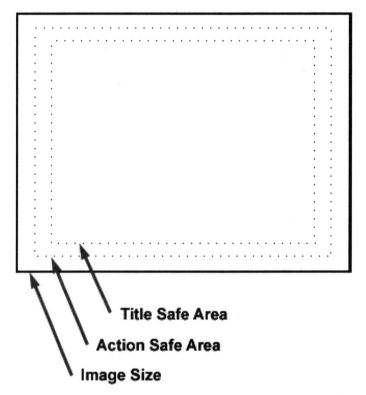

Title Safe Area

Action Safe Area

Image Size

Figure 9-2 Action Safe and Title Safe areas.

FROM CREATION TO IMPLEMENTATION

Once you have created your title in the Title Tool, there are still a few steps you must do before you are able to see it in your timeline. With your Title Tool window active:

❶ Select Save As from the File menu.

❷ Name your file and save it in a location that you will be able to easily find. (See my tips on creating and naming files and folders in Chapter 2).

❸ Click Save.

❹ Inside your Project window, select a bin where you want to import the text file you just created.

❺ Select Import from the File menu.

❻ Select File from the pop-up menu or use the keyboard shortcut Control-I (Windows) or Command-I Macintosh).

❼ Locate the file you saved and click OK.

Once the clip has been imported into your project (inside of a bin), you can edit the title into your timeline just as you would any other type of file.

GETTING TEXT TO APPEAR CORRECTLY

When you create a title in Premiere's Title tool, you may have to make a few modifications to get it to look exactly the way you intended it to appear. When you type your text in the Title tool and bring it into your project, or more specifically your timeline, it probably has a default white background (depending on how your last settings were left). If you place your text in Video Track 1, it will pretty much remain as your text (with whichever attributes you applied to it) over the white background. If you want your text to appear over other images, you need to do the following:

❶ Edit the text into Video Track 2 or higher. This gives you access to keying and transparency controls.

❷ Click on the text segment in your timeline to select it.

❸ Select Video from the Clip menu.

❹ Select Transparency from the pop-up menu or use the keyboard shortcut Control-G (Windows) or Command-G (Macintosh).

Or

Right click (Windows) or Control-Click (Macintosh) to display the pop-up menu. Select Video>Transparency.

❺ Apply one of the appropriate key settings, depending upon your text and the desired effect you're looking to create.

Most often, if your text you created is initially displayed with a white background, selecting Alpha Channel or White Alpha Matte should do the trick. If your text has a black background, try the Black Alpha Matte. Premiere automatically generates an alpha channel around the text you create. All you have to do is go in and select how you want that background to appear (or disappear in this case) (Figure 9-3).

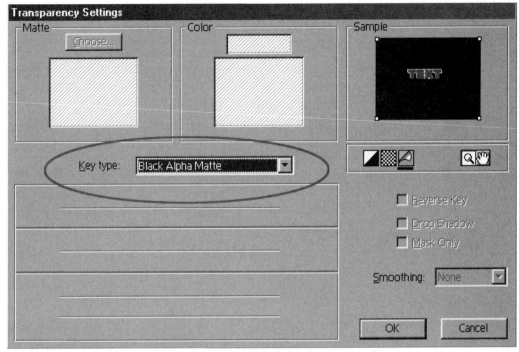

Figure 9-3 Applying a Black Alpha Matte to drop out the black background.

EDITING EXISTING TEXT

I can't think of a project where I didn't have to go back into a text clip that I had created earlier and make a few modifications. Making corrections and updates to text clips already edited into your timeline is extremely easy.

❶ Double-click on a text clip in the timeline that you want to change. The Title tool window should appear with the text in an editable format.

❷ Make any necessary changes.

❸ Save the new text changes.

The text changes should update automatically upon saving. The new corrections will appear in the timeline as well as in the source clip file.

To keep the original version of a text file while updating one in the timeline, simply save the new corrections using the Save As option and supplying a new file name.

APPLYING TEXT ATTRIBUTES

Now that you've typed your text, I'm sure there are a few things you would like to do to improve the way your text appears on screen. Depending upon what type of project you are editing and what style appeals to you, you probably are going to want to change the font, color, size, or other text attributes. To change text attributes:

❶ Select the Type Tool (if not already selected).

❷ Highlight the text you typed.

❸ Click on Title from the menu choices or use the keyboard shortcut Alt-T (Windows) or Option-T (Macintosh). A drop-down menu should appear, listing all of the text attribute choices available with Premiere (Figure 9-4).

Figure 9-4 A list of the Text Attributes.

The following are some ways to change the characteristics of your text:

◆ Font—This displays all of the font choices available for use in Premiere's Title tool. You can purchase and install other fonts for use in Premiere.

◆ Size –You can either choose from one of the preselected sizes or choose Other to enter your own custom font size.

◆ Style—The default is Plain. You can change that to Bold, Italic, Underline, and Emboss. You can select multiple styles for a single word. Click on the same choice to toggle that selection off.

◆ Justify—This selection determines which direction the text comes from and how it lines up. Left justification keeps all the words lined up on the left margin, with no defined edge on the right. Right justification keeps all of the words lined up on the right margin, with no defined edge on the left. Center lines up each line of text to be centered down the middle of the bounding box (Figure 9-5).

◆ Leading—You can change the amount of space between lines of text using the Leading option. Choose from More Leading (increasing the spacing), Less Leading (reducing the spacing), or Reset Leading to return to the normal, default line spacing (Figure 9-6).

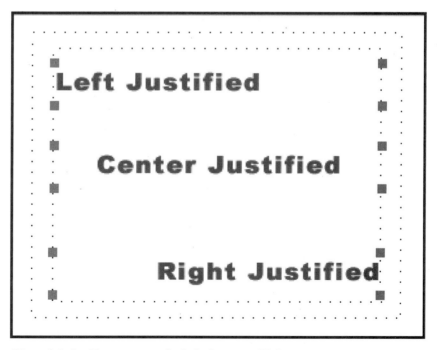

Figure 9-5 Justify your text to the Left, Center, or Right.

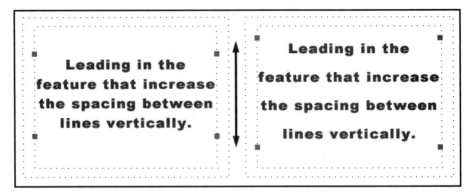

Figure 9-6 Leading increases the spacing between each line of text.

◆   Orientation—This determines the direction that the text will flow. Normal writing
     (including this book) is written horizontally from left to right. For creative aspects,
     you can change the direction to write from top to bottom (Figure 9-7).

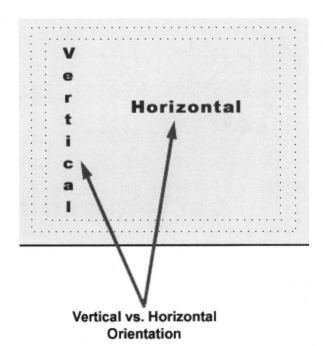

*Figure 9-7 Use the Orientation aspect to change the direction of the text from left to right to
top to bottom.*

◆ Rolling Title Option—Use this option to create rolling titles (similar to the way credits move at the end of a movie) or scroll text across the screen (similar to the way a breaking news update moves across the bottom of your screen) (Figure 9-8). See the section on Creating Rolling Titles below.

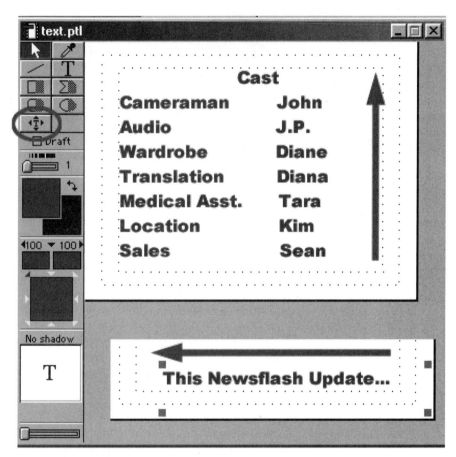

Figure 9-8 Rolling titles can either scroll bottom to top or right to left.

◆ Shadow—This option determines the type of shadow that is applied to your text. The Single shadow selection adds a basic hard-edged drop shadow. The Solid shadow selection connects the shadow to the actual text. This gives a three-dimensional look to the text. The Soft shadow selection gives the edges of the drop shadow a feathered, more natural look and feel (Figure 9-9).

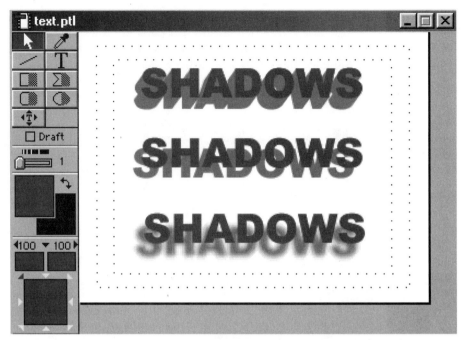

Figure 9-9 Apply shadows to text to give it the appearance of depth.

◆   Bring to Front—This option brings the text or object you have selected in front of any other text or object you have created within the same text file. Each text block or object that you create is placed on top of the last text or object you created. Bring to Front allows you to move the desired text or object to the front, overlapping any other objects.

◆   Send To Back—This aspect works in the opposite manner as Bring To Front. This option brings the text or object you have selected and places it behind any other text or object you have created within the same text file.

◆   Center Horizontally—This selection positions your text or object in the center of the screen on the same line that it is vertically, with the beginning and end of the text or object equally spaced from the left edge and right edge of the screen (Figure 9-10).

◆   Center Vertically—This selection positions your text or object in the center of the screen on the same line that it is horizontally, with the top and bottom of the text or object equally spaced from the top edge and bottom edge of the screen (Figure 9-11).

◆   Position in Lower Third—This selection moves the text or object to the lower portion of your screen. This is a common screen position used for placing text and objects while identifying people, places, or things on screen (Figure 9-12). See the section on Creating High Class Lower Thirds below.

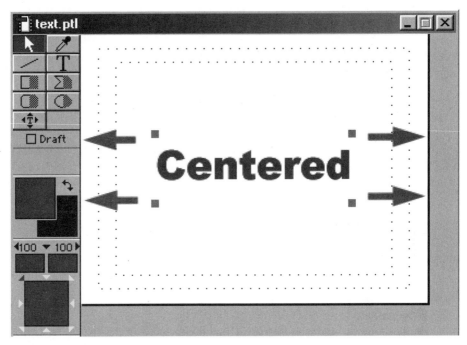

Figure 9-10 Center your text perfectly in the center of your screen, balanced left to right.

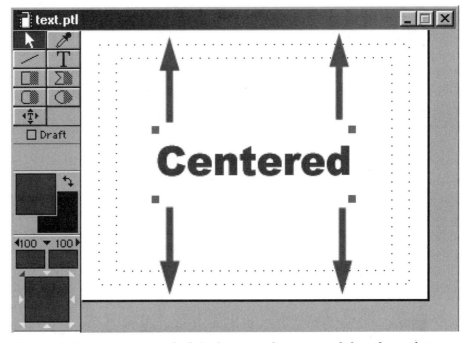

Figure 9-11 Center your text perfectly in the center of your screen, balanced top to bottom.

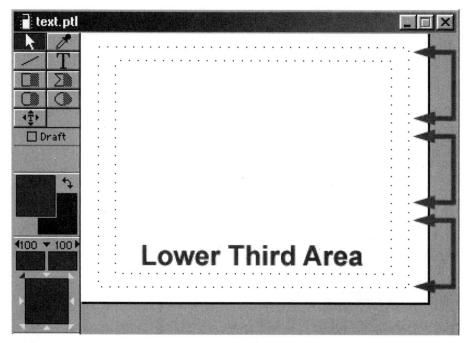

Figure 9-12 Position your text as a Lower Third for quick identification titles.

BRINGING TEXT TO LIFE WITH COLOR

When you begin typing in Premiere for the first time, you'll notice that the default text color is solid black. This may be what color your project requires, but keep in mind that you have the ability to change the fonts to any shade of the 16 million colors available through a standard color picker. You can change your text to either a solid color or create a gradient blend between two colors you select. To change the color of your text:

❶ Highlight the text you want to change its color.

❷ Click on the Object Color swatch (Figure 9-13). The Color Picker window should open.

❸ Select the color that you prefer or enter the RGB color values in the appropriate fields.

❹ Click OK.

This will change any of the text you highlighted to the new color value, a solid color change. You can also make the text appear having a gradient between two color values:

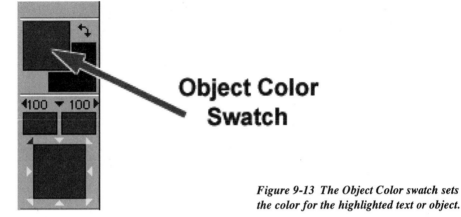

Object Color
Swatch

Figure 9-13 The Object Color swatch sets
the color for the highlighted text or object.

❶ Highlight the text that you want to change to a color gradient.

❷ Click on the Gradient Start Color swatch. The Color Picker window should appear.

❸ Select the color that you prefer or enter the RGB color values in the appropriate fields.

❹ Click OK.

❺ Click on the Gradient End Color swatch. The Color Picker window should appear.

❻ Select the color that you prefer or enter the RGB color values in the appropriate fields.

❼ Click OK.

Premiere automatically updates the text that you have selected and changes its color attributes to display the new color gradient, evenly blending from the first color selected to the second color from one end of the font to the other. You can now change the direction of where the gradient color starts and ends. To change the starting position of the color gradient:

❶ Highlight the text you want to change.

❷ Click on one of the directional triangles in the Gradient / Transparency Direction area (Figure 9-14).

If you do not see the gradient colors in your preview window, make sure you do not have Draft check box selected in the tool palette.

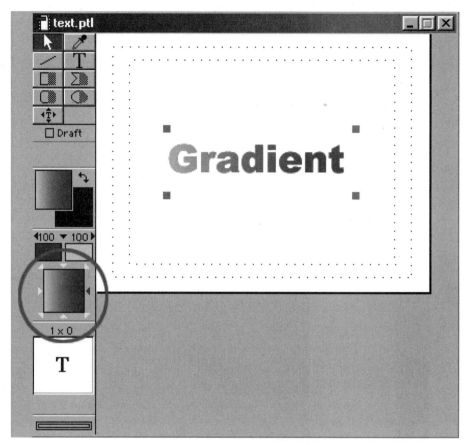

Figure 9-14 Set the direction of a color or transparency gradient using the directional arrows.

ADJUSTING TEXT TRANSPARENCY

Putting text on screen today is more than just conveying information. Editors spend about as much time typing the info as they do coming up with creative ways to display the text. Displaying the text creatively may also involve making the text partially transparent. You can use partially transparent text to bring across a more subtle message than plastering the text on-screen fully opaque. Applying multiple layers of text in combinations of varying transparencies gives a very modern and creative look and feel. To adjust the transparency level of your text:

❶ Highlight the text that you want to alter.

❷ Click on the Overall Transparency triangle. The Opacity window should appear (Figure 9-15).

❸ Click on the opacity scale or drag the triangle sliders up and down until you select the desired transparency level.

Premiere also allows you to create a transparency blend within your text. You can customize your text to start at any transparency level and evenly fade into another transparency level. This is a great effect when using words or phrases in the background of your images. To change your text to have a transparency blend:

Figure 9-15 The Opacity window sets the overall transparency level.

❶ Highlight the text that you want to alter.

❷ Click on the Start Transparency triangle. The Opacity window should appear for the starting level.

❸ Select the desired transparency level.

❹ Click on the End Transparency triangle. The Opacity window should appear for the ending level.

❺ Select the desired transparency level.

The position of your starting transparency level is determined by the position you set using your Gradient/Transparency Direction indicator (Figure 9-16).

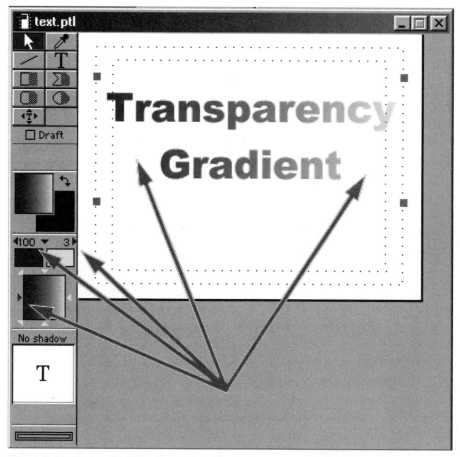

Figure 9-16 Change the direction of the transparency gradient of an object with the Gradient/Transparency Direction indicators.

When changing the transparency level of your text, be aware that the transparency level of your shadow does not change. Therefore, if you lower the level of your text to 10% opaque, your shadow may wind up being more visible (Figure 9-17).

Figure 9-17 Shadows do not change accordingly as you lower the transparency level of the text.

MANIPULATING SHADOWS MANUALLY

If you want your text to have a three dimensional look, you'll need to add some type of shadow. Adding a shadow to your text is as simple as clicking and dragging your mouse around to set the desired position of the shadow.

❶ Highlight the text you want to adjust.

❷ Click in the Shadow Position box. Your cursor should turn into the hand icon.

❸ Drag your cursor around the box to set the desired position of your shadow.

Notice a numeric indicator located above the Shadow Position box. This gives you the exact position of your shadow. This is extremely helpful when you want to keep all of your shadows in the same exact position throughout your entire project. The first number in the position indicator tells you the distance the shadow appears from the font in a left-right direction. A negative number indicates that the shadow is displayed to the left while a positive number indicates that the shadow is displayed to the right. The second number indicates the position of the shadow in reference to whether it appears above or below the font. A negative number indicates that the shadow appears above the font while a positive number indicates that the shadow appears below the font.

The default shadow is displayed as a soft drop shadow. Throughout your project, the type of shadow that is applied is determined by the shadow setting type you selected the last time you created text. To change the type of shadow that is applied:

❶ Highlight the text you want to adjust.

❷ Click on Shadow from the Title menu.

❸ Select from one of the three types of shadows that Premiere can create in the Title Tool: Single, Solid, or Soft.

 See Shadows under Applying Text Attributes above to get a description and see a sample of the three different types of shadows.

CREATING ROLLING TITLES

If you've ever stuck around at the end of your favorite movie, you've probably noticed the credits come rolling up, listing the stars of the movie. The same feature in Premiere also creates those ticker news bulletins that come scrolling across the bottom of your television. You can add these professional text features to your productions. Rolling Titles and Scrolling Text features are easy to create in Premiere:

❶ Select New from the File menu.

❷ Select Title from the pop-up menu. The Title tool window should appear.

❸ Click on the Rolling Title tool icon or hit the Y key on your keyboard.

❹ Drag a box outlining the area where you want your rolling text to cover (Figure 9-18).

❺ Type in the desired text.

❻ With the text selected, click on Rolling Title Options under the Title menu. The Rolling Title Options window should appear (Figure 9-19).

❼ Change the attributes as desired. This is where you can choose the direction and flow of your text.

 You do need to hit the Enter key (Windows) or Return key (Macintosh) to begin typing on the next line. Premiere does not automatically add Word Wrap.

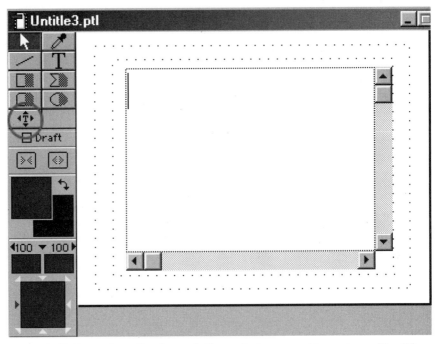

Figure 9-18 Drag a bounding box to indicate where you want to create a rolling title.

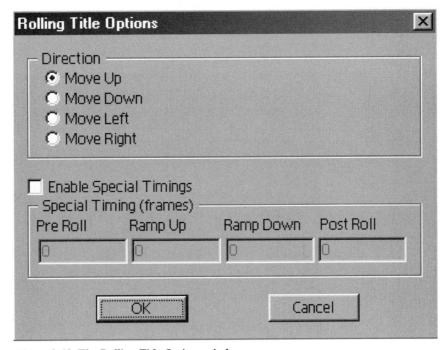

Figure 9-19 The Rolling Title Options window.

Use the Ramp Up and Ramp Down features to alter the speed at which your text begins to move or comes to a halt. The larger the value you enter in the appropriate field, the longer (slower in speed) it takes to get your text in motion at full speed. The Pre Roll and Post Roll features determine the number of frames it takes for your text to actually remain motionless either at the beginning or end of the segment respectively. Pre Roll keeps the text stationary from the starting frame of the clip for the number of frames that you determine and then begins its motion. Post Roll works in the same manner on the back end of a clip. The motion of your text will stop at its final resting place and remain motionless for the number of frames that you select until the ending frame of the clip.

To preview a Rolling Title that you have just created inside the Title tool, click on the slider located in the lower left corner of the Title Tool window (Figure 9-20). Keep in mind that the preview will not display any special times entered into the Pre Roll / Post Roll or Ramp Up / Ramp Down fields. To see the effect of these special timings, you need to edit the title into your timeline and preview your timeline as you normally would playback your movie.

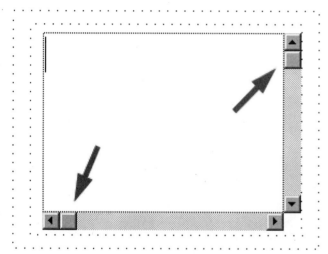

Figure 9-20 Use the slider to scroll through a Rolling Title.

CREATING HIGH-CLASS LOWER THIRDS

Whether you are cutting a news story for broadcast or a corporate video containing interviews of selected key individuals from the company, you usually need to identify the people that appear on screen. The most common way to bring a person's name (and any other information about them) up on screen is known as positioning the text as a "lower third." This name comes from the position of the text on screen, where it is

Figure 9-21 "Lower Thirds" are placed in the lower portion of the screen.

physically placed (Figure 9-21). Keep in mind, there are no rules that require you to identify someone using a lower third title. It works out as the best place on the screen because it does not interfere with the person's face or other areas of interest when placed on screen. Premiere includes a menu choice to position your text as a lower third. Click on Position in Lower Third found under the Title menu choice while in the Title tool.

Putting just text as an identifier can be very boring however. I recommend watching some of your favorite news programs to see how much more complex their lower thirds have become over the years. I personally like the ones found on CNN and ESPN. The point is that you can add layers of graphics, multiple font choices, animations, and even moving video clips for your lower thirds. Here are a few ideas that you can play around with, from simple, quick fixes that you can completely create in Premiere to the more professional and advanced ones that require a bit more time and effort.

Simple Example (Figure 9-22)

◆   Use graphic tools found in Premiere Title Tool

More Elaborate (Figure 9-23)

◆   Play with Transparency levels
◆   Add many different levels of graphics

Figure 9-22 Simple lower third can be created in Premiere.

Figure 9-23 Use more layers and animation features to enhance the appearance of a lower third.

Figure 9-24 Use third-party applications to create real high end lower thirds.

◆   Add motion to text or images

Professional (Figure 9-24)

◆   Use matte keys for custom shapes and designs
◆   Add animations
◆   Add moving video

IMPORTING BACKGROUND IMAGES FOR POSITIONING

Many times, text attributes such as font style, size, and color are determined by their position on screen. The last thing you want is to place text over a key area of interest in your video, blocking the most important part of your video. The hard part is guessing where the text should be placed. So why guess? Premiere has an option that allows you to import a frame of your video or still graphic as a background image for your text. This is extremely handy in determining the positioning and attributes for your text. It saves a tremendous amount of time by taking the guesswork out of deciding which fonts and which colors might look good over a clip that you can't see. Now you can place the appropriate frame in the background to size up your titles perfectly every time. To add a visual frame in the background of your Title tool (for positioning):

❶ Click on the video clip that you want to use for the background.

❷ Go to the frame of the clip that you want to use for text positioning.

❸ Select Set Marker from the Clip menu.

❹ Select 0 (zero) from the pop-up menu. This identifies the frame Premiere uses for the Title tool.

❺ Open the Title tool.

❻ Drag the selected frame from your source clip monitor into the Title tool window. The selected frame should appear in the Title tool window.

You can change the background image or update the frame displayed in the Title tool at any point. Just set a new frame for Marker 0 and Premiere will automatically update the selected frame represented as the background of the Title tool. To delete the frame from the Title tool display altogether, simply select Remove background Clip from the Title menu.

The frame you import is used only for text positioning and is not included as part of the saved text file. This frame will not appear when playing back the text file in your timeline.

ANIMATING YOUR TEXT

I'm not talking about bringing each letter to life and having them dance around on screen to some swing music. That's left for 3D animators (Figure 9-25). What I'm talking about is moving your text around on the screen and flying it in from different positions. Animating text in Premiere works the same way as adding motion to video clips works. Moving text is a great effect for opening titles, key words during a motivational video, and descriptions during a training video.

To add motion to your text:

❶ Edit the text into any video track.

❷ Click on the clip to select it.

❸ Select Video from the Clip menu.

❹ Select Motion from the pop-up menu or use the keyboard shortcut Control-Y (Windows) or Command-Y (Macintosh).

❺ Adjust the variable in the Motion Settings window to control the speed, rotation, and overall direction of the movement of your text.

Figure 9-25 3D animation programs are used to create high end animated text scenes.

GETTING TEXT TO BOUNCE

One cool trick that I try to incorporate into my video (when applicable) is to get the text to look and act like the word it's describing or emulate the movement of the scene it's in. For instance, during a highlight sports video, I wanted the word BASKETBALL to appear to be dribbling across the screen like a real basketball. The real trick to giving your animated text some validity is to pay special attention to the little nuances. These little adjustments can make or break your animation.

❶ Edit the text into any video track.

❷ Select the text.

❸ Select Video from the Clip menu.

❹ Select Motion from the pop-up menu.

❺ Set the keyframes in the Motion Settings window to create a zig-zag pattern (Figure 9-26).

❻ Add a keyframe just before and just after every low point on the pattern (Figure 9-27).

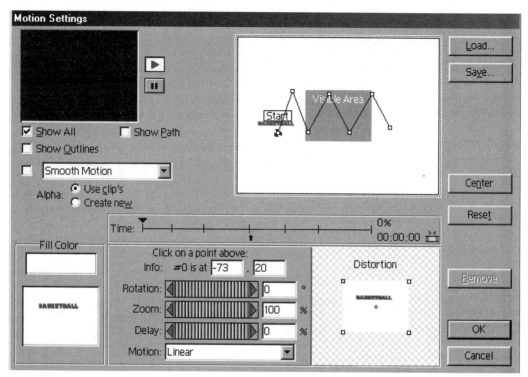

Figure 9-26 Use keyframes to add motion to your text.

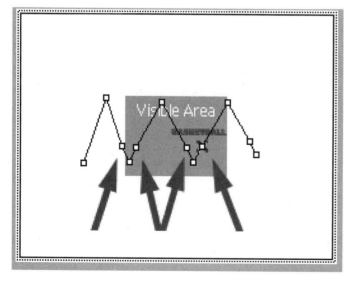

Figure 9-27 Add a keyframe just prior to original keyframes.

❼ Click on the bottom keyframe to select it.

❽ Use the Distortion window to squish the text.

❾ Click on the keyframe directly after the lowest one.

❿ Set the Motion to Decelerate. This makes the image appear to "bounce" off the ground with some added zing to the movement.

Play with a few of the other adjustments to see if you can create some of your own twists and turns to add life to your text animations. There are so many ways you can fine-tune the movements to get a realistic action from the text's motion settings.

CREATING GRAPHIC OBJECTS IN TITLE TOOL

Having a full blown paint/graphics package inside of Premiere would make life very easy. Then again, I guess that's why Adobe sells Photoshop. Since you can export and import images pretty seamlessly between Premiere and Photoshop, I guess I can't complain. The good thing about the Title tool in Premiere is that you can create some basic graphics and images to use in your movies. Granted, it takes a bit of playing around and some creativity, but you can actually create enough of the most commonly used graphic elements directly within Premiere's Title tool. The following is a list of some basic elements that you will probably use in many of your projects and how to create them:

◆ Lines—Every project needs lines, somewhere somehow. Lines work great to separate various lines of text (Figure 9-28).

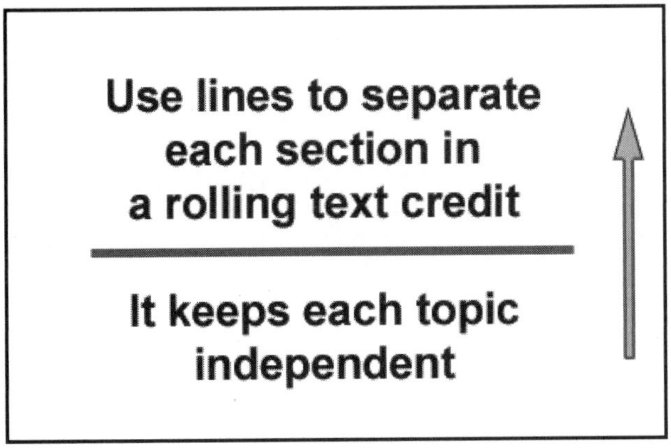

Use lines to separate each section in a rolling text credit

It keeps each topic independent

Figure 9-28 Using lines works well for separating blocks of texts.

❶ Click on the Line Tool icon or hit the L key on your keyboard.

❷ Click in the work area and drag your mouse for the desired length. You can always click on either end of the handles to relocate the line's position (starting and ending points).

❸ Adjust the colors, shadows, and so on, the same as you would for text.

 Hold down the Shift key to lock the line as a straight horizontal or vertical line.

◆ Rectangles—Use rectangles for masking areas that need to be covered up or as a background portion for text (Figure 9-29).

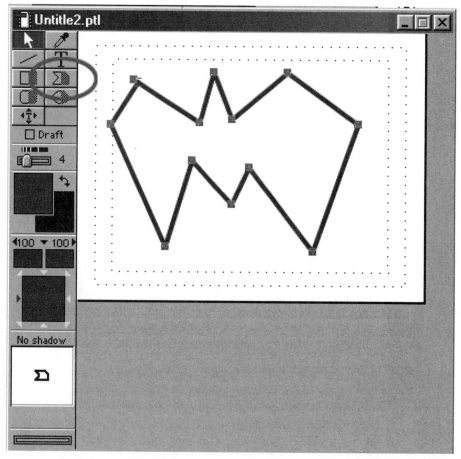

Figure 9-29 Rectangles work well for making text stand out on busy backgrounds.

❶ Click on the Rectangle tool icon or hit the S key on your keyboard.

❷ Click in the work area and drag your mouse for the desired box size. You can always click on one of the end handles to resize or reposition the rectangle.

❸ Adjust the colors, shadows, and so on, the same as you would for text.

 Hold down the Shift key to constrain the proportions of the rectangle to be a square (equal sides).

◆ The Oval tool and Round Rectangle tool—These tools work the same way that the Rectangle tool functions. You can use the keyboard shortcut O or R keys respectively. The Polygon tool (or P key) allows you to draw any custom shape object by continually click where you want the corners or "anchor points" to appear (Figure 9-30).

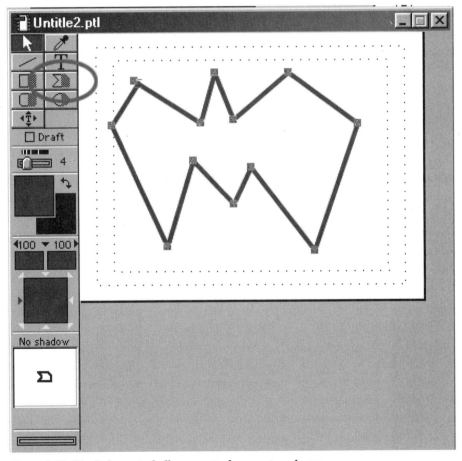

Figure 9-30 The Polygon tool allows you to draw custom shapes.

Select Smooth Polygon from the Title menu to "round out" the edges on the images you create (Figure 9-31). You can still manipulate the handle to truly customize the shapes.

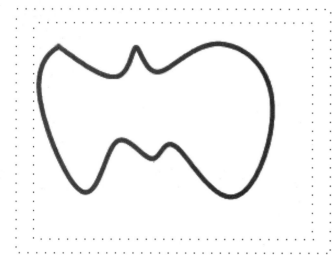

Figure 9-31 Apply the Smooth Polygon to round out your object's edges.

SUMMARY

It's almost impossible not to use any text or graphic elements in your productions these days. The ones you do use need to compete with the high-class quality of the ones you see on television. People have become exposed to high quality graphics and text images on screen, so you need to make sure you spend time coming up with some creative ways to get your text to match its subject content while making it look as good as it can be. My last tip for this chapter is to try to emulate the good ideas you see on television, but always try to make them one step better.

OUTPUTTING

YOUR WORK

Here's what you've been waiting for. You went out and shot all of your footage, digitized it into Premiere, added all the bells and whistles, and now have this Academy Award-winning production. Well, unless you plan to lug around your computer everywhere you go to show off your editing masterpiece, you need to output your project. One of the great things about Premiere is that you have several different options for outputting your movie. Whether you choose the traditional route of going to tape or jumping onboard with the new media channels of distributing your movies, Premiere helps you prepare for any one of the methods.

PREP YOUR TAPE

Before you actually output your program to tape, there are a few last minute details that need to be addressed. These are the vital portions of your program (especially if you're editing for broadcast). Whether you are outputting your program for air or just making your protection master to store in the archives, it's always a good idea to prepare your tapes with all the "tech specs" before your program. By this I mean adding the correct amount of black space before the program starts. Nothing is more frustrating to work with than a tape where the program begins as soon as the tape is inserted into the deck (at the very beginning of the tape). One of the standard methods (check with each facility to find out their specific requirements) includes:

❶ At least 10 seconds of black at the beginning of the tape.

❷ 30 seconds to one minute of SMPTE color bars with a 1 kHz tone.

❸ At least 10 seconds worth of slate information. (See below).

❹ 10 seconds of black.

❺ A 10-second countdown. (See below).

❻ The program.

There are several ways to add black to your timeline (before or after your edited program). One method is to digitize black from a tape or from a black burst generator. Another technique that I have used is to edit in an audio clip but mute the volume completely. The easiest process is to create a black matte in Premiere. To create a black matte to use as filler:

❶ Select Create from the Project menu.

❷ Select Color Matte from the pop-up menu.

❸ Use the Color Picker and select black or enter 0,0,0 in the RGB value fields (Figure 10-1).

❹ Click OK.

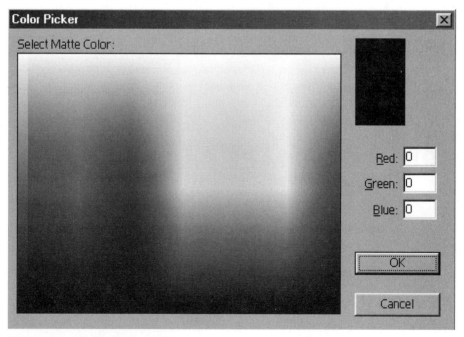

Figure 10-1 Standard Color Picker.

❺ Enter a name to identify the color (black) matte you've just created.

❻ Click OK.

> **If you have device control and a timecode generator, you typically want your first frame of your movie to begin on the one-hour mark of your timecode (01:00:00:00). This means your prep materials will start prior to the one-hour timecode, say 00:58:30:00.**

BARS AND TONE

It's a good habit to put bars and tone, a slate, and a countdown at the beginning of every tape. Standard SMPTE color bars are used as a measurement tool for balancing the deck and monitors so that the program that is about to follow plays at its best (Figure 10-2). Similar to when you are digitizing footage into the system, you use the color bars to adjust and balance the video signal. If you didn't put bars on your edited master tapes, no one would be able to correctly balance the signal. All the guesswork would only be able to be done by eye.

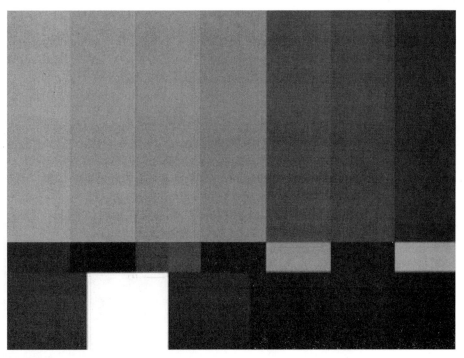

Figure 10-2 SMPTE Color Bars.

With the SMPTE bars generally goes an audio tone. This is usually a 1kHz (or 1,000 hertz) tone set at zero on your VU meters. This too is used as a calibration signal to adjust the proper playback levels once your signal has been recorded onto tape. What you must do is set the level of the tones to be the same level as your loudest portions of your movie's audio level. Hopefully, if you mixed your audio well throughout your editing, the majority of your movie should remain consistent and ride around the zero VU meter mark. It is perfectly acceptable, if your movie contains softer portions, to let the meter drop below zero VU, but try to refrain from going too much past +1 or +2 on your VU meter (Figure 10-3). If your signal goes much past that point, you may begin to experience audio distortion, clipping, or complete signal dropout (depending on whether you are outputting to analog or digital formats). This is generally referred to as "pinning the needles."

If your audio tracks are very dynamic (vast differences between high- and low-volume levels), you may want to look into using a compressor/expander. A compressor takes any signal over a certain threshold (that you set) and "compresses" the signal, reducing the dynamic range. This keeps signals more even and balanced, avoiding the real loud surges. A good example would be if a scene in your movie contained a person screaming or a bomb exploding, these loud (dynamic) sounds would not send the needles off your meters. The expander works in exactly the opposite fashion. It takes signals below a certain threshold and raises them accordingly to try and balance out the softer portions of your movie.

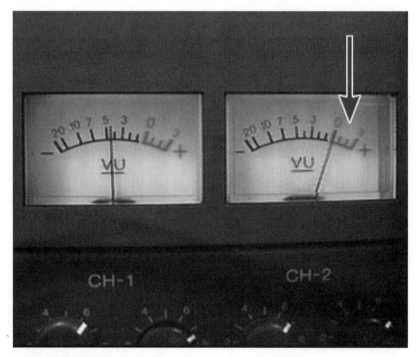

Figure 10-3 A VU Meter gauges the level of the audio signal.

You can use external, outboard audio gear found at most professional music equipment stores or use some third-party plug-ins becoming available to integrate right within your editing software.

THE SLATE: WHO, WHAT, WHEN, AND WHERE

You don't have to get overly fancy with this. Some people include the slate information in with their countdown screen. I generally keep it separate. (It makes it easier to make any kind of text changes that seem to always occur). Slate information is especially helpful in many situations. You never know if a label gets ripped off or written over. How many times does a tape wind up in the wrong box? How many times are there multiple versions of the same program? By having the slate information right at the beginning of the program, you can quickly cue up the tape to the slate and verify whether it is the correct version you are looking for. The following lists some basic information to include. Again, check with each facility to obtain a list of their specifications. A slate may include (but is not limited to):

◆ Program Title—the name of the movie or program

◆ Client—who the program was edited for (i.e., who paid the bill)

◆ Episode or Version—weekly shows or commercials which may have specific names or numbers to identify slightly altered versions

◆ Date—the date the final master edit was completed and output to tape

◆ Total Run Time—the overall duration of the program from the first frame to the last.

◆ Production Company—who produced the program

◆ Executive Producer—the key person who was in charge of the project

◆ Post Production Facility—where the program was edited

◆ Contact Information—address and phone number of key individual or studio in case there is a problem with the tape

Making a slate is as easy as typing white letters on a black screen (Figure 10-4). Feel free to get as creative as you want, but keep in mind, the general public almost never sees the slate. It's designed for information only, not artistic expression. Only the guys in the tape room who cue up your program get to view it. My advice is not to spend too much time or money trying to make a fancy slate.

TEN, NINE, EIGHT, ...

Creating a countdown is important if your material is going out for broadcast. The countdown does exactly what you would think it does. It signifies how much time is left until your movie starts. Generally you start off at ten seconds and count down all

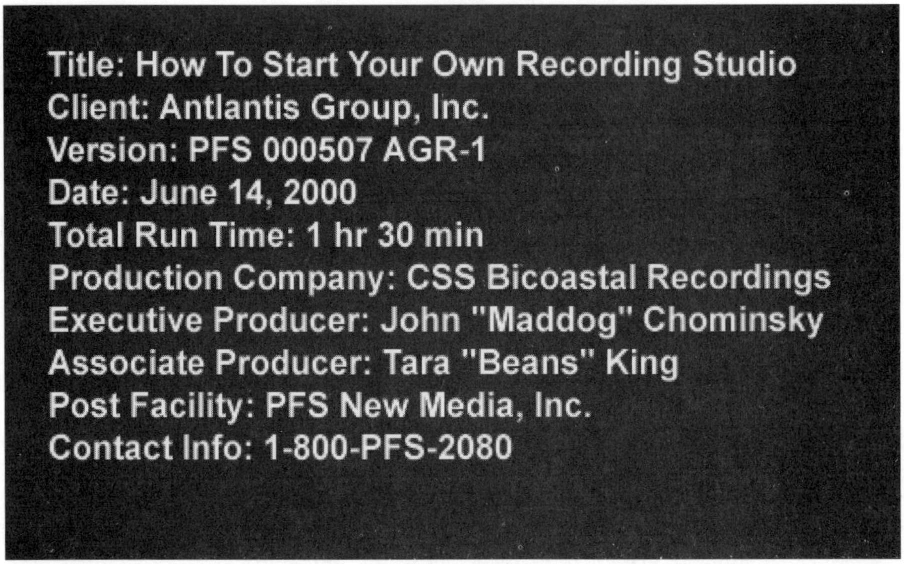

Title: How To Start Your Own Recording Studio
Client: Antlantis Group, Inc.
Version: PFS 000507 AGR-1
Date: June 14, 2000
Total Run Time: 1 hr 30 min
Production Company: CSS Bicoastal Recordings
Executive Producer: John "Maddog" Chominsky
Associate Producer: Tara "Beans" King
Post Facility: PFS New Media, Inc.
Contact Info: 1-800-PFS-2080

Figure 10-4 Sample Slate information screen.

the way to two seconds, leaving exactly two seconds blank (just black video) before your program starts (Figure 10-5).

Do you know why you don't actually count all the way down to one second? This goes back to live television (before computers controlled our world). The two seconds of black gave the program directors enough time to switch between video sources and fade up audio levels without seeing or hearing any portion of the countdown. Now, with frame-accurate computer controlled sources, countdowns are almost not as necessary but I'd still advise you to keep it in. Check out Chapter 3 to find out how to create your own custom countdown.

OUTPUT BOARD SETTINGS

The make and model video capture card you have installed on your system will determine which type of output controls and settings you will have available when outputting your movie from Premiere. I have a miroVIDEO DC-50 board from Pinnacle Systems installed in my computer. Here are a few of the settings I can control that will affect the output quality of my movie (Figure 10-6):

◆ Standard—Select the format that you want to output your movie as (mine is set to only output NTSC).

◆ Pixel Ration—Select between square and nonsquare pixels.

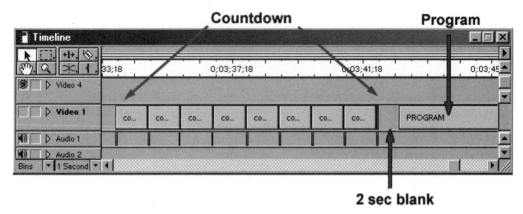

Figure 10-5 The timeline indicates 2 seconds of black before the main program begins.

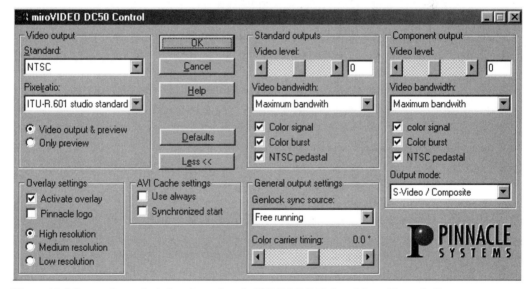

Figure 10-6 Output Control window from the miroVIDEO DC-50 board from Pinnacle Systems.

 Going into detail about pixel ratio specs goes beyond the scope of this book. There are many video technical reference books on the market that covers this, and other technical specifications, in greater detail.

◆ Video Level—one last fine adjustment globally affects the video level of your movie.

◆ GenLock Setting—used to sync up your video sources. Ideally, you should use one standard black burst signal to sync up all of your gear. This is often referred to as House Sync."

◆   Output Mode—this determines where the signal is being sent to, either composite, s-video, or component.

Your video card may have more or fewer controls and settings than my board. Whichever board you are using, make sure it offers enough control and flexibility so that you can check and correct any signal flow coming out of your computer. After all the time you spent editing your program, the last thing you want is a poor-quality output.

OUTPUTTING TO TAPE (WITHOUT DEVICE CONTROL)

If you're like most editors, the majority of your projects will wind up going out to tape. Even if your final destination is a clip for a CD-ROM, you'll probably want to make a protection master on video tape and throw it in the library archives.

To output your edited timeline to tape:

❶   Check all of the Settings under the Project menu to make sure that they are set for full screen, full motion output.

❷   Make sure your video deck is ready to record.

❸   Select Export from the File menu.

❹   Select Print to Video from the pop-up menu.

❺   Set any playback options in the Print to Video window, such as Full Screen Playback, Color Bars, etc (Figure 10-7).

❻   Click OK in Premiere and manually press Play and record on your video deck.

You can record any clip in Premiere to tape, regardless of whether it is in your timeline. Individual clips can play using the settings saved within the clip.

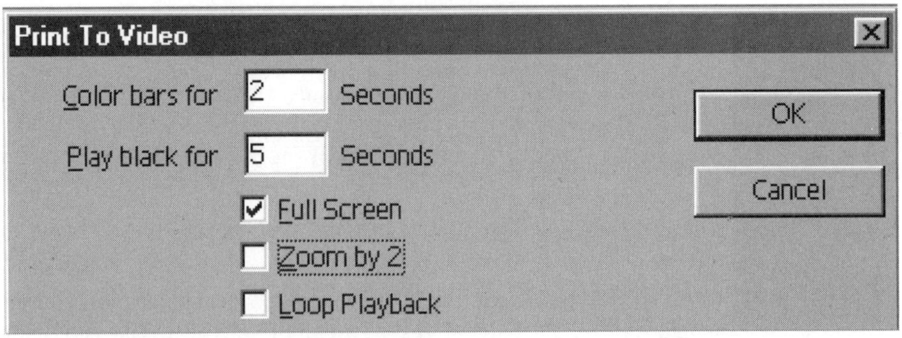

Figure 10-7 The Print To Video window.

Without deck control, you will not be able to frame accurately with your output nor can you insert edit (adding a clip to a middle section of material already on tape).

As far as output settings go, if you want to control the final look and feel of your video, you need to understand which settings affect which type of output. When outputting your timeline to tape, the settings in the Project Settings windows (Video Settings, Audio Settings, and Keyframe and Rendering Options) determine the output quality and features of your video. If you're outputting your video to disk for digital multimedia platforms, you'll use the settings found under the Export Settings found under the File menu.

To record your sequence directly to tape from your computer (your timeline), check the documentation that came with your video capture card to make sure that it can generate television scan rates (NTSC, SECAM, or PAL). Even though the majority of standard capture cards are capable, it's a good idea to check before you purchase a card.

RECORDING TO TAPE USING DECK CONTROL

Ideally, having full deck control offers many more advantages when outputting your movie to tape than not having device control. Depending upon your deck, having deck control probably means having full control of your deck completely from within Premiere. If your deck has frame accuracy control, you can begin recording your program onto tape at a specific point you select. This is important especially when outputting your program for broadcast. It's recommended to start the first frame of your movie at the one hour timecode mark (01:00:00:00).

Another advantage of decks that run on device/remote control from Premiere is that it allows you to Insert edit. Insert editing is the ability to frame-accurately add a video clip to the middle of an existing program already on tape (obviously covering up what was previously there). The difference between frame-accurate insert editing and assemble editing is what happens at the end of the recording process.

Insert editing pops out of record mode at the exact frame the clip you're adding is finished, seamlessly continuing on with the next frame on the tape (Figure 10-8). Assemble editing adds a few frames to a few seconds of garbage at the end of the clip, including destroying your control track. Therefore, you wind up not having a clean edit point at the end of the edit (Figure 10-9). In addition, Insert editing allows you to control which tracks you want to record to the master tape. Do you want to just output

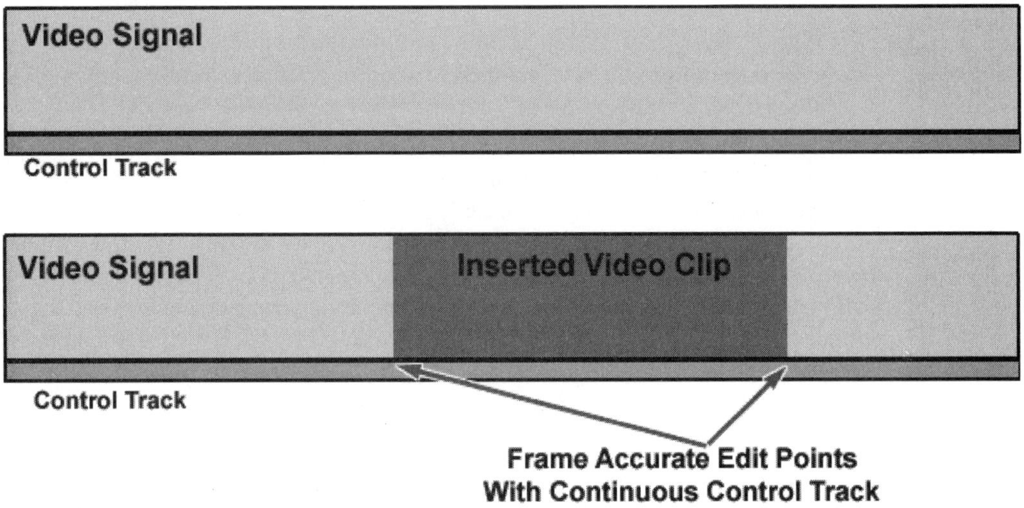

Video Signal

Control Track

Video Signal   **Inserted Video Clip**

Control Track

**Frame Accurate Edit Points
With Continuous Control Track**

Figure 10-8 Insert Editing allows for frame-accurate editing.

video? Do you want Audio Track 1 only, Audio Track 2 only, or both? Now you can begin to see the advantages of having device control for output.

To record to tape using device control:

❶ Check all of the Settings under the Project menu to make sure that they are set for full screen, full motion output.

❷ Make sure your deck is properly connected. Check the Device Control settings under File>Preferences>Scratch Disk/Device Control.

❸ Select Export from the File menu.

❹ Select Export to Tape from the pop-up menu.

The Export to Tape feature is functional only if you have installed the proper plug-ins that support device control.

❺ Select Activate Recording Deck in the Device Options section.

❻ Select the options you need for outputting your movie, including type of editing (i.e., Insert editing), which tracks (i.e., Video, Audio 1, Audio 2), and timecode.

❼ Click OK. Premiere should then take control and record your movie to tape at the specific location you set.

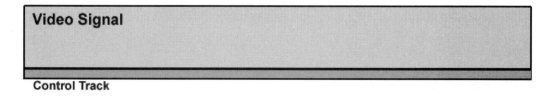

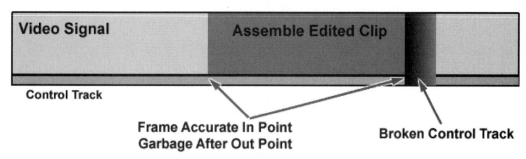

Figure 10-9 Assemble Editing is used only to build a program from the beginning and breaks the control track signal after editing.

EDLS: HOW TO "READ" A MOVIE

This section is not only for those of you who have device controlled deck with time-code, but that sure does make a huge difference. I'll show you ways that those less fortunate can benefit in emergency situations from an Edit Decision List, more commonly referred to as an EDL. An EDL is nothing more than a database file that contains all the relevant information about all of your edits in your timeline (Figure 10-10). Every time you add a clip to your timeline, a new entry is made to the EDL. For each transition placed in your movie, the information about that transition is added to the EDL. First we'll cover the main reason you would use an EDL and then we'll look at a few time-saving tips that anyone can use, even people without timecode on their tapes.

There are many different formats that you can use to save your EDL. These are based on the type of online edit controller that you will use (and it can read) to reconfigure your movie, exactly replicating the edits you made in Premiere. Some of the most common formats include:

◆ CMX

◆ Grass Valley

◆ Sony

```
┌─ Text: C:\WINDOWS\Desktop\edl.edl ──────────────────────────────── _ □ ☒ ┐
│TITLE: DEMO VIDEO                                                        ▲ │
│FCM: NON-DROP FRAME                                                        │
│001   UND006    AA/V   C         00:00:00:00 00:00:05:27 01:00:00:00 01:00:05:27 │
│REEL UND006 IS CLIP RADOCD.AVI                                             │
│AUDIO GAIN IS 0.00DB AT 01:00:00:00                                        │
│AUDIO GAIN IS 0.00DB AT 01:00:05:27                                        │
│002   UND007    AA/V   C         00:00:00:00 00:00:00:02 01:00:05:27 01:00:05:29 │
│REEL UND007 IS CLIP BIGEXPL.MOV                                            │
│AUDIO GAIN IS 0.00DB AT 01:00:05:27                                        │
│AUDIO GAIN IS 0.00DB AT 01:00:05:29                                        │
│003   UND008    AA/V   C         00:00:00:00 00:00:03:10 01:00:05:29 01:00:09:09 │
│REEL UND008 IS CLIP EXPLO1.MOV                                             │
│AUDIO GAIN IS 0.00DB AT 01:00:05:29                                        │
│AUDIO GAIN IS 0.00DB AT 01:00:09:09                                        │
│004     BL      V      C         00:00:00:00 00:00:32:08 01:00:09:09 01:00:41:17 │
│005   UND006    AA/V   C         00:00:00:00 00:00:08:00 01:00:41:17 01:00:49:17 │
│REEL UND006 IS CLIP RADOCD.AVI                                             │
│AUDIO GAIN IS 0.00DB AT 01:00:41:17                                        │
│AUDIO GAIN IS 0.00DB AT 01:00:49:17                                        │
│006   UND006    AA/V   C         00:00:00:00 00:00:29:17 01:00:49:17 01:01:19:04 │
│REEL UND006 IS CLIP RADOCD.AVI                                             │
│AUDIO GAIN IS 0.00DB AT 01:00:49:17                                        │
│AUDIO GAIN IS 0.00DB AT 01:01:19:04                                        │
│007   UND006    V      C         00:00:00:00 00:00:00:01 01:01:19:04 01:01:19:05 │
│REEL UND006 IS CLIP RADOCD.AVI                                             │
│008     BL      V      C         00:00:00:00 00:00:02:25 01:01:19:05 01:01:22:00 │
│009   UND008    AA/V   C         00:00:00:00 00:00:02:19 01:01:22:00 01:01:24:19 │
│REEL UND008 IS CLIP EXPLO1.MOV                                           ▼ │
└────────────────────────────────────────────────────────────────────────┘
```

Figure 10-10 Sample display of a typical EDL layout.

The traditional way EDLs were used was to rough-cut your movie on an off-line system or low resolution nonlinear system, save your edited sequence as an EDL, and take that disk to an online facility to repurpose your movie at the highest quality. The EDL works the same way the Batch Capture feature works. The EDL looks at the time-code of the clip you edited and recreates that edit by finding the starting timecode frame, the duration of the clip, and the end frame of the clip and records that to your new master tape. What EDLs do is so much more. They also recreate any audio changes for each audio track, any transitions that were used, and tally the names of each clip and source tape (as it was noted during the logging or digitizing process).

Always check what format your online studio can read before creating an EDL. There's nothing more frustrating than trying to finish a project, book editing time, and find out you don't have the proper formatting.

To view and save an EDL in the desired format:

❶ Open an existing edited timeline or edit a new one in the timeline.

❷ Select Export from the File menu.

❸ Select from one of the EDL formats from the pop-up menu that come with Premiere.

❹ Set the particular settings in the EDL Output window.

❺ Click OK.

❻ Save the EDL file and any other files (such as a B-Roll list).

❼ Click OK.

The EDL Output window should appear (Figure 10-11). It contains various options for creating an EDL, depending upon the format you selected. For example, if you choose CMX 3600 (one of the most common formats), you can add the following information to your EDL:

◆ Specify a name for the EDL

◆ Starting Time Code and Frame Rate

◆ Audio Processing (whether the audio information is listed with the video information)

◆ Level Note for Audio and Keys (Figure 10-12)

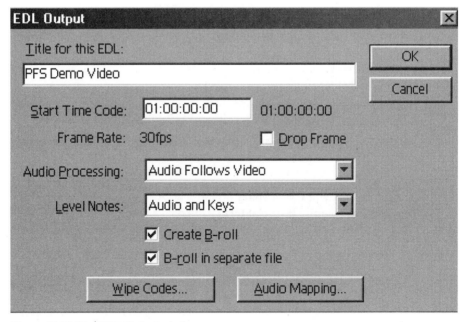

Figure 10-11 The EDL Output window.

```
 Text: C:\WINDOWS\Desktop\edl.edl

TITLE: DEMO VIDEO
FCM: NON-DROP FRAME
001  UND006    AA/V   C           00:00:00:00
REEL UND006 IS CLIP RADOCD.AVI
AUDIO GAIN IS 0.00DB AT 01:00:00:00
AUDIO GAIN IS 0.00DB AT 01:00:05:27
002  UND007    AA/V   C           00:00:00:00
REEL UND007 IS CLIP BIGEXPL.MOV
AUDIO GAIN IS 0.00DB AT 01:00:05:27
AUDIO GAIN IS 0.00DB AT 01:00:05:29
003  UND008    AA/V   C           00:00:00:00
REEL UND008 IS CLIP EXPLO1.MOV
AUDIO GAIN IS 0.00DB AT 01:00:05:29
AUDIO GAIN IS 0.00DB AT 01:00:09:09
```

Figure 10-12 View any audio level changes that occurred during editing.

◆   B-Roll Tape information (You may need a B-Roll tape if two shots you edited in Premiere with a transition come from the same source tape. You cannot add transitions between shots on the same "linear" source tape; therefore you create a copy of that tape, known as a B-roll Tape.)

◆   Wipe Code information (displays how the online switcher will interpret any transitions in your movie) (Figure 10-13)

◆   Audio Mapping (which audio tracks are related to which audio channels) (Figure 10-14)

CMX and Grass Valley do not work off of a MS-DOS formatted disk, and require a special format. The best option is to request a copy of that disk from your online house to ensure compatibility.

My advice to every editor (whether or not you have timecode and device control) is to create, save, and print out a copy of the EDL of your edited timeline sequence. This may come in handy in case you ever have to recreate a project from scratch (which always happens to those of you who forget to back up a copy of your project files). You may not remember the exact scenes you used, but at least you will have the source tape names from where you pulled the clips, their duration, which transitions you used, and

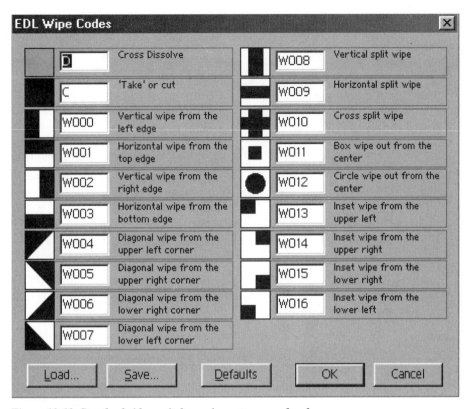

Figure 10-13 Standard video switchers wipe patterns and codes.

Figure 10-14 The Audio Mapping window allows you to set the audio output tracks.

any notes about audio levels. Whether you decide to finish your project in Premiere or somewhere else, it always helps to have a hard copy of your EDL in your hand.

DESTINATION: COMPUTER (EXPORTING FOR MULTIMEDIA)

Exporting a movie as a digital (computer) file for multimedia is easy. The hardest part is understanding all of the different types of variables that come in to play when creating digital files. To Export a movie:

❶   Open an edited sequence or create one in the timeline.

❷   Select Export from the File menu.

❸   Select Movie from the pop-up menu or hit Control-M (Windows) or Command-M (Macintosh).

❹   Set desired settings in the Export Movie window by clicking on the Settings button (Figure 10-15). The Export Movie Settings Window appears (Figure 10-16).

❺   Click OK.

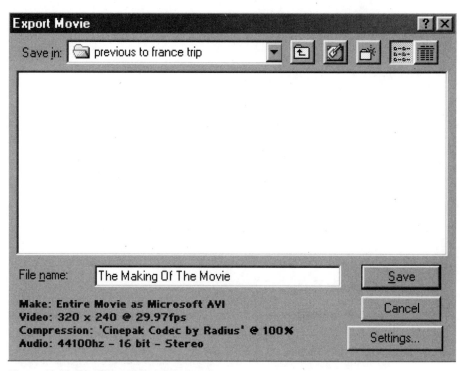

Figure 10-15 The Export Movie window.

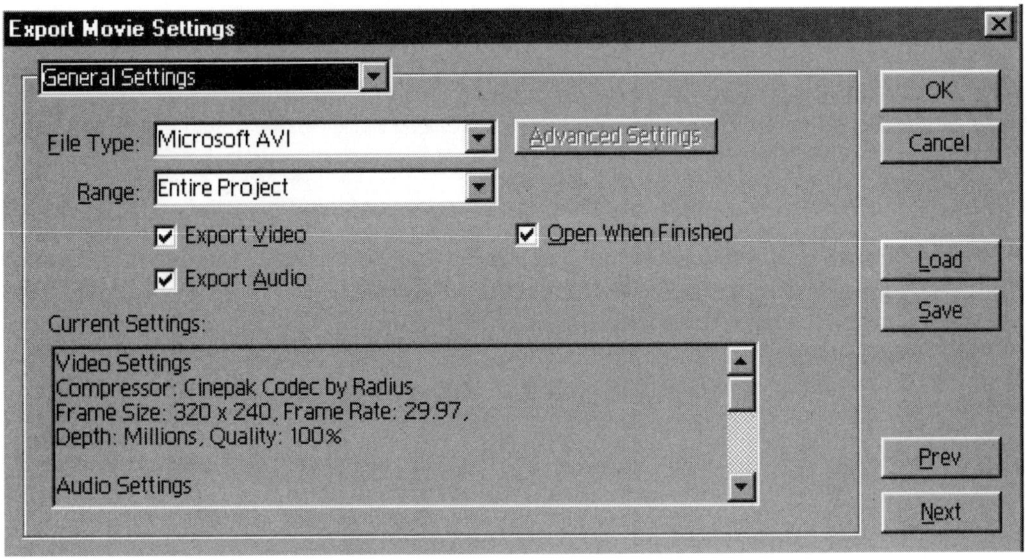

Figure 10-16 The Export Movie Settings window.

The following are the types of files you can export in Premiere:

◆ AIFF Audio (Macintosh only)

◆ Audio Video Interleaved (AVI) (Windows only)

◆ Animated GIF

◆ GIF Sequence

◆ Filmstrip

◆ FLC/FLI (Windows only)

◆ PICT Sequence (Macintosh only)

◆ QuickTime

Now comes the fun part: trying to figure out what each control is and how its settings affect the final output quality of your media. Depending upon which file type you choose to export your movie, various options and controls will be available. These controls determine the file type, size, and quality of your movie.

CODECS

The greatest challenge for any digital video editing system is to reproduce the highest-quality video signal. The problem is that it takes high-end computer systems to capture and play back high-quality video. Therefore, many companies have introduced various forms of compression technologies that allow standard computers to play back video files. The compression and decompression applications are known as Codecs, short for **C**ompression **Dec**ompression.

 To learn more about codecs and compression formats, check out the Web site www.CodecCentral.com.

Codecs have the the ability to compress large files into the smallest possible components while conversely trying to preserve the best possible quality. When exporting your movie from Premiere for multimedia use, you use one of these compression formats to compress your original video digital video file to reduce its size and optimize it for playback on your computer. Then, using the same technology, you play the video clip back on your computer using the decompression portion of the application. There are several different types of codecs, including:

◆ Cinepak

◆ Animation

◆ MPEG 1 and 2

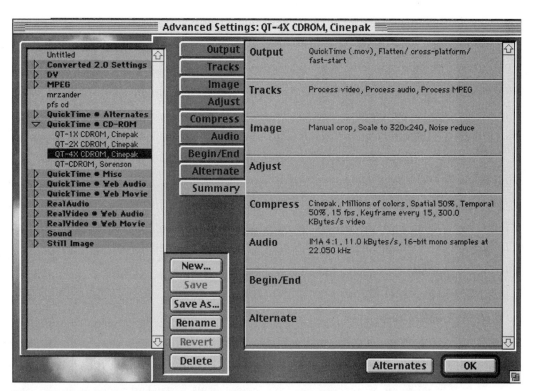

Figure 10-17 Terran Interactive's Media Cleaner Pro's Settings and Control window.

◆ Intel Indeo

◆ Video

◆ Sorenson

◆ Motion JPEG

Creating the best-quality movie is important. My advice is to export your movies without any compression. This will take a great deal longer to complete and use up a tremendous amount of hard drive space. Then I recommend using a program like Terran Interactive's Media Cleaner Pro. It is by far the best compression application out on the market. You can choose to repurpose your movie into just about any type of digital media format that exists (Figure 10-17). This easy to use program is a must if you want flexibility and control to produce the best quality digital media files. Check out Media Cleaner Pro at www.Terran.com.

Having complete control over your movie's settings, as found in Media Cleaner Pro, allows for ideal file size, especially in today's push for video over the Internet. It even writes out the HTML embed tags for you non-Web programmers out there.

DATA RATE

After choosing the desired codec, the next most important aspect that will determine quality and playback capability of the file is the Data Rate. Every computer is configured slightly differently and distributing digital media can be a challenge. Because some of your end users will not have the latest and greatest system, optimizing your movie for playback is an important consideration. The Data Rate determines the amount of information that the computer system can process for that file. If the Data Rate is set higher than the playback capability of the computer, the video file will either play slower than it was set to play, drop frames randomly, or freeze up altogether. Determine how you want your end users to optimally view your movie. If they will be playing the movie from their hard drive, you can set a high data rate (over 300 KB per second). If they will be viewing the clip from a smaller bandwidth channel, such as a CD-ROM or an intranet, drop down to 100 to 200 KB per second.

The lower the Data Rate, the lower the quality of your image will appear.

KEY FRAMES

Some codecs offer you the ability to set keyframes. Keyframes act as a starting point for the compression processes taking place. This type of compression is referred to as Temporal compression. Temporal compression basically works by compressing

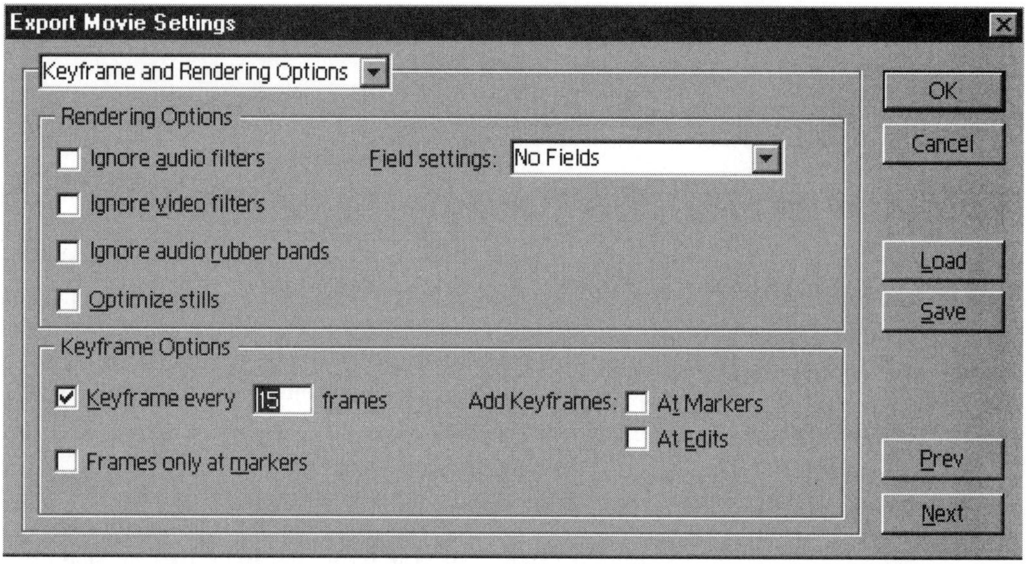

Figure 10-18 The Keyframe and Rendering Options window.

the changes frame by frame from a given point. Therefore, if a keyframe is set every fourth frame, the next three frames are using the previous keyframe to compare patterns or repetition of pixels.

Setting a keyframe every frame would allow for higher quality playback but at the cost of increasing the overall file size. If you had a scene that held pretty static, with very little movement, you could leave a greater number of frames between keyframes. For quick movement in clips, set a lower interval between keyframes.

> When exporting your movie, set keyframes in the Keyframe and Render Options window under the Export Movie Settings menu choice (Figure 10-18).

EXPORTING STILL IMAGES

There may be times when you want to export only a single frame from your movie. Premiere allows you to quickly and easily select the desired frame and save it to your hard drive. The frame that is exported is the frame that you are parked on, where your playback bar is currently positioned. This frame can be from your source monitor or your edit monitor (timeline view). Exporting from your edit monitor will carry through any filters or layering applied to your timeline as it appears on screen.

To export a single video frame:

❶ Position the playback bar on the frame that you wish to export.

❷ Select Export from the File menu.

❸ Select Frame from the pop-up menu or use the keyboard shortcut Control-Shift-M (Windows) or Command-Shift-M (Macintosh). The Export Still Frame widow should appear.

❹ Click the Settings button in the lower right portion of the window.

❺ Select the type of file you wish to export from the General Settings option under the Export Still Frame Settings window (Figure 10-19).

❻ Select Special Processing from the pull-down menu.

❼ Click on the Modify button.

❽ Make final adjustments, including Cropping, in the Special Processing window (Figure 10-20).

❾ Click OK twice.

❿ Name the file and save it in the location you choose.

⓫ Click Save.

Premiere can export:

◆ TIFF

◆ Targa

◆ Bitmap (windows)

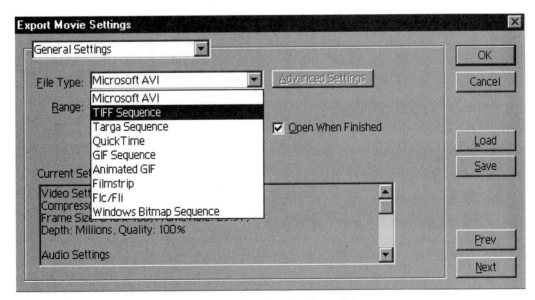

Figure 10-19 The General Settings option window for exporting still frames.

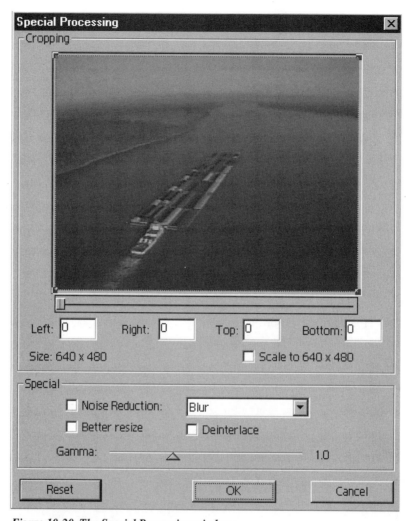

Figure 10-20 The Special Processing window.

- ◆ GIF
- ◆ Pict (Macintosh)

A NEAT LITTLE EXTRA

Exporting to tape can be a hassle once in a while, especially if you're only outputting to verify how something is going to look on a standard television (compared to a computer monitor). One little gadget that I recently came across and found very valuable is a small box called the MultiPro 2000 by AITech. This little device actually comes in handy for many applications. It is designed to convert computer (VGA) signals into television (NTSC or PAL) signals. One use that I find works rather well is to connect this unit to your computer monitor and a television. Now, when you select Export to tape, the full screen image plays on your television set as well as your computer monitor. This saves the time and cost of outputting to tape and then bringing that over to your VCR, and so on. Here, you can instantly see what your program will look like on television. Check out the MultiPro 2000 and some of AITech's other products at www. AITech.com (Figure 10-21).

Figure 10-21 The MultiPro 2000 from AITech.

This unit can also be used for input. Hook up the video signal to a VCR and record your computer screen in use (mouse movements and all). This is great for producing training and educational pieces for computer applications.

SUMMARY

That's it. It's that easy to get your final edited movie out to tape or digital format for multimedia distribution. Keep in mind, capture cards are going to vary with the export features and controls they offer. Look around and find the one that offers you the most flexibility within your price range. Here's one area that you don't want to pennypinch. The quality of your work, after all that time digitizing and editing, depends on your output settings. Good luck and have some fun with your movies.

INDEX